ABETTING BATTERERS

ABETTING BATTERERS

What Police, Prosecutors, and Courts Aren't Doing to Protect America's Women

Andrew R. Klein
and Jessica L. Klein

ROWMAN & LITTLEFIELD
Lanham • Boulder • New York • London

Published by Rowman & Littlefield
A wholly owned subsidiary of The Rowman & Littlefield Publishing Group, Inc.
4501 Forbes Boulevard, Suite 200, Lanham, Maryland 20706
www.rowman.com

Unit A, Whitacre Mews, 26-34 Stannary Street, London SE11 4AB

British Library Cataloguing in Publication Information Available

Library of Congress Cataloging-in-Publication Data

Names: Klein, Andrew R., author. | Klein, Jessica L., author.
Title: Abetting batterers : what police, prosecutors, and courts aren't doing
  to protect America's women / Andrew R. Klein and Jessica L. Klein.
Description: Lanham : Rowman & Littlefield, [2016] | Includes bibliographical
  references and index.
Identifiers: LCCN 2015050842 (print) | LCCN 2016006666 (ebook) | ISBN
  9781442248274 (cloth : alk. paper) | ISBN 9781442248281 (Electronic)
Subjects: LCSH: Abused women—United States. | Wife abuse—United States. |
  Family violence—United States. | Abusive men—United States.
Classification: LCC HV6626.2 .K5947 2016 (print) | LCC HV6626.2 (ebook) | DDC
  364.15/550973—dc23
LC record available at http://lccn.loc.gov/2015050842

∞™ The paper used in this publication meets the minimum requirements of American National Standard for Information Sciences—Permanence of Paper for Printed Library Materials, ANSI/NISO Z39.48-1992.

Printed in the United States of America

CONTENTS

INTRODUCTION

The Right of Chastisement, A Husband's Responsibility

THEN

Mr. and Mrs. Black were estranged, living apart in North Carolina in 1864. Mr. Black happened to pass by his wife's dwelling. She yelled out to him, questioning whether he had "patched Sal Daly's bonnet," a woman described in the court record as being of "ill-fame." Mr. Black proceeded to follow his estranged wife back into her house and accused her, in turn, of having a connection with a "Negro," according to subsequent court documents. She retorted that Mr. Black was nothing but a "hog thief." At this point, he grabbed her by her hair and forced her to the ground, where he held her for a long time. Perhaps he also strangled her, because she sustained injuries to her head and suffered a sore throat that lasted several weeks, although, we are told, she was fully recovered by the time of her husband's trial for assaulting her.

The trial did not last long. In fact, it never began, as the trial court summarily dismissed the charges against Mr. Black because he had the right to beat his wife, known as the Right of Chastisement.

The court ruled: "A husband is responsible for the acts of his wife, and he is required to govern his household, and for that purpose, the law permits him to use towards his wife such a degree of force as necessary." The court concluded that the law "prefers to leave the parties to themselves as the best mode of inducing them to make the matter up and live together as man and wife should." Anything—like a trial—that opens up the matter to the public "widens the breach, makes reconciliation impossible and encourages insubordination."[1]

Besides, the court noted, Mr. Black acted in the heat of passion, provoked by his wife's verbal abuse. In fact, the court went on to praise Mr. Black for showing restraint in his assault.

The Civil War ended the year after this decision. A new, liberal, reconstructed North Carolina Supreme Court returned to the issue of domestic violence in 1874, several years before the North abandoned its occupation of the state. This time it was a drunken Mr. Oliver who came home for a morning work break to his wife. He claimed that the bacon she served him had "skippers" on it, and he threw their coffeepot on the floor in protest. He then went outside and cut two switches, which he brought inside and placed on the floor. He announced he was going to beat his wife with them because she and her "d—d mother had aggravated him to death."

The switches were four feet long, half filled with branches and leaves. One was as large as a man's small finger. The other was smaller. Mr. Oliver struck his wife five times with the switches. According to a witness, he hit her as hard as he could. He only stopped as a result of outside intervention.

At a subsequent trial, Mr. Oliver was found guilty. The new, improved North Carolina Supreme Court, typical of courts across the country in the 1870s, allowed his conviction to stand. The court declared: "We assume that the old doctrine that a husband had the right to whip his wife, provided that he used a switch no larger than his thumb, is not the law in North Carolina." However, lest its decision be misinterpreted, it hastened to add: "But from motives of public policy, in order to preserve the sanctity of the domestic circle, the Courts will not listen to trivial complaints. If no permanent injury has been inflicted, nor malice, cruelty, nor dangerous violence shown by the husband, it is better to draw the curtain, shut out the public gaze, and leave the parties to forgive and forget."[2]

NOW

Fast-forward to May 13, 2014. More than 140 years later, North Carolina NFL star Greg Hardy attacked his partner in his apartment, picking her up and throwing her into the tiled tub of the bathroom, causing bruises to her head, neck, back, shoulders, arms, legs, elbow, and feet, according to the victim. Hardy then pulled her from the tub by her hair, declaring that he was going to kill her, break her arms, and other threats that she subsequently admitted she "completely believed." He dragged her across the bathroom into the bedroom where he strangled her with both hands around her throat while she was lying on the floor. Hardy picked her up over his head and threw her onto a couch covered in assault rifles and/or shotguns that Hardy bragged were loaded. Landing on those weapons caused more bruises to the victim's neck and back. Hardy then summoned an employee to come into the room and hold her, which the assistant did. They then took her into the hallway outside the apartment while she begged for her freedom and promised not to reveal their violence. In the hall, they pushed her down and then returned back inside the apartment. The victim crawled to the elevator, escaped to the street, and ran to the Charlotte-Mecklenburg police department.

On June 15, a judge found Hardy guilty of assaulting a female and communicating threats. She imposed a sixty-day jail sentence, but then suspended it so that Hardy would serve no time at all in jail. Hardy appealed. Prosecutors subsequently dropped the charges because they said the victim had disappeared, and under the state's archaic trial *de novo* system, the first trial before a judge is not recorded and doesn't count if the defendant claims his right to a jury trial. According to the *Charlotte Observer*, Hardy reached a private settlement with the victim.[3]

Although some may suspect that Hardy received special consideration as a sports celebrity, in fact the maximum sentence allowed under North Carolina law for what prosecutors charged Hardy is only 150 days in jail. For Hardy to be charged with the more serious offense of strangulation, the state would have had to prove "physical injury," which is difficult to establish short of the victim dying from asphyxiation.

Short as the maximum sentence is, North Carolina takes domestic violence a bit more seriously than South Carolina, where the maximum penalty was only sixty days in jail until May 2015 when the legislature finally increased it by thirty days—and more for repeat convictions, if the victim is pregnant, or if the offenses occurred in the presence of children or involved strangulation. The maximum sentence for violation of a protective order remained at thirty days. Of course the maximum punishment for a domestic assault, strangulation, or violation of a protective order is only theoretical. Rarely do prosecutors recommend or judges impose actual jail sentences for domestic violence crimes. Hardy's sentence is typical in that respect; any jail sentence imposed is usually suspended, if the case even gets that far in court. Most are diverted or dismissed.

The reform legislation finally toughening South Carolina's domestic violence penalties also included a provision allowing prosecutors to plead down the domestic violence charges to assault and battery so that convicted violent abusers wouldn't lose their firearms as the new law requires.[4]

The curtains have still not opened, at least not all the way, when it comes to domestic violence, although the definition of "domestic violence" has expanded over time beyond wife beating.

Domestic violence, or intimate partner violence, has come to include violence and abuse between current and former married couples, cohabitating couples with or without children, and, in most states, boyfriends/girlfriends. The understanding of what constitutes domestic violence has also moved beyond physical assaults (wife beating). Even the current U.S. Supreme Court has come to recognize that domestic violence is a constellation of behaviors designed to coercively control intimate partners. In *United States v. Castleman*, writing for the majority in 2014, Justice Sotomayor wrote, "[W]hereas the word 'violent' or 'violence' standing alone 'connotes a substantial degree of force,' that is not true of 'domestic violence.' 'Domestic violence' is not merely a type of 'violence,' it is a term of art encompassing acts that one might not characterize as 'violent' in a nondomestic context. Indeed, most physical assaults committed against women and men by intimates are relatively minor. . . . [T]he accumulation of such acts over time can subject one intimate partner to the other's control (footnotes omitted)."[5]

Generally, all of the following make up what is commonly called "domestic violence" or "intimate partner violence": 1) sexual abuse, from rape to unwanted sexual contact, 2) physical violence, from pushing to burning and strangulation, 3) psychological abuse, from name-calling and humiliation, threats and intimidation to coercive controlling behaviors, 4) stalking, from harassment to threatening behaviors that cause fear, 5) reproductive and health abuse, from sabotaging birth control to withholding medication and health care, and 6) financial abuse, from controlling family finances to prohibiting employment. In terms of what behaviors result in abusers being arrested and prosecuted in court, most arrests under state-specific domestic violence statutes or offenses involving the requisite relationships are for physical assaults, simple or aggravated.

Between 2007 and 2011, in South Carolina, for example, out of a quarter million domestic violence incidents recorded by police, 177,157 were for simple assaults and 42,699 for aggravated assaults. The only other domestic violence crime reported that came close was "intimidation" with 32,196 reports. The most serious domestic violence crime reported was homicide with 412 reports. Although most of the assaults resulted in victim injuries, they were reported as "minor." Only 10 percent were reported as a "severe laceration" or "major injury." South Carolina law lumps family violence and intimate partner violence or domestic violence together. Two-thirds of the crimes reported as domestic violence involved intimates, spouses, ex-spouses, and "romantic" partners. The rest were miscellaneous family members.

The South Carolina incident report breakdown is consistent with what victims reveal in national crime victim surveys. Between 2003 and 2012, the majority of domestic violence was reported by victims to have been simple assaults (64 percent), while the remainder constituted more serious crimes, including rape or sexual assault, robbery, and aggravated assault.

Simple assaults are those assaults that do not leave observable injuries and are misdemeanors, lesser crimes tried in lower criminal courts and punishable by time in local or county jails as opposed to state prisons. Aggravated assaults are those that leave observable injuries, or where a weapon is used other than fists, and are felonies, considered more serious crimes tried in circuit or superior courts (or supreme courts in New York) and punishable by time in state prisons. While domestic violence is by no means limited to physical attacks, it is rare that physical attacks are absent in domestic violence. As an experienced domestic violence victim advocate related, she knew of only one case of domestic violence where the victim had never been physically assaulted by her abuser. In that situation, however, the abuser had previously been imprisoned for murdering a former intimate partner. In place of a physical assault, all he had to do was say to his current victim, "You are beginning to remind me of Ann" (his deceased partner).

When it comes to domestic violence, the lasting and most severe damage is not physical. It is also true that abusers are *not* directly responsible for most victim fatalities. As the 2010 Washington State Fatality Report rightly realized, far more women victimized by their partners die by suicide each year than are murdered by them. In that state, three times more women died by suicide than were murdered by their partners. The precise percentage of suicides directly tied to domestic violence is not known, but it is the lion's share.

1

COUNTING DOMESTIC
VIOLENCE VICTIMS

Really, we have no idea how many women or men are abused by their intimate partners, notwithstanding annual reports issued by the U.S. Department of Justice.[1] Crime in general has declined across the country over the last several decades, and no doubt domestic violence has too. But how much is uncertain, particularly because how much domestic violence there was before is not known either. Whatever the number is, though, it is too high for the individual victims, their families, and the community in general that spends billions of dollars a year treating the injured, repairing the damages, and policing the perpetrators. If domestic violence were a contagious disease like the flu or measles, it would be called an epidemic. The media went into a tizzy in 2014 over one Ebola death in the United States. On average, at least twenty people are victims of physical violence by an intimate partner every minute of every day in the United States. That equals more than ten million men and women every year.

Traditionally, crime has been tracked through police report statistics. The problem is these statistics tell more about what police, not criminals, are up to. It is fairly widely agreed, for example, that when it comes to domestic violence, a significant percentage of victims, 40 to 50 percent, do not call police. To get a more accurate count, the U.S. Justice Department turned to crime victim surveys in the early 1990s so that police response no longer mediated the results. Every year the U.S. Justice Department releases its National Crime Victim Survey (NCVS).

Something like 13,000 interviews, representative of the entire U.S. population, are conducted each month for this continuing survey. According to victim surveys, domestic violence has declined by two-thirds, mostly between 1994 and 2002. It has stabilized since. The domestic violence homicide rates have also dropped, mostly between 1993 and 2001, according to the FBI.[2]

But there are reasons to doubt the actual numbers of domestic violence victims the survey comes up with annually—even domestic violence homicides, which should be pretty clear-cut. The problem is that many victims of intimate partner violence, no matter how much they may suffer, don't consider their abuse to be a crime or their partners to be criminals. Asked if they were victims of crime, when it comes to domestic violence, they say "No." The surveys report no consistent decline in domestic violence involving weapons or resulting in injuries. The surveys have found that the use of weapons by abusers has fluctuated since 1993 between 13 and 25 percent, but not declined. Reported injuries have also been fairly constant. In other words, the abuse that one suspects most victims would more readily recognize as "criminal" shows no decline.

Even if all victims understand domestic violence to be a crime, many would still be reluctant to admit to their victimization as the interviews may be conducted in the presence of their abusers!

In regard to domestic violence homicides, the statistics are mostly based on FBI reports. The largest category of FBI-reported homicides falls under "victim/offender relationship—unknown." While the relationship involved in a murder of a wife by her husband is easy to determine, the relationship involved in a murder by a former boyfriend is not.

It has also become apparent that different surveys, using different methodologies, find different results. A lot depends on how broadly domestic violence is defined. Does it include the full panoply of abuse-related crimes including robbery, threats, cyberstalking, intimidation, thefts, and so on? It also matters whether potential victims are questioned via telephone or face to face. Some national victimization surveys have documented domestic violence rates to be many times higher than others. The National Intimate Partner and Sexual Violence Survey (NIPSVS) data from January through December 2011, for example, found 2.3 percent of the population experienced severe physical violence by intimates that year. At the same time, the NCVS found the rate of serious intimate partner violence (IPV) to be much less at 1.4 percent. And state surveys have found still higher rates than either national survey. An Ohio State University survey in partnership with the Health Policy Institute of Ohio and the Health Path Foundation of

Ohio found, for example, 115,000 adults in that state to be physically abused by a current or former intimate, higher than the rate found in NIPSVS.[3]

In 2013, the number of emergency calls for help in California for domestic violence was roughly equal to the total number of all other violent crimes in the state put together. A state portrait for 2014–2015 concluded, after collecting this and other domestic violence–related data, that domestic violence "is central to any discussion of a long and healthy life. Its toll on the physical and mental health of victims and their families in California, as in every U.S. state, is staggering."[4]

Whatever the number, domestic violence remains much too large for a preventable crime.

The domestic violence murder statistics, incomplete as they may be, do allow us to peer a bit behind the curtain. At first glance, they show a dramatic drop in domestic violence–related homicides since such murders were first identified and tracked by the FBI in the early 1990s. A closer examination of domestic violence homicide statistics tells a more disturbing story. While domestic violence murders are down, most of the decline is men not being murdered by their female intimate partners, most of whom were victims of their male partners' abuse.

Since 1976, the number of men murdered by female intimates declined by almost three-quarters, while the number of women murdered by male intimates dropped only a quarter. At the same time, the number of homicides in general declined by more than a third, according to the FBI. In other words, compared to the overall decline in lethal violence across the country, the murder rate of women by their male intimates has actually risen in the last several decades.

Battered or abused women (terms used synonymously in this text) face a Hobbesian choice. Stay and risk death. Leave and risk death. As made evident by state fatality reports, lethal violence does not end with separation. The Washington State fatality report, for example, reveals that 46 percent of the homicides occurred after the victim had divorced, separated from, or left her abuser, or was in the process of breaking up and leaving her abuser. The 2010 fatality report admits that the information on relationship status is often incomplete, so the number of victims in the process of leaving is undoubtedly higher.[5]

Ironically, while the growth in domestic shelters and other assistance has encouraged battered women to escape their abusers, at the same time, it has increased their likelihood of being stalked and even murdered by their abusers. In short, the country is getting safer for almost everyone, except women who have or have had abusive male intimate partners.

2

VICTIM ADVOCACY AND SERVICES
HELPFUL, BUT INSUFFICIENT

While the number of abused intimates is not easy to track, services for domestic violence victims are. They began in the 1970s. The first shelter for battered women opened in Chiswick, England, in 1970. Three years later, the first American shelter opened in St. Paul, Minnesota. By the end of that decade, there were over 250 domestic violence shelters across the United States. By the end of the 1980s, there were 1,200 battered women programs in the United States providing shelter to 300,000 women and children. Passage of the Violence Against Women Act (VAWA) in 1994 added billions of federal dollars, a quarter earmarked for domestic violence victim services. By 2005, the feds had allotted $5 billion to fund VAWA.

In 2013, the National Network to End Domestic Violence surveyed all but 250 of the 1,649 identified local domestic violence programs across the country to create the latest annual *National Census of Domestic Violence Services*. It illustrates what all the funding and work by committed advocates and service providers have produced. Over the twenty-four-hour period on September 17, 2013, 66,581 victims received some services provided by these agencies. Of those, 36,348 found refuge in emergency shelters or transitional housing (excluding abused women and their children housed in nondomestic violence–specific shelters). Another 30,233 adults and children received nonresidential assistance and services, including counseling, legal advocacy, and children's support groups. During that same twenty-four-hour period, various state and local domestic violence hotlines answered 20,167 calls. The national domestic violence hotline answered another 550 calls. Together they averaged fourteen calls per minute. The domestic violence programs also offered 1,413 training sessions on domestic violence that day to 23,389 individuals.

However, not every abused adult or child who contacted a domestic violence program that day was provided services; 9,641 service requests that day were unmet, with most, 5,778, being requests for shelter. It is reported that most, 60 percent, of those requesting services that weren't available returned to their abusers, while another 27 percent became homeless and 11 percent ended up living in their cars, according to information provided by the domestic violence programs.

Throughout that year, all of the domestic violence programs provided individual support or advocacy, 95 percent provided court advocacy or legal accompaniment to victims in court, 94 percent children's support and advocacy, 92 percent related to child welfare/protective services, and 91 percent provided transportation, group support or advocacy, advocacy related to public benefits like TANF/Welfare, and advocacy related to mental health. Eighty-five percent provided emergency shelter, but only 42 percent provided transitional housing and only 18 percent provided safe houses, although 63 percent provided funding for temporary hotel or motel stays and 90 percent provided advocacy related to housing offices or landlords. Most, 79 to 88 percent, provided advocacy for other services, from substance abuse to health care to immigration to technology use (to counter cyberstalking, etc.). A little over half, 54 percent, provided day care.

According to the experts, all of these domestic violence services that aim to enhance victims' internal resources and improve their social support, including counseling, support groups, advocacy, and shelter services, have been found to be beneficial.[1] For many victims, participation in community-based advocacy services has been found to result in higher quality of life and greater social support and less difficulty obtaining community resources compared to battered women who do not receive such services.[2] In fact, just disclosing abuse has been found to decrease victim distress.[3]

It is also true that not all available domestic violence services are equally effective for all victims. One study, for example, suggested the most effective service components for IPV victims include domestic violence emergency shelters, support groups, information sessions, resource referral, and participation in individual counseling. Psycho-educational group counseling did not play an equivalent significant role nor did group counseling focusing on empowerment and information about domestic violence. Based on these findings, the domestic violence service agency under study substituted a trauma recovery counseling program.[4]

It is also understood that most victims are satisfied with most of the services generally offered, even if the services don't meet all of their needs.[5] As the saying goes, any port in a storm will do. Well, almost—there are some exceptions. General mental health counseling has been found to be unhelpful. Those seeking mental health treatment complain that many typical providers fail to focus on the abuse, are quick to provide medication but not support, and do not appreciate or understand the trauma that victims experienced.[6] On the other hand, the individual counseling offered by domestic violence programs was reported to be helpful. The verdict was more mixed for individual counseling obtained outside of domestic violence programs. While some found it helpful, others did not. Those who found the counseling unhelpful reported that therapists urged them to reconcile with their abusers or attend couple counseling.[7]

According to victims, their typical unmet needs are financial in nature (e.g., acquiring a job, transportation, rent, and other cash assistance), which is generally beyond the scope of the assistance offered by nonresidential domestic violence programs.

Even if all domestic violence service providers offered exactly what victims need and in ample amounts, the vast majority of domestic violence victims do not partake. Whether prevented from reaching out for assistance or unaware that such services are there for them, most victims, including the most vulnerable victims, never connect with these service providers or advocates. In general, the national crime victim surveys find only a quarter of respondents who identify themselves as victims of domestic violence report receiving assistance from victim service providers. That figure rises only a little, to 28 percent, for victims of more serious abuse. And this figure pertains only to victims who self-identify as crime victims. A review of state domestic violence fatality studies reveals how deep the chasm between victims and victim services is. In 2012, for example, according to the Washington State fatality report, only five of eighty-eight domestic violence homicide victims received services from a certified domestic violence service provider agency, ranging from a call on a hotline to emergency shelter. In Florida, a similar 2013 fatality study found that only 14 percent of homicide victims had known contact with victim support services. In New Hampshire, between 2011 and 2013, only 4 percent of homicide victims had accessed crisis center services.[8]

Calling police, not domestic violence hotlines or service providers, is one of the most commonly employed help-seeking strategies by women in abusive relationships. Accessing domestic violence services occurs much less often.[9]

But here's the bottom line, and why subsequent chapters of this book don't focus on victim services and advocacy, though they are welcome and needed. Victim services and advocacy offered to victims do not result in victims' long-term safety and escape from abuse.[10] After all, if victims were in control, they wouldn't be victims. Victim safety requires an engaged and competent criminal justice system, including law enforcement, prosecutors, judges, probation and parole officers, and corrections.

That engagement is relatively recent in American history.

PRYING OPEN
COURTHOUSE (BACK) DOORS

It wasn't until the late 1970s that state and then federal legislators began to enact laws to encourage police, prosecutors, and judges to take domestic violence seriously. While preexisting assault laws, for example, made no exception for the relationship of the parties involved, in practice they rarely were applied to intimate partners by criminal justice officials. The curtain remained shut. This began to change as advocacy pressed legislators to make it crystal clear that domestic violence was, indeed, a crime. Enactment of specific domestic violence assault and related statutes, they believed, would send a clear message that these assaults should be taken as seriously as stranger assaults and other crimes.

The advocates were tremendously successful, except when it came to marital rape. Marital rape was not even theoretically covered by existing rape statutes in all states until 1993. To this day, a little more than a dozen states still treat marital rape less severely than stranger or acquaintance rape. Nineteenth-century justices of the North Carolina Supreme Court would feel right at home in Idaho, for example. The law there holds that "No person shall be convicted of rape for any act or acts with that person's spouse, except . . . [w]here she resists but her resistance is overcome by force or violence; and [w]here she is prevented from resistance by the infliction, attempted infliction, or threatened infliction of bodily harm, accompanied by apparent power of execution; or is unable to resist due to any intoxicating, narcotic, or anaesthetic substance."[1]

Ironically, the first great wave of domestic violence legal reform to protect victims of domestic violence targeted civil, not criminal law.

PENNSYLVANIA ADVOCATES OPEN
COURTHOUSE BACK DOOR

In the 1970s, advocates were well aware that courthouse doors were shut
for victims of domestic violence, unless they were arrested for defending
themselves or retaliating against their batterers. Police were not arresting
men for battering their wives or girlfriends. In fact, at the time, police training taught officers to defuse the situation, not arrest perpetrators.

However, on another front, battered women could rely on some government intervention.

As a result of President Johnson's War on Poverty, launched in 1964 with
the passage of the Economic Opportunity Act, poor people were provided
legal services. Unlike older versions of legal aid, legal service lawyers were
also charged with advocating for reforms in statutes, regulations, and administrative practices. In the words of its first director, legal service attorneys were to "do no less for their clients than does the corporation lawyer
checking the Federal Trade Commission for sloppy rulemaking, the union
lawyer asking Congress for repeal of 14(b), or the civil rights lawyer seeking an end to segregation in bus stations." Although by the time of Richard
Nixon's election there was growing opposition to the program, President
Nixon failed in his attempt to dismantle it, and Congress continued it by
passing the Legal Services Corporation Act in 1974.

Legal service attorneys in Philadelphia found that many of the female
clients they were representing in divorce proceedings were arriving in
their offices beaten and bruised at the hands and fists of their estranged
husbands. Together with the state's half dozen women's shelters, they successfully lobbied the Pennsylvania legislature in 1976 for the creation of a
special court protective order that these women could secure from judges
to stop the beatings.

Protective orders, also commonly called restraining orders, are designed
to be simple and straightforward. A victim of abuse, which is usually defined
as physical violence and/or threats of violence that would result in an average
person being fearful, goes to court and tells her story to the judge. This is
called an *ex parte* hearing because only one side is represented at this point.
If the judge believes her evidence to be more likely than not (a civil standard
of evidence), the judge issues a temporary order, generally requiring the

respondent, the abuser, to refrain from abuse and stay away and have no contact with the victim. Other conditions may be included, but these are the most common. The temporary order goes into effect as soon as the abuser is served with the court order, usually by police. At the same time, the abuser is invited to court, where a hearing is shortly scheduled allowing the accused abuser a chance to refute the charges or the conditions of the order. If there are children involved, for example, while the abuser may agree to stay away from their mother, he may want visitation or, more likely, to contest having to pay child support since he is no longer allowed in the family home. If the judge finds for the victim, the judge issues a final order, one that is extended from a year to forever depending upon the circumstances and the state law.

Since first enacted, protective orders have become more complicated and diverse. Some are automatically imposed upon a domestic violence arrest, not initiated by victims. These are generally referred to as "criminal protective orders." They generally end when the abuser is tried or, more likely, the criminal charges are dismissed. Protective orders generally cover current or former cohabitating couples, but some do not cover current or former girl/boyfriends. Some cover physical abuse, but not stalking. In California, at present, there are eight different kinds of protective orders, including 1) domestic violence restraining orders, 2) criminal protective orders, 3) civil harassment restraining orders, 4) elder or dependent adult restraining orders, 5) juvenile orders, 6) school violence prevention orders, 7) workplace violence restraining orders, and 8) emergency protective orders. Apparently, California legislators are convinced that there is no abuse that cannot be made better with court orders. Many states also have protective orders specifically for stalking victims. Unlike domestic violence protective orders, the alleged stalkers do not have to be current or former intimate partners of the victim, although most are.

In 1976, setting an enduring and unfortunate precedent, the Pennsylvania legal and shelter advocates and the legislators who responded to their concerns all failed to appreciate the true nature of batterers. They assumed that would-be batterers would either respect the court orders or, at least, be cowed by them. In the 1976 law, there was no provision for order enforcement, or what to do if the batterer did not obey the orders. Advocates had to return to the legislature within a year to amend the law to make violation of the order a form of criminal contempt carrying a possible jail sentence. What they did not understand in 1976 has become clear since. Abusive men brought to court for civil protective orders are at as high if not higher risk to reabuse than abusive men brought to criminal court under arrest by police. The notion of "civil" abuse, after all, is oxymoronic.

Massachusetts became the second state to follow suit two years later. In its version, it made violation of a protective order a separate crime, punishable by up to two and a half years in the House of Correction, an anomalous punishment for a misdemeanor in that state (more than twice as severe as most states' misdemeanor punishments). Eventually every state in the union and the District of Columbia followed suit with its own version. State laws vary, as do the penalties for violating them. As of 2015, twenty-nine state protective order codes included provisions to extend orders to explicitly protect the victim's pets, giving the victim "exclusive care, possession, or control of any animal owned, possessed, leased, kept or held by either" party or child in the residence and prohibiting the abuser from "taking, concealing, molesting, physically injuring, killing or otherwise disposing of the animal and limiting or precluding contact . . . with the animal."[2] These laws reflect the fact that some abusers use pets as proxy victims to intimidate, punish, or harass victims. Many victims specifically remain with batterers fearful of their pet's safety if they leave.

In most states the penalty is a standard misdemeanor penalty of up to one year in the local jail. Virginia is typical. The penalty for violating a protective order without a prior violation conviction is a Class 1 Misdemeanor,[3] maximum punishable up to twelve months in jail and a fine up to $2,500, the same as that for littering.[4]

As more and more states enacted laws establishing protective orders for domestic violence, their use increased across the nation. In many states, law enforcement officers began providing information cards to domestic violence victims explaining to them how they could request protective orders from courts. While the exact number of orders issued is unknown, the Institute for Law and Justice estimates that 860,000 orders were granted in 2002 across the country.[5] In New York State, the number of orders increased from 176,000 in 2006 to more than 300,000 in 2013. In 2012, 11,137 abusers were arrested for violating orders in that state alone.[6] According to the FBI, which maintains a national registry of orders in the National Crime Information Center (NCIC), up to 700,000 final orders are entered every year.[7] However, eight states do not participate in the NCIC registry at all, and many other states have incomplete coverage. For example, in Texas, twenty-five counties do not report. In California, seventeen counties do not have a reliable procedure to enter orders into their databases.

The number of temporary restraining orders issued across the country is unknown. But breakdowns on temporary (emergency and *ex parte* orders) versus final orders are available from several states. In Connecticut, 9,390 restraining orders were issued in 2004, of which 66.5 percent were temporary and the remaining 33.5 percent were permanent. In Pennsylvania,

57,316 Protection From Abuse orders were issued in 2004, consisting of 39,997 temporary orders and 17,319 final orders. In Virginia, 84 percent of all restraining orders are emergency or temporary, 16 percent are permanent.[8] In Vermont, 34 percent of the petitions for orders requested between the spring of 2010 and spring of 2011 resulted in final orders.[9]

Based on these data, it appears that there are at least several temporary orders for every final order issued. The initial, temporary orders can last from several days to months.

PROTECTIVE ORDERS' ACHILLES' HEEL

There are two widely acknowledged Achilles' heels of protective orders: getting them served and getting them enforced.

Unserved Orders

A surprising number of orders are issued but never served. Sometimes, abusers know the orders are coming and hide out or evade service. But usually they don't have to, because the system in place to serve the orders breaks down before it gets near the abusers. The responsibility for serving orders varies. At worst, some put the onus on the victim to see that the order is served. In several of Hawaii's circuit courts, for example, the judge will issue an order, but the victim has to pick it up from the clerk's office and then find a process server and hire him or her to serve it.

Across Kentucky there is what researchers describe as a "relatively stable" nonservice rate of almost a quarter (22 percent) of all orders issued in urban areas of the state. That rate more than doubles to over half (56

LACK OF SERVICE HAS CONSEQUENCES

Sheila Nash, in Bowling Green, Kentucky, was granted a protective order after Gary Thompson threatened to burn down her apartment. He had broken into her home before. The order was unserved when he was charged with shooting and killing her on June 9, 2015.[*]

Note

[*]Highland, D., "Man Could Get Death Penalty in Domestic Shooting Case," *Bowling Green Daily News*, July 17, 2015.

percent) in the rural areas of the state. Like most other activities when it comes to the criminal justice system and domestic violence, the nonservice rates vary depending upon the competence and commitment of each county's sheriff's department charged with serving the orders. As a result, even in rural counties where service requires more effort, service rates range from as high as 78 percent to as low as 20 percent.[10]

The *Seattle Times* exposed poor service rates in that city back in 2007. Police failed to serve more than 40 percent of the orders. The story came to light because Rebecca Griego, twenty-six, had secured an order against her former boyfriend. The order, as well as an accompanying criminal complaint arising from the same domestic violence, were still not served several weeks later when he murdered her and then committed suicide. At the time, the police department had assigned only two detectives to serve orders. In fact, court clerks advise victims to take their orders to the county sheriff for more dependable service. The sheriff had thirteen deputies assigned to deliver the more than eight thousand orders it served each year back then. Presumably, the exposé in the local press prompted reform. At least, the *Times* has not raised the issue of service since. Like most criminal justice agencies, department priorities continue to ebb and flow—today's triumph is tomorrow's scandal and, fortunately, vice versa.

WRAL News investigated complaints about lack of protective order service in Durham, North Carolina, in early 2015. It found that it was impossible to know how effectively the sheriff's office was doing because neither the courts nor the sheriff's office kept any records. However, the reporters followed two weeks of orders and found that deputies served orders about 68 percent of the time in an average of six days. Officials explained that because the orders are civil, deputies do not have the legal authority to bust down doors to serve them.

The *Hartford Courant* similarly revealed in 2014 that it estimated that 40 percent of orders issued by New Haven judges between 2010 and 2011 never got served. Given that about 9,000 orders are requested, that means as many as 3,600 are not served each year. In Connecticut, marshals serve orders. After Lori Gellatly was killed by her husband in May 2014 after she had obtained an order, a legislative panel was charged to investigate order service. At its first public hearing, it heard about a long list of problems, including bureaucratic delays, communication problems, inadequate information, the method of paying state marshals, and failures by some marshals to meet required deadlines, all contributing to the high failure rate for serving restraining orders. The state only pays marshals a set fee for service: $30 and travel expenses after successful service. For that limited amount of money, marshals can't afford to make repeated attempts to service orders.

Connecticut is not alone in trying to improve its service delivery, even though jurisdictions have had decades to get their acts together. Tennessee's legislature, for example, finally amended its laws in 2014 to allow courts to fax protective orders to another county for service when the abuser does not live in the court's jurisdiction. Up until then, the orders were mailed to local law enforcement for service—not the fastest response time for a victim in immediate crisis.

Unenforced Protective Orders

Of all the domestic violence homicides in Oklahoma from 2001 to 2011, almost one in five victims had a protective order in place at the time of their death. Protective orders are particularly not very protective in much of Oklahoma. The Tulsa District Court inadvertently explains why in a brochure provided to victims seeking protective orders. It reads: "If your abuser is convicted of a Protective Order violation, he will probably be placed on probation and may be ordered to counseling at domestic violence or an alternative program." It continues: "If he violates it again, you may request his probation be revoked and that he be charged with the new violation. Abusers tend to obey the Protective Order. Only a few want to test your resolve and very few violate a second time. However, if you are not consistent with prosecution of violations, the effectiveness is reduced and you will again be in danger. A small percentage of abusers continue to ignore Protective Orders, even after convictions. The most frequent multiple violators are ex-convicts who have no fear of the system. The most serious and dangerous violator is the suicidal abuser. Alcoholics tend to obey the order but have faulty judgment when drunk and continue to violate. Occasionally an abuser ignores the order repeatedly because he believes he owns his partner and children and the system has no right to interfere. An advocate can help you decide what options remain if the Protective Order fails you."

In short, the onus is on the victim to hold the abuser accountable for repeatedly violating orders, not Tulsa's police, prosecutors, or judges. Other than place the violator on probation, Tulsa's courts have apparently absolved themselves of any responsibility for victim protection. Apparently, the brochure applies to the rest of the state as well. Not only did almost one in five victims who were murdered by their intimate partners in Oklahoma from 2001 to 2011 have a protective order at the time, but in two-thirds of those cases, the order had been violated, on average, three times, with the last violation proving lethal!

WITHOUT ENFORCEMENT, PROTECTIVE ORDERS ARE JUST PIECES OF PAPER

Leo Henry and Brandy Moreno had begun dating a couple of years earlier. They blended their respective families, her then eleven-year-old daughter and nine-year-old son, and his five-year-old son and two daughters, ages six and eight. Although Henry might have been unfaithful and made her quit her job so he could be the "man of the house," the breakup didn't occur until Moreno found out from Henry's own mother that she had witnessed Henry molesting his own daughter. Each of the girls then confirmed to Moreno that they'd been violated by Henry. Moreno went to the Oklahoma City Police Department, but to her surprise, they did not arrest Henry. Instead, the Department of Human Services removed all the children from the home.

When she learned the police said their investigation would take time, as she later told the *Oklahoman*, "My heart just about stopped. I was like, 'Oh my God, you realize what kind of situation we're going to be in?'" Henry called her repeatedly, telling her to drop the charges. She filed for and got a protective order. She regained custody of the children. She changed the locks and hoped the protective order would protect them all.

Leo Henry stabbed his ex-girlfriend, Brandy Moreno, twelve times in September 2014. The attack ended when the victim's eleven-year-old daughter shot him. He had broken into her and her children's house at 4 a.m., shattering a sliding glass door and pushing aside a dresser that had been used in an attempt to barricade the door. Moreno survived, blinded in one eye by the knife.[*]

Note

[*]Sutton, J., "Girl, 11, Shoots Man Attacking Mother in Southeast Oklahoma City," *The Oklahoman*, September 24, 2014.

Oklahoma legislators have provided that order violators can be sentenced up to a year in jail and a $1,000 fine. Subsequent violations carry a minimum of ten days in jail with maximum fines increasing to $5,000. If the protected person is caused physical injury, there is a minimum of twenty days

DAUGHTER SAVES MOTHER WHEN PROTECTIVE ORDER VIOLATED

Brandy Moreno was relatively lucky, at least in surviving the assault, thanks to her sister. Before the assault, her sister brought her a gun for protection against Henry. Brandy asked a friend how to use it. Her friend suggested she also show her eleven-year-old daughter how to use it. Brandy told her daughter that if Henry came, she should not be scared because Henry would attack her mother first. However, at the time, she was pregnant by Henry and didn't really believe Henry would hurt her. She was disabused of this belief a short time later. Although she could no longer see after being stabbed, she heard Henry promise the eleven-year-old that if she gave him the gun he would leave. The little brother called 911. The daughter fired and Henry fled the house. He was later arrested and charged with assault and battery with intent to kill, maiming, and burglary. A judge denied his bail. Henry had been shot in the face.

According to the newspaper, after the baby is born, Moreno hopes to terminate Henry's parental rights and move her family out of Oklahoma.[*]

Note

[*]Sutton, J., "Girl, 11, Shoots Man Attacking Mother in Southeast Oklahoma City," *The Oklahoman*, September 24, 2014.

in jail. However, judges have to actually impose the sentences for violators to be jailed. In the same year that Moreno was stabbed, the estranged wife of Allen Marshall Kester, forty-eight, also of Oklahoma City, got a protective order against him.[11] In the next several months, Kester was charged with violating the protective order three times and once for an additional domestic abuse crime. It turned out that his estranged wife was only one of at least seven people who had filed protective orders against Kester since the mid-1990s, according to court records. Kester was finally imprisoned, but not for the protective order violation. In the interim, he had also been arrested for a number of nondomestic violence charges, which apparently the court had more trouble ignoring than the repeat order violations.

The *Columbus Dispatch* did a four-part series on domestic violence, including a detailed look at how violations of protective orders were enforced
in Franklin County, which includes the state's capital, Columbus.[12] Generally, under Ohio law, a first violation of a protective order is a misdemeanor,
punishable by up to six months in jail and/or a fine of $1,000, except if the
violation involved the commission of a felony, then the order violation is
also a felony. A second or subsequent violation is a felony, punishable by
up to one year in jail and/or a fine of $2,500.

The paper found that about a third of the orders were violated. About
40 percent of the violations were dismissed. Not much more happened to
the rest. The paper highlighted the case of an abuser, who, after spending
a year in jail for a felony order violation, got out and violated the order
two more times. Both were charged as misdemeanors, notwithstanding
the state's enhancement statute. In fact, the paper found that in about 80
percent of the cases involving abusers with at least *five* domestic violence–
related arrests since 2000, protective order violations were prosecuted as
misdemeanors. As a result, even if judges wanted to sentence recalcitrant
violators to prison, they could not. Not that many were interested in doing
so, according to the *Dispatch*. In another example, an abuser was charged
with violating an order nine times. The victim reported she could not recall
how many times she awakened to find her abuser in her house, hovering
over her, having unplugged the phones so she could not call police. He also
punched her, beat her with an ax handle, twisted her wrist until it snapped,
and broke her nose five times. With support from advocates, she obtained
a protective order. When it expired, she got a new one. But he continued to
haunt her, taking her car so she couldn't go to work, sleeping in her garage,
threatening to crush her skull into the ground. Police arrested him nine
times, but a judge found him guilty in only four of the cases, still exposing
him to two years in jail. He spent a grand total of seventeen days in jail.
The victim, according to the newspaper, doesn't bother to call police much
anymore. She sleeps with a knife under her pillow.

On the other hand, the seventeen days were more than that spent by
another abuser also charged with nine violations. He spent no time in jail.

Some state laws reinforce lack of commitment to protecting victims with
orders. The following item was reported in the *National Bulletin on Domestic Violence Prevention* in July 2015. Headlined "Florida Considers Making
Third Violation of a Protective Order a Felony," it explained: "So let's see,
the average victim is abused repeatedly for up to a year or two before deciding to even petition for an order. She finally musters the resolve to get
an order. Then it is violated. She then learns that her abuser has neither

concern for her or what the court has ordered. Her abuser then violates the order again and she learns something else, the state legislature isn't concerned for her yet either!"[13]

PROTECTIVE ORDERS FOR SAME SEX DOMESTIC VIOLENCE

In many states, unmarried same sex victims are not eligible to receive protective orders. However, with the legalization of same sex marriages, more and more states should be following Montana's lead. In 2013, it repealed the provision in its protective order statute that a person could only get a protective order against an intimate partner "of the opposite sex." Historically, victims of abusive same sex partners have found protective orders to

ABUSER SECURES PROTECTIVE ORDER TO ACCESS VICTIM IN HIDING

Tomas and Juan (not their real names) had been dating and then living together for over a year when the latter started becoming verbally and then physically abusive. Eventually, the abuse escalated to a point where Tomas could no longer take it. He was lucky enough to get away from Juan and find his own place, the address of which he kept hidden from his abuser.

At least, Tomas thought he had escaped Juan's abuse. In retaliation for the breakup, Juan went to court and got a protective order against Tomas. Not only did this drag Tomas into court, but it also dragged him out of the safety of his own home. Tomas received phone calls from Juan prior to his court date, threatening that if Tomas went to court, Juan's cousins would be waiting for him outside, ready to inflict physical violence. This left Tomas with a terrible dilemma—come to court and face assault, even death, to clear his name, or stay at home and be legally vulnerable at the mercy of the criminal justice system.[*]

Note

[*] This material comes from a personal conversation with the author. Names and other details have been changed to protect those involved.

be a mixed blessing at best. Like police, as will be discussed in the subsequent chapter on law enforcement, judges have trouble distinguishing victims from abusers when both are male, female, or one is transgender.

For this and other reasons, the National Coalition of Anti-Violence Programs (NCAVP), which conducts surveys of its member agencies that offer services to LGBTQ survivors of violence, reported that only 17 percent of victims served applied for protective orders in 2013. However, this represented a huge increase of just over 4.9 percent the year before. The survey also found that 41.9 percent of the requests for orders were denied. This represented an improvement over 2010 when 55 percent of the requests were denied.[14]

Unlike heterosexual petitioners for protective orders, LGBTQ victims may not have domestic violence service agencies, where staff understands

ISOLATION COMPLICATES SAME SEX VICTIM ESCAPE

Rahim's abusive live-in partner Esa (names changed) took advantage of the fact that Rahim had no support system outside their relationship. No one else knew about his sexual orientation. The first major signs of Esa's abuse came out when he started stealing Rahim's pain medication and selling it for his own profit. Rahim was disabled, and the medication allowed him to get by on a daily basis. In addition to the medication, Esa stole money and Rahim's vehicle, stranding Rahim as he was not mobile without it. Fortunately, Rahim lived in a major city with LGBTQ services.

When the abuse escalated to physical violence, Rahim reached out for help to an LGBTQ-friendly organization. He was reluctant to do so because he hadn't told anyone about the abuse before, as no one knew he was gay and living with another man. Rahim's disability compounded this isolation. The fact that Rahim came from a cultural background that heavily discriminated against LGBTQ-identifying people certainly didn't help either. Still, his location provided him with services he could use to protect himself.*

Note

*This material comes from a personal conversation with the author. Names and other details have been changed to protect those involved.

their special needs, to assist them. Staff at such agencies may not be aware of the issue of "outing." Many LGBTQ victims don't report domestic violence because doing so would also mean reporting their sexual orientation, which they may not have done in many facets of their lives. People who don't identify as straight still face discrimination by service providers, employers, coworkers, and even family members and friends, let alone the entire criminal justice system, from police to judges. There is also the stigma they may face from others who identify as LGBTQ. Disclosing their status as a victim is another form of "outing" of their ex- or current partners.

Isolation is a problem for anyone dealing with domestic violence, and abusers exploit this. Rampant homophobia, biphobia, and transphobia allow abusers of LGBTQ people to manipulate their isolation on yet another level.

Not all LGBTQ victims of intimate partner violence live in a major metropolitan area with services targeted toward their needs. Even when they do, those services are numbered. Thus, other abuser tactics include co-opting the limited services for LGBTQ people, especially if victims live in more isolated or rural areas, where there are few accessible services that aim to help those who do not identify as heterosexual and/or cisgender. If the abuser gets to one of these services first, they've already locked their partner out of the one good chance they might have had to get the help they need. Navigating courts to secure protective orders and confronting abusers before the judge are both scary propositions, especially for victims under stress. Deprived of support, many victims, LGBTQ or not, will opt out.

POLICE CONDUCT COMPLIANCE CHECKS

While horror stories abound, not all law enforcement agencies abandon victims after orders are served. They realize the obvious problems in putting the onus on victims to enforce their own orders. To expect a victim to monitor the restrained abuser and then notify police of any violation are tasks many, if not most, victims are unable and ill-equipped to carry out. Many police departments, like the Pima County sheriff's department's domestic violence unit in Arizona, have taken the onus of order enforcement off the victim. Since August 2014, the domestic violence unit has conducted compliance checks. An example was captured in local media. Three sheriff's detectives make a call at night at the trailer home of a domestic violence victim. Her abuser, recently released from jail for aggravated assault and criminal damage, was not supposed to be there. The detectives are just checking. They see the suspect in the window. He either does not see them or, because they are dressed as civilians, does not believe they are cops. Covering all exits just in case, the detectives knock on the door and soon arrest the abuser. The unit's goal: "to disempower the offender." Rather than leave it to victims to police court orders, the unit takes the initiative. The Pima County sheriff's department gets four thousand domestic violence calls a year. According to the sheriff, by the time a victim calls 911 with an order violation or new abuse, someone is terrified, injured, or worse. Emotions and tensions are sky-high. The threat of more violence is always there.[15]

PROTECTIVE ORDERS CARRY POISON PILLS

Serving orders and enforcing them are the least of the problems posed by protective orders.

This first great wave of legal reforms designed to protect victims of domestic violence continues to play a tremendous role in addressing domestic violence, but not all of it positive. The civil protective orders continue to allow victims to bypass indifferent or hostile police and get at least through the back door of the courthouse to get a judge's assistance. It also allows victims to seek assistance without having their partners arrested. However, in terms of holding batterers accountable for their behavior, all it allows the judge to do, in effect, is to order the batterer not to do it again.

Women don't rush to court to ask for protective orders the first time they are struck or threatened. Most sustain multiple episodes of abuse over months or years before seeking orders. They are consequently able to testify to a litany of assaults, threats, stalking, sexual abuse, and the like. But all the judge is asked to do is sign his or her name to a piece of paper that may or, in many jurisdictions, may not be served on the abuser. And all the paper generally says is stay away from the victim, don't contact her, and don't do it again.

After almost every other court hearing, if the court has probable cause (a lower standard of evidence than is required for the court to issue a protective order) to believe such behavior had occurred, the court would charge the defendant with multiple crimes and order his immediate arrest. But inadvertently, thanks to protective order laws, instead the courts hear of the most horrendous accounts of abuse and do less than they would at a probable cause hearing for shoplifting. As a result, although the revolution begun in Pennsylvania has succeeded spectacularly in gaining victims entry into courthouses across the country, it has also shielded batterers from any accountability for their abuse.

Judges would probably howl in protest if the infamous bank robber Willie Sutton were brought before them and all they could do was issue an order instructing him to stay away from banks and refrain from robbing them.

Worse, if abusers do it again, and at least half do, they will invariably be treated as first offenders because the issuance of a civil protective order does not count as a prior criminal conviction. As described subsequently, this legal technicality combined with common police and prosecutor practices has helped to create a new class of criminal abuser defendants, "perpetual first offenders."

Ironically, even as police have transformed their response to domestic violence, mandated by law in many jurisdictions to hunt down batterers and arrest them, courts continue to provide sanctuaries for batterers, substituting civil protective orders for criminal charges and prosecutions. They miss any opportunity to hold batterers accountable for their crimes and impose greater measures to protect their victims afforded by criminal prosecution. Further, as mentioned, the use of protective orders as a primary criminal justice response to domestic violence puts the onus on the victim to act, ignoring another fundamental principle of domestic violence: If a victim's abuser were under her control, she would not be a victim!

Advocates rightly argue that one of the advantages of civil protective orders is that victims don't have to call police and get their partners arrested. Many want peace, not prosecution. If faced with having their partners arrested or doing nothing, many would choose the latter. Protective orders give them a good alternative. However, as state domestic violence fatality reports reveal, it is an alternative that most women who are eventually murdered by their intimate partners forego. The percent that had taken out orders against their subsequent murderers ranged from a low of 4 percent in New Hampshire (2011–2013), 8 percent in Oklahoma (2013), 12 percent in Utah (2003–2008), 17 percent in Florida (2013), and 20 percent in Washington to a high of only 35 percent in New Mexico (2012).[16]

Giving battered women the option to ask for a protective order in lieu of calling 911 for police assistance also carries within it another fundamental flaw with protective orders. Victims can choose to ask for orders; they can also choose to drop them, and most do. When a victim first comes to court to ask for an order, she comes alone, fills out an affidavit, and tells her story to the court. After the initial temporary order is obtained, victims can choose not to return to court and the order automatically expires, or they can return at any time and ask that the order be dropped. In fact, most victims do not request subsequent or final orders as indicated by the far greater number of temporary orders issued over final orders.

As a result, any benefits accrued by the orders are short-term, and some benefits don't kick in until final orders are issued. One of the major protective attributes of orders is a federal law prohibiting court-restrained abusers from possessing or being sold firearms. However, the federal law only takes effect with the final order, not the temporary order.

Why do so many victims drop out? Perhaps the abuser has reformed, learned his lesson, kissed and made up, and a final order is not needed. But perhaps the abuser has successfully intimidated or threatened his partner, or manipulated or beaten her into submission.

Examples of the latter are all too common.

Other victims want to believe their batterers have changed. Some may, others will not. Samuel Baker's girlfriend wrote in her affidavit requesting an order that the jailing of her former boyfriend for his last bloody assault on her had made her finally realize "that things will never change." Despite the order, he was arrested again for assaulting her, severely enough to require hospitalization. Despite a lengthy criminal record, he was released pending trial for the violation and new assault. After he promised to marry her, Baker's girlfriend returned to court and got the order dropped. She

COLLABORATING WITH ABUSERS TO DEPRIVE VICTIMS PROTECTION

Scott McAlpin was repeatedly arrested for beating and threatening his girlfriend. She took out a succession of nine protective orders against him. Although she had left him, she continued to drop orders against him. Her actions did not reflect changes of heart and reconciliation with her violent abuser. According to what law enforcement authorities later revealed to the press, when his threats got too scary, she would go back to him "so as not to stir his anger." In 2008, it ceased to work. The twenty-eight-year-old strangled her, killing her.*

Note

*"Nine Strikes and Then Out," *National Bulletin on Domestic Violence Prevention*, July 2009, 14(7), 5.

testified that she was no longer afraid, and they would shortly be moving in together. A few weeks before the trial was scheduled, Baker's father turned his son in for murdering his fiancée.[17]

The failure of the criminal justice system to take actions against abusers, including those specifically brought to their attention by victims in sworn court affidavits, leaves victims particularly defenseless when their abusers succeed in getting them to withdraw or not extend protective orders.

WHEN PROTECTIVE ORDERS ARE OBVIOUSLY INSUFFICIENT

For months, Michael Robles, forty-three, relentlessly harassed and stalked his former girlfriend after she broke up after eight years of an on and off again relationship. It got worse after she began dating again. Robles escalated his abuse by increasing his stalking, hiding in the bushes outside the apartment she shared with her thirteen-year-old daughter. Although his ex-girlfriend revealed this history and all the danger signs and red flags it included, the judge did nothing more than issue a temporary order. A week later, just before midnight on the eve of Thanksgiving 2011, Robles crept inside her home to lie in wait. Early that morning, the day of his former girlfriend's thirty-fourth birthday, he strangled her while her daughter slept upstairs. Her body was later buried in a shallow grave. Although he never admitted guilt, Robles led investigators to her body; he hanged himself in his jail cell four months later.*

Another Example of Judicial Learned Helplessness

Michael Hart, forty-one, had five protective orders taken out against him by four different women in Pierce County (Tacoma), Washington, between 2000 and December 2014. All had dated him and testified he had threatened to kill them and harm their families. Of the first three orders granted, two were never served. Hart was only charged with a crime in connection with the abuse related to one of the petitions. In 2008, he was convicted of felony harassment. In that case, the victim showed police a news report she had found about him stalking another girlfriend and her family in London. Hart had sent the former girlfriend 166 texts and forty voice messages in five days, including one that threatened: "You're dead. Leave your work now and go somewhere safe where I can't find you."

The fourth petition for a protective order was filed in 2013 by a woman who shared a child with Hart. She reported that he had abused her and threatened to kill her and burn down her parents' house while they were inside. He also had sent lewd photos and videos to her family and her work. Hart contested that petition, writing the court that the woman was manipulating the court to keep him away from his child. Nevertheless, the court granted that protection order and made Hart complete a domestic violence treatment program. No criminal charges were lodged against him.

Less than a year later, a new girlfriend reported being beaten up by Hart. The next day, police were at her home to investigate her allegations when they saw Hart drive by and requested him to stop. He didn't, and a high-speed chase ensued. He allegedly had a police scanner in his car that probably allowed him to avoid spikes other officers placed in the roadways to stop him. The car's rear license plate frame also had a profane insult to police, according to a report in the *News Tribune*. Police finally caught him and charged him with assault, resisting arrest, and attempting to elude police. The woman whose report prompted the chase filed for a protection order the next day. This one, the fifth filed against him, was also granted.[†]

Notes

[*]Figueroa, T., and Sifuentes, E., "Suspect in Schabarth Slaying Found Dead," *North County Times*, March 4, 2012.

[†]Krell, A., "5 Requests for Restraining Orders against Man Accused of Fleeing Police," *News Tribune*, Tacoma, WA, January 5, 2015.

Hart was able to terrorize intimates for fourteen years straight because apparently it never occurred to the judges that persistent, seemingly pathological stalkers such as Hart, who had repeatedly violated the law for months, even years, might not be deterred by pieces of paper, even with a genuine judge's signature. It apparently did not occur to any of the judges involved that the abuser be arrested for the many crimes he had committed, which the judges had found *on the preponderance of the evidence*. Nor did any judge alert the police or prosecutors to investigate further what could be done to stop these criminal campaigns by such an abuser.

In so many cases, the judge has to be a dewy-eyed optimist indeed to believe the abusers before him will be deterred by an order of protection. Yet few take any action beyond signing the orders.

IGNORING SEXUAL PREDATORS

Perhaps the most egregious example of how the protective order reform prying open courthouse doors for domestic violence victims also provides batterers "get out of jail free" cards is found across the state of New York. In 2008, that state expanded its protective order laws to allow teens to secure orders of protection for dating violence even if they did not have a child in common with their abuser. A few years later, researchers looked at all the orders requested by teens for dating violence across the state in 2009 and 2010.

In these first two full years after the law's expansion, New York teens requested 1,200 orders of protection for dating violence. In an overlooked appendix of the study, researchers noted a small subgroup of fifty-four abusers brought to court by their female teenaged victims. Unlike most of the other petitions, these teens specifically alleged sexual abuse as the reason for the petition. Their alleged abusers were also older, a quarter of them five years or more. They also had much more extensive prior criminal histories than the other alleged abusers, averaging more than five prior sets of criminal charges as opposed to a little less than two for the others. More startling, all their prior criminal histories included sex offenses. All this led the researchers to suggest that "this subgroup of respondents (abusers) may more accurately be characterized as 'sexual predators,' not dating violence perpetrators."[18]

The good news: Two of these abusers brought to court by their teen victims were also arrested for sex offenses. The first, who had a prior record for sexual misconduct, was arrested again for the same offense. The second, who had a prior record for rape, was arrested for failure to register as a sex offender. But the rest? The New York judges ordered them to refrain from further abuse and stay away from their teen victims.

In what other court forum would fifty-two sexual predators with under-age victims (!) be brought to the attention of the court and be so totally ignored? What kind of responsible adult, much less one trained in the law and sworn to uphold it, could believe, on the preponderance of the evidence, that these young girls were sexually abused and not direct the court bailiff to escort the alleged abusers to the holding cells below the courtroom, or issue a warrant for their arrest if it was an *ex parte* hearing, or at least call for the police or prosecutor to investigate? One would expect more from a Good Samaritan, much less a judge.

It is not veniality on the part of the judges that makes for this behavior. They suffer from learned helplessness. The civil nature of protective orders makes them blind to consideration of the crimes being alleged and the criminals they are being alleged against. As a result, the judges become accomplices, inadvertent collaborators with abusive criminals, even sexual predators of children. The chasm between civil and criminal has even led judges to ignore information they need to do their job. After a court-restrained abuser murdered his partner in Massachusetts, investigators found out that the judge who had issued the protective order against him did not look at the abuser's criminal record. If the judge had, he would have seen that there was an outstanding warrant for his arrest for a prior domestic assault against another victim issued from that very same courthouse!

Alabama legislatures have enacted legislation to bridge the gap between civil and criminal law when it comes to protective orders. Unfortunately, their actions do nothing to protect the most vulnerable victims, including victims like Kelley Rutledge-Johnson, who inspired the legislation. In 2000, she was murdered by her estranged husband. At the time, she had a protective order against him. He subsequently pled guilty and was imprisoned, but the plea deal made him eligible for parole after a little more than a decade. The victim's brother-in-law and others successfully convinced the legislature, after twelve years of campaigning, to make murdering someone with a protective order a capital offense, requiring either the death sentence or imprisonment for life. While the new law is too late to change Kelley's murderer's sentence, it will apply to the next convicted court-restrained abuser who murders his victim in Alabama. One legislator who voted against the law argued, "If someone is dangerous enough to need a (protective order), we need to have additional steps for protection and safety that need to be available before the crime ever happens."[19]

The violation rate of protective orders is, not surprisingly, consistently high, from a third to two-thirds.[20] It would no doubt be much higher, but most orders only last several weeks or months, giving even the most active abusers little time to violate them![21]

But abusers are not the only ones who ignore civil protective orders. So do judges.

IGNORING PROTECTIVE ORDERS

Judges in criminal sessions routinely ignore civil protective order histories, resulting in preventable fatalities. Some judges sitting in criminal sessions may not have access to civil court files, while others don't think they are relevant. Two judges in Albuquerque, New Mexico, for example, allowed Ralph Montoya, thirty-seven, to remain free on bond after he was arrested on charges of kidnapping, aggravated battery, and aggravated assault after allegedly forcing his way into the home of his ex-girlfriend's current boyfriend, a popular University of New Mexico professor, and assaulting the couple. His bond was set at $100,000 cash or surety in an arrest warrant signed by a district court judge. Montoya posted bond and was released the next day. The next month, he appeared before another judge who let him remain free. Six days later, he murdered the ex-girlfriend, who was a high school teacher, and the professor.

A subsequent investigation found that all the judges had before them in making their decision was a record of a conviction fifteen years earlier for attempted arson and breaking and entering. Without looking at the defendant's civil file, they did not understand that those crimes stemmed from his stalking, threatening, intimidating, and burning the car of a former girlfriend who had taken out two protective orders against him. The judges were also not aware that since then, another woman had taken out an order against Montoya for stalking her. He had, according to the affidavit in the court file, called her fifteen to twenty times a day, pretending to be her father to get her to take his calls at her work.

A gubernatorial domestic violence advisor at the time admitted to the *Albuquerque Journal* that "[i]n most courtrooms in New Mexico, the likelihood is that the judge wouldn't have all the information in front of them with someone who has a history of domestic violence." She added, "We need to do a better job of making everyone within the system aware of what they're dealing with."[22]

Most state legislatures have enacted statutes requiring enhanced sentences for repeat abuse. However, the statutes require prior convictions, not prior abuse, even if that abuse was adjudicated by a judge who then issued a protective order against the defendant.

4

MAKING DOMESTIC VIOLENCE A REAL CRIME

Creation of domestic violence protective orders was only the beginning. State legislatures and eventually Congress moved on, adding an avalanche of new domestic violence–related laws. Much of the new legislation was influenced or adopted from the Model Code developed by the National Council of Juvenile and Family Court Judges, funded by the Hilton Foundation. The Model Code incorporated the best of what individual states had already pioneered and added what an array of progressive practitioners, advocates, and feminists advised.[1] When unveiled in 1994, the Model Code not only represented a consensus on the best legislation relative to domestic violence but also a state-of-the-art policy framework for best court practices and the ideal community response, or at least what was believed to be best back then. The Model Code has been frequently cited as the nation's seminal legislative policy document on the subject. At least large chunks of the Model Code have been enacted in every state of the union.

The Model Code calls for aggressive criminal justice intervention, beginning with arresting perpetrators regardless of victim desires. It calls for arrest "based solely on probable cause, and the decision may not be informed by extraneous, extralegal factors."

The Code defines the crime of domestic violence as the occurrence of one or more of the following acts, not including acts of self-defense: a) attempting to cause or causing physical harm to another family or household member, b) placing that member in fear of physical harm, or c) causing a member to engage involuntarily in sexual activity by force, threat of force, or duress. Family and household members included adults or minors who are current or former spouses, persons who live or lived together, persons who are dating or dated, persons who are engaging in or have engaged in sexual relations, persons who have a child in common, as well as other family members including relatives. The Code recognizes that violence does not end when the formal relationship, including marriage, ends. It also recognizes that domestic violence includes assaultive and non-assaultive conduct that includes injury that "might not typically be identified as a medical injury." In terms of relationships, the Code does not require cohabitation and recognizes that the relationship does not have to be current. The Code calls for enhanced penalties for second or subsequent crimes involving domestic violence. It does not create a new crime of "domestic violence," but provides a list of crimes that may be included depending upon the parties involved.

It spells out duties of police officers responding to allegations of domestic violence. It requires police to use all reasonable means to protect the victim and prevent further violence, including confiscating weapons, assisting the victim and any child in obtaining medical treatment and safety, and providing victims with notice of their rights. These rights include asking the prosecutor to file a criminal complaint and securing a protective order.

It offers two alternatives regarding arrest. The first reads that if police have probable cause to believe a person has committed a crime, whether they saw it or not, and whether a misdemeanor or felony, the officer "should presume that arresting and charging the person is the appropriate response." If the officer receives conflicting claims, the officer is supposed to determine the primary aggressor. Officers should not make the determination of arrest based on the victim's consent, and the officer should be required to write up a report justifying his decision if no one or multiple parties are arrested. The second option provides for mandatory arrest upon probable cause. In addition, mandatory arrest is called for in violations of protective orders. The Code also provides police with broad authority to seize weapons from suspected abusers.

Addressing pretrial release, the Code requires the court or party charged with determining pretrial release to make a finding regarding the danger of the suspect and then fashion conditions of release to mitigate that danger. Those conditions are then to be communicated to law enforcement and the victim. If any of the prerelease conditions are violated, arrest is mandatory. The Code did not include mandatory detention pending arraignment or for a designated cooling-off period.

Next, the Code addresses prosecutors, beginning with a requirement that each prosecutor's office develop or adopt written procedures for attorneys prosecuting domestic violence to advance effective prosecution and protection of the victim. While it is not possible to require prosecutors to prosecute every domestic violence arrest because the legal standards for arrest (probable cause) are far lower than those for conviction (beyond a reasonable doubt), the Code substitutes other duties, including that prosecutors must notify victims if they decline prosecution or enter into a plea agreement with the suspect. If the prosecutor dismisses domestic violence charges, the reasons must be reduced to writing and placed in the court file. In an accompanying commentary, the Code pleads with prosecutors not to dismiss cases "as a matter of course" when a victim, even under subpoena, fails to appear in court. The prosecutor is advised to ascertain the basis for the victim's absence, as it may be due to coercive conduct by the defendant.

Judges are prohibited from dismissing domestic violence cases for the sole reason that a civil compromise or settlement is reached. Victims are also given the right to provide the court with a victim impact statement as well as attend the court sessions. Spousal privilege is barred. Judges are barred from confining abusers in the homes of the victims. Diversion is also barred, but judges can defer sentencing. In such cases, the defendant pleads or is found guilty, but the guilty finding, much less a sentence, are not immediately imposed, giving the defendant a chance to complete conditions imposed by the court. Upon successful completion, the court dismisses the case.

The Code also addresses probation. Probationary sentences are to be imposed only after the court finds it safe to do so. Conditions to be mandated are the same as available in protective orders, including no contact and stay away orders. The Code also calls for a perpetrator to participate in and complete, to the satisfaction of the court, a program of intervention for perpetrators, treatment for alcohol or substance abuse, or mental health treatment. Probation is required to enforce the conditions and immediately report back to the court and victims if they are violated. Similar conditions are set for paroling agents.

Probationary sentences are generally in lieu of jail, handed down by judges, and parole generally applies to time cut short from a defendant's jail sentence, granted by parole boards or other paroling authorities.

Jails are directed to establish programs for education and counseling of incarcerated abusers.

The Model Code also addresses civil orders of protection, issues pertaining to family, child custody, and visitation where domestic violence is involved, as well as domestic violence treatment and prevention. The latter calls for training of the various criminal justice officials, including police, prosecutors, judges, and probation officers as well as attorneys.

In the first year after its release, forty-one states added new domestic violence laws to their books. These included introduction of a new crime, stalking; creation of state registries for protective orders; mandated training for police officers; establishment of custody presumptions; development of domestic violence fatality reviews; and more. That same year, 1994, Congress enacted the Violence Against Women Act (VAWA).

And the new laws have kept coming since.

In 2013, as in every year since 1995, almost every state continued to enact new or amend existing domestic violence laws, many still harkening back to the recommendations in the Model Code. The new laws demonstrate that some states have come farther than others. New Jersey finally got around to barring abusers charged with domestic violence in its municipal courts from being diverted. Iowa enacted a law barring judges from diverting domestic violence offenses a *second* time! Georgia just got around to requiring courts and guardian *ad litems* to consider evidence of domestic violence in determining the best interests of a child. Kansas mandated that defendants convicted of domestic violence undergo an assessment for a batterer intervention program. Mississippi expanded the definition of simple domestic violence to include negligently causing injury or physically menacing to put another in fear of imminent or serious bodily injury. North Carolina finally came into compliance with the federal Violence Against Women Act enacted in 1994 and amended its protective order statute to prohibit courts from charging victims seeking orders. Oklahoma prohibited courts from imposing terms or conditions in protective orders that compromise victim safety! These include ordering couples counseling, mediation, parenting classes, or victim-offender counseling sessions. And Oklahoma judges were also given allowance to consider victim safety in setting bond for protective order violations.

Other states continued to chart new ground. Michigan, for example, authorized courts to require abusers to wear electronic monitoring devices. Colorado declared domestic abuse not only to be limited to physical threats of violence and harm but also to include mental and emotional abuse, financial control, document control, and property control. It also made domestic violence defendants ineligible for diversion programs with limited exceptions.

Twenty-three states were still fiddling with their protective order laws. The most significant trend was expanding the conditions judges could impose, including terms aimed at supporting a family's separation from an abuser. Colorado, for example, authorized judges to stop abusers from halting rent, mortgage, utility, transportation, insurance, and child care payments or disposing of property to diminish support payments, all tactics commonly employed by abusers. California lawmakers added conditions that forbid court-restrained abusers from changing beneficiaries of insurance policies. New York and Vermont added the return of passports, health insurance cards, and the like to victims.

A number of states specifically included stalking as abuse, qualifying a victim to obtain a protective order. Others added prohibition of stalking as a condition of an order. California authorized judges to bar an abuser from engaging in false impersonation. Four states allowed judges to add animal protection to orders. As other states have already done, Utah authorized orders for dating violence, but only for parties eighteen years and over.

As abusers often justify no contact or stay away violations by claiming that their victims invited them, which is sometimes true, New York required that all orders state that the protected party (victim) cannot consent to contact with the subject and is not subject to arrest for violating the order. Other states addressed penalties for violations. South Dakota made it a felony if the abuser violates an order by stalking the victim. Texas enhanced penalties for repeat violations.

Ten states passed stalking statutes outside of protective orders. Washington expanded what counts as a stalking felony and created pretrial conditions for accused stalkers. Virginia made repeat stalking a felony, and made intentional deceptive use of electronic tracking a stalking crime. Arkansas added strangulation to its aggravated assault statute and stalking as a misdemeanor.

A bunch of states tried to fashion more specific legislation to limit judges' discretion in deciding custody and visitation when domestic violence is involved. Hawaii passed a law to establish qualifications for child custody evaluators and for filing complaints against them for doing poor jobs. The intent no doubt was to stop judges from hiring underemployed attorneys they like and making them custody evaluators, a common practice across the country.

Many expanded firearms prohibitions for abusers. In addition, Connecticut created a new form that allows victims to indicate whether or not the abuser has a firearm. Obviously the courts could have created their own form to assist judges in determining whether gun prohibitions were in order, but they hadn't so the legislature mandated it. New York required sentencing judges to demand the surrender of firearms and firearm licenses if they determine there is a danger the firearm will be used against a party covered by the order. Further, and importantly, New York mandated that gun owners who live with someone prohibited from possessing firearms keep their firearms locked up away from the prohibited party. Colorado made it a crime for a prohibited party to attempt to purchase a firearm or failure to surrender one. The former is important because it is relatively easy for prohibited parties to buy firearms given the many loopholes created by Congress in current national procedures designed to prevent such purchases.

On the other hand, three states made things worse for victims, lowering the barriers for gun ownership for abusers. Texas lifted the bar on obtaining a gun license for persons with a domestic violence deferred prosecution that is more than ten years old. North Dakota eliminated the requirement that an application for a firearm license provide documentation of incidents of domestic violence in order to pass a background check. In a dubious move, Oklahoma decided to allow domestic violence victims who have protective orders to obtain, at no cost, six-month temporary firearm licenses. Given the case that spurred this legislation (Leo Henry stabbing Brandy Moreno, shot by the latter's daughter, as described in chapter 3), it is surprising these solons did not mandate all eleven-year-old daughters be armed.

California regressed, repealing mandatory provisions that police have written policies and standards for an officer's responses to domestic violence and making them discretionary. And South Carolina required police to use uniform traffic-like tickets for select domestic violence offenses so that they could be disposed of by court magistrates and not bother judges.[2]

5

ENCOURAGING DOMESTIC VIOLENCE ARRESTS

Even the best, most well-intentioned laws are not self-enforcing. It is easier to enact laws than see them enforced. When it comes to domestic violence criminalization, the laws must be implemented by police, prosecutors, judges, attorneys, and probation officers to work. With scattered exceptions, thanks to advocates and enlightened legislatures, the necessary laws to protect victims of domestic violence and hold their abusers accountable are on the books. What is mostly lacking is a commitment and the competence of criminal justice practitioners to implement them.

SPURRING ON POLICE TO ARREST ABUSERS

Up until the 1970s, police were explicitly trained to avoid arresting perpetrators of intimate partner violence, keeping that curtain drawn tight. Lieutenant Howard Black of the Colorado Springs Police Department began his law enforcement career in 1978. Since then, he has become a leader in fashioning effective domestic violence policing. Asked about the reforms since 1978, he describes that "when I first became a cop thirty-five years ago, I was told to get in and get out of those houses as a new recruit—this is not our business."[1] The police response back then was based on two widely believed propositions, notwithstanding the fact that they were, on their face, mutually exclusive. First, domestic violence calls were the most dangerous calls police faced, and second, domestic violence did not constitute a serious crime worthy of police intervention. (While traffic accidents account for more police deaths than domestic violence, between 1996 and 2009, 106 police officers were killed responding to domestic violence incidents, most when approaching the scene and almost all, 97 percent, with firearms.[2])

There were also legal barriers that police faced. Historically, given our revolutionary origins, states have been reluctant to grant police too much power, fearful of its arbitrary exercise. Our founding fathers did not want to give police too much unbridled authority over citizens. They wanted an impartial non-police magistrate to intervene to grant police arrest authority on a case by case basis. They made exception for the more serious crimes like felonies. Requiring police to obtain warrants to arrest misdemeanants proved to be of little inconvenience because most misdemeanor arrests were the result of activities police were able to witness in person.

Take the crime of drunk driving, for example. Police see the drunk driver in action before arresting him or her. Or disorderly conduct: Police witness the culprit yelling and disturbing the peace of third parties who have a legitimate expectation of tranquility and quiet before police make a disorderly conduct arrest.

As result, American police historically did not have the legal authority to arrest most persons accused of domestic violence because their purported crimes, most often classified as misdemeanors, occurred behind closed doors before police arrived. To arrest these suspected abusers, police had to go before a neutral magistrate and obtain a warrant, which the magistrate would only issue upon a finding of probable cause that the suspect had committed the crime. In contrast, alerted by a terrified bank teller that the bank had just been robbed, police could arrest the suspect robber even if they did not personally witness the robbery because bank robbery is a felony. However, alerted by a terrified wife or girlfriend, police could not arrest the suspected batterer unless they had been alerted in time to witness the assault, as the average "simple" domestic assault is generally classified as a misdemeanor.

Generally, by the time officers arrive at the scene of a domestic violence incident, the actual crime is over. If anything, upon arrival the only crime they may be in time to witness is a hysterical victim striking out at her abuser or the responding police officers. In fact, when victims are arrested, it is generally for disorderly conduct, for not being well-behaved victims. In Connecticut, for example, where police typically arrest both domestic violence victims and perpetrators in almost half of all incidents, the couples are arrested for disorderly conduct and breach of the peace!

When the majority of domestic violence incident reports in a state are *not* identified as assaults, it is evident that police and prosecutors are either intentionally or incompetently misunderstanding the nature and reality of domestic violence. Fortunately, Connecticut and only a handful of states like Wisconsin represent such outliers.

Through most of the 1980s, police just weren't arresting for domestic violence even if the crime constituted a felony. As late as 1989, for example, D.C. police were not arresting in more than 85 percent of the incidents where the victim was found bleeding from her wound.[3] All of that changed dramatically by the 1990s. In 1988, for example, California police arrested 32,000 persons for its basic domestic assault statute covering spouses and cohabitants. That more than doubled by 1997. The same held true in most jurisdictions around the country. Not only were more people being arrested for domestic violence, but the rate of such arrests rose too. Denver police, for example, only arrested 20 percent of persons brought to their attention for violating protective orders in the 1980s. That rose to 87 percent by the end of that decade.

Increased arrests were the result of several different factors: reforming arrest laws, lawsuits, arrest research, and victim advocacy. The factors fed on each other, providing an insurmountable momentum by the end of the twentieth century, a momentum that has since petered out in many states and localities.

ALLOWING POLICE TO ARREST IN UNWITNESSED CRIMES

With Indiana joining the rest of the country in 2000, every state in the union now authorizes warrantless arrest for misdemeanor domestic violence based on probable cause. At least twenty-one states and the District of Columbia go further and mandate it. In addition, thirty-one states mandate arrest for violations of protective orders. These legal reforms were critical because most abusers commit their crimes behind closed doors and drawn curtains. In Kansas, which tracks these data, in 2013, for example, police responded to 23,508 domestic violence incidents. A little more than 54.18 percent occurred in a single family home, with another 15.83 percent in multi-unit dwellings (apartments). Less than 10 percent occurred in public (streets). Most occurred on weekends and in the wee hours of the morning.[4]

However, this explains why police still make so many domestic violence disorderly arrests; unlike the preceding domestic assault, disorderly conduct is committed in their presence, providing an open and shut charge. Because they witnessed the crime themselves, the charge requires no more investigation or effort on the officer's part. Thinking ahead too, the prosecution will not have to rely on one of the parties to testify in court. Returning to Kansas, for example, in 2013, of the 23,508 incidents, police coded about 17,000 as domestic assaults (and/or batteries as Kansas breaks down the offense) and a little over a thousand for "disorderly conduct" or "disorderly conduct, offensive language, noisy conduct."

So to get police to arrest domestic violence perpetrators, state legislatures had two options. Make domestic assaults and other common related criminal behavior a felony or amend the laws to allow police to arrest for domestic violence offenses without warrants even for crimes classified as misdemeanors. Unfortunately, they uniformly opted for the weaker alternative, leaving most crimes against intimate partners as less serious, misdemeanor offenses.

Giving law enforcement the authority to arrest abusers for unwitnessed misdemeanor crimes was only the first step. It took lawsuits to convince many departments to exercise their new powers.

SUING POLICE TO PROTECT VICTIMS

A succession of lawsuits against police for the failure to arrest abusers followed. One of the more infamous cases arose in Connecticut in 1983 when Torrington police not only refused to arrest Charles "Buck" Thurman for repeatedly assaulting his wife, but watched him assault her, including kicking her on the head and breaking her neck, crippling her for life. The crippling assault followed multiple notifications to police of repeated violations of a protective order his estranged wife, Tracey Thurman, had taken out against him, which they also did nothing to enforce.

Police finally arrested Thurman only when he approached her as she was being led away in a stretcher by medics. Tracey Thurman subsequently sued the City of Torrington for the police conduct. The U.S. District Court allowed the suit to go forward even though police generally have discretion when it comes to decisions to arrest or not. The court ruled the police did not have discretion to discriminate against any class of citizens, including battered women. Harkening back to the North Carolina Supreme Court in 1874, the court admonished the City that any notion of a husband's prerogative to discipline his wife was an "outdated misconception." The court, however, felt compelled to discuss whether it was best to close the curtain and save the marriage. It pointed out that police inaction could not promote "domestic harmony" because Tracey Thurman had no desire to stay with her husband. While the City could not be held responsible for every action of a police officer in its employ, the number of different officers involved over the eight months of Charles's campaign of terror against Tracey showed the police response to constitute an official department policy. Although the court cited an article indicating that noninterference was at the time found in at least thirty other police departments, it concluded that the failure of this police department to perform its duty to protect all its citizens constituted a denial of equal protection of the laws.[5]

Eventually the City settled with Tracey Thurman and paid out $2.3 million. Charles was convicted of the assault and imprisoned. The Connecticut legislature, equally concerned for victims of domestic violence and the costs of future judgments against its cities and towns, enacted a mandatory domestic violence arrest law, removing any discretion from police. The state's police chiefs supported the legislation because, they argued, it took their towns and cities off the hook from future suits as a result of poor judgment or biases of officers. Unfortunately, to this day, many of the state's police officers continue to interpret the law as a mandate to arrest all parties, victims as well as offenders, just to make sure. Subsequently, the legislature amended the law by adding that victims defending themselves should not be arrested. However, Connecticut still leads the nation in mutual arrests, increasingly rare elsewhere.

There is a postscript to the Charles "Buck" Thurman story. Sixteen years later, nine years after he was released from a Connecticut prison, Thurman was convicted of violating another protective order, this time in Massachusetts. The order was taken out by the mother of their six-year-old son. In applying for the order, Thurman's latest victim wrote that Thurman began abusing her in January 1993, forcing her to have sex. On September 15, 1998, she wrote, "Thurman choked me in the presence of our son and proceeded to threaten my life if I should ever leave."' The woman fled to Florida after the assault and sought the protective order when she later returned to Massachusetts. The order barred any contact with the victim, while mandating $85 a week in child support and supervised visitation with the son for two hours every other Saturday at an area YWCA.

The violation, according to the police report, was Thurman pulling alongside the victim and her son in his car when she was at a stoplight and honking his horn at them. The court released Thurman after he was charged because the judge at arraignment said that although he believed Thurman to be dangerous, he also believed the meeting was by chance.

At trial, the prosecutor asked that Thurman be imprisoned for two years for violation of the order, with six months suspended after that so he would be released on probation, calling the violation a "re-initiation of an abusive situation." The defense counsel argued that Thurman had paid his debt to society, the order violation was technical only as his client was simply waving at his son. The judge found Thurman guilty and put him on probation for a year.

A local advocate questioned: "If Charles Thurman can be simply put on probation for violating a restraining order, what does that say to other batterers? I think the community should be outraged, but they should also be scared, because he's wandering around in our area." Thurman's lawyer declared that his client was sorry for his prior abuse, quoting his client as telling him, "Nobody will ever know how much pain that causes me, what I did when I was a kid seventeen years ago." According to a press report, while Thurman goes to work every day in Massachusetts, Ms. Motuzick (Tracey Thurman remarried) in Connecticut struggles just to get out of bed in the morning and had recently developed problems with her vocal cords that doctors believe stem from Thurman's attack. The right side of her body is partially paralyzed and she can't lift her right hand above her head. "The everyday things that you took for granted before—you know, blow-drying your hair—I can't do that anymore."[6]

Suits against police for their inaction did not end with *Thurman v. Torrington*. In 2002, for example, history repeated itself in Sonoma County, California. This time, the county sheriff and district attorney were sued for their failure to respond to repeated protective order violations and stalking.

CALIFORNIA COUNTY AND SHERIFF SUED FOR IGNORING ORDER VIOLATIONS

Avelino Macias's estranged wife, according to the wife's family, had called the sheriff for help more than twenty-two times. The wife could not testify in the suit because Avelino had followed her to the house where she was employed to clean and shot and killed her, injured her mother who was also there, and then shot and killed himself. At the murder scene, officers found two notebooks recording all of the abuse the victim had suffered. Previously, a deputy had advised her to keep a log of the abuse, even though the deputy refused to arrest the husband. The officers also found tapes of threatening phone calls from him that she had recorded.

According to the sheriff, although his deputies never arrested Avelino despite such evidence, his office had asked the district attorney on three separate occasions to prosecute Avelino, but the prosecutor had refused. The victims' family sued the county. The federal district court threw the suit out, ruling that the state had no duty to protect Mrs. Macias. On appeal, the 9th Circuit Court overturned the district court, ruling that the issue was not duty to protect, but equal protection. Mrs. Macias, it ruled, had a constitutional right to have the same police services as everyone else. Whether or not she had been discriminated against was the issue. The case was returned to the district court to decide. On the second day of the trial, the county caved and agreed to pay $1 million to the family as long as the county did not have to admit either negligence or wrongdoing. The family took the money to support Mrs. Macias's three children.[*]

Note

[*]*Estate of Macias v. Ihde*, 219 F.3d 1018 (9th Cir. 2000).

In 2013, the supreme court of the State of Washington upheld a jury award of $1.1 million against the City of Federal Way for a police officer's failure to protect Baervel Roznowski.[7]

WASHINGTON CITY SUED

Ms. Roznowski had gone to court and gotten an anti-harassment order against Chan Kim. The order issued by the judge included a specific warning that Kim would probably react violently once he understood the order. It also ordered Kim to stay five hundred feet from Roznowski's home. Police, notwithstanding the written warning and the order itself, served the order on Kim in the presence of Roznowski in her home and then left the premises. A few hours later, Kim stabbed Roznowski eighteen times, killing her. A jury found in favor of the victim's daughters. The City appealed.[*]

Note

[*]Pulkkinen, L., "Supreme Court Faults Police for Failing to Protect Murdered Federal Way Woman from Abuser," *Seattle Post Intelligencer*, October 17, 2013.

Sadly, lawsuits against police continue even in Connecticut, demonstrating how some battles are never won permanently. Getting police and the rest of the criminal justice system to take domestic violence seriously is unfortunately one of those battles.

CONNECTICUT POLICE CONTINUE TO SHOCK THE CONSCIENCE

The City of Waterford, Connecticut, settled such a case against it in 2011, which had begun in 2007, two and a half decades after *Torrington*.

ANOTHER CONNECTICUT CITY SUED

Carrie Arteaga sued the Waterford, Connecticut, police department for its failure to protect her from her abusive ex-husband.* The suit gained traction when a superior court judge ruled that the Waterford police officers' responses to the escalating violence against her by her ex-husband were "so egregious that they shocked the conscience." The judge scheduled the trial for the next year. Arteaga charged that police failed to protect her from the chronic abuse she suffered after divorcing her husband (whom she had married as a pregnant teen) that culminated in a life-threatening and crippling attack in 2004. In that attack, the ex-husband, Michael, dove through a locked window into her house and attacked her and a male friend with two butcher knives. Police were able to intervene before anyone was killed, but Michael stabbed the male friend twenty times and Carrie twice.

It was the failure of police to prevent that attack that prompted the suit, because they had had years of opportunities. The month before, the ex-husband had broken into Carrie's house and stood over her while she slept. Although he disabled her phone, she was able to call 911 from a secret phone she had had installed. Michael fled the house, and police searched for him through the night to no avail. However, when she left her house a few hours later with her children, he showed up and forced them into a car. He told her to drive to a wooded area, but she drove to a gas station instead and leaned on the horn. He fled again. She called police again and told them where Michael was, but they went to her home instead and berated her for getting into his car. Finally a concerned neighbor came over and told the police to stop harassing her. Although the police officers assured Carrie they would get a warrant for Michael's arrest, they didn't bother.

Two days later, Michael struck again, forcing their eight-year-old daughter into his car, driving around for hours while threatening to kill her and then himself. Finally, he released her.

And these were just a few of the most recent incidents. The very first time Carrie called police, after serving Michael with divorce papers, the responding police officer ordered her to stay in the house even though Michael was threatening her. Finally, a sergeant arrived and told her she could leave but had to stay in Connecticut. In the months that followed, Michael pushed her down the stairs during a custody exchange, breaking a rib. She told her children to call the police, but Michael told the children he would break their fingers if they did.

Carrie also faulted the police for bringing her ex-husband to her house twice, supposedly to get his belongings nearly a year after their divorce was finalized and months after he had released any claim to the home. Police also did not arrest Michael when he entered Carrie's house to call the daughter, in violation of a protective order, because they chose to believe the father over the daughter who reported the violation.

Police also, according to Carrie, failed to tell her ex-husband's federal probation officer about his behavior. Since he was on probation for federal drug convictions, the federal courts could have imprisoned Michael for his abuse because it constituted a violation of his federal probation.

In short, Carrie charged that the police were on Michael's side from the moment she first called 911 in January 2003. Carrie further alleged that the police also failed her ex-husband, because, if he had been punished adequately for previous crimes against her, he would have had an opportunity to "cool his jets." Michael was sentenced to twelve years in prison as a result of the 2004 attack. After the state sentence, he will serve another thirty-three months for violation of probation for his federal offenses.

At the time of the 2004 attack, Michael had at least two outstanding warrants for his arrest. Overall, Michael Arteaga had been arrested at least three times in the period between the divorce and the stabbing, but was released on bail each time.

Note

Carrie Arteaga v. Town of Waterford et al., No. HHD X07 CV 5014477S (March 16, 2010).

The case, *Carrie Arteaga v. Town of Waterford et al.*, went further than most such lawsuits against municipalities (judges usually dismiss lawsuits against municipalities and police who work for them, deeming them "immune" from such civil actions). The lawsuit initially named individual police officers, including the police chief, but the court dismissed the individuals from the suit on the town's motion for summary judgment. The judge also dismissed four out of five counts of the lawsuit, but allowed Arteaga to sue the town because "there are genuine issues of material fact as to whether the defendants implicitly but affirmatively encouraged (Michael) Arteaga's domestic violence or enhanced the danger to the plaintiff because they conveyed to Arteaga that he could continue to engage in domestic violence with impunity."

As a result of Tracey Thurman's successful suit against Torrington, in addition to mandating that police officers arrest for domestic violence, Connecticut also required police officer trainees to receive twenty hours of instruction on family violence, followed by two hours of in-service training every three years to maintain their certification. However, a deposition of Waterford police taken in connection with Arteaga's suit revealed that most of the Waterford police were unable to recall their domestic violence training. It was also found that Waterford police had not updated policies on domestic violence for more than a decade.

In 2011, the Town of Waterford settled the lawsuit. The settlement was for an undisclosed amount of money, and all parties were barred from revealing the amount to the media.

ANOTHER CONNECTICUT SUIT SETTLED IN 2015

The estate of the wife of Selami Ozdemir and her children sued West Haven, Connecticut, and its police officers and dispatchers a few years after *Arteaga v. Waterford.*

Ozdemir's murdered wife, Shengyl Rasim, was from Turkey and did not speak English well. While West Haven police had translation services for 911 callers, they did not bother to use them. The first time Ozdemir was arrested on charges of beating, kicking, and knocking his wife into their child's crib, prosecutors diverted his case on the condition that he enter into a family violence education program. Four months later, when he was arrested for hurting her again, Ozdemir was released without posting any cash bail. He returned to his home and killed his wife, then himself. At the time, he was still on the waiting list to attend the family violence education classes ordered after the first assault.

The 911 operators failed to relay key information to police who were at the family's home six minutes before the murder-suicide. The dispatchers did not tell the officers that Ozdemir was intoxicated, dangerous, and coming back, so they left the scene. The lawsuit claims that when police arrested Ozdemir the day before the shooting, he was barred from returning to the wife's home. After posting bond to get released, Ozdemir violated that order. The next morning, at 3:30 a.m., Rasim called police and said her husband had shown up at the home. West Haven officers were dispatched to the residence, but Ozdemir was gone before police arrived and they left.

About thirty minutes later, police got another call from Rasim's home, and over the phone line they heard crying and banging noises. The lawsuit says Rasim was shot multiple times while holding her young child. The couple's second child, seven, was in an upstairs room sleeping. When officers arrived, they found Ozdemir and Rasim dead. Said the estate's lawyer, "You have a person who is crying out for help. [Police] know exactly who she is, they know exactly where she is and they know that they have police officers readily available to help her. Yet they don't tell the police officers to go and help her. It's inconceivable."[*]

NOTE

[*]*Grenier et al. v. West Haven et al.*, U.S. District Ct, Case 3:11-cv-00808-JAM, September 17, 2012.

Connecticut has a state victim advocate appointed by the governor, which at the time of the Ozdemir incident was Michelle Cruz. She publicly criticized the prosecutor and court for allowing Ozdemir a second chance, charging that the family violence education program is intended for low- or moderate-risk offenders. Ozdemir had been before the court before for a nondomestic assault, and that case too had been diverted for participation in an anger management program. Subsequently, two West Haven police officers and two dispatchers were docked one to three days of vacation time after internal affairs determined they mishandled the response to the murder-suicide. That report, which a newspaper obtained through a Freedom of Information Act request, cited an overall lack of communication and faults the police officers and dispatchers for multiple procedural errors, including failing to relay "critical" information about 911 calls, not trying to find suspect Selami Ozdemir, and failing to dispatch a street sergeant to the scene despite Ozdemir's having violated a protective order twice in twelve hours before the final call.

In 2014, U.S. District Judge Jeffrey Meyer ruled in *Grenier et al. v. West Haven et al.* that the case could proceed to trial as a federal civil rights claim against West Haven police officers, combined with other claims of neglect against the City of West Haven, arising from the death of Rasim and the orphaning of her two children. The judge ruled that the conversations between Officer Stratton and Dispatcher Guthrie—who were involved in the incident leading to Rasim's death—which were captured and recorded on police communication equipment, could be found by the jury to be "derogatory" and show "discriminatory animus" and by so conducting themselves the officers involved "neglected their responsibilities in a manner that could have prevented Rasim's murder."

In 2015, the City settled the lawsuit, agreeing to pay the victim's family $3 million. The lawyer for the City denied negligence or discrimination by the police but said the City agreed to pay because of uncertainty of what a jury might do. The lawsuit included two specific police officers and two dispatchers. One of the dispatchers committed suicide in 2013 after being charged in a child sex slave case. After the murder, the victim's children left Connecticut and are living in Turkey. The probate court must now approve the settlement.

Unfortunately, in 2005, the U.S. Supreme Court did its best to end suits against police for failures to enforce domestic violence laws and protect victims in federal courts. In *Castle Rock v. Gonzales*, 545 U.S. 748 (2005), the court ruled, 7–2, that a town and its police department could not be sued for failing to enforce a protective order that had led to the murder of a woman's three children by her estranged husband, notwithstanding that the state statute required police to arrest alleged violators of protective orders.

CASTLE ROCK, COLORADO, SUED UNSUCCESSFULLY

During divorce proceedings, Jessica Lenahan-Gonzales, a resident of Castle Rock, Colorado, obtained a final protective order on June 4, 1999, against her husband, Simon, who had been stalking and controlling her, requiring him to remain at least one hundred yards from her and her four children (son Jesse, who is not Simon's biological child, and daughters Rebecca, Katherine, and Leslie) except during specified visitation time. On June 22, at approximately 5:15 p.m., Simon took possession of his three daughters in violation of the order. Jessica called the police at 7:30 p.m., 8:30 p.m., and 10:10 p.m., and at 12:15 a.m. on June 23, and went to the police station in person at 12:40 a.m. on June 23 begging them to enforce the order and retrieve her children. The police took no action, despite Simon having called Jessica prior to her second police call and informing her that he had the daughters with him at an amusement park in Denver, Colorado. At approximately 3:20 a.m. on June 23, Simon drove to the Castle Rock police station and shot at police. He was killed in a shootout with the officers. A search of his vehicle revealed the corpses of the three daughters in the trunk, all of whom had been shot to death, either by their father or by the police. It was either never determined or, if determined, revealed.[*]

NOTE

[*]Leung, R., "Gonzales Vs. Castle Rock, Supreme Court to Decide If Mother Can Sue Her Town and Its Police," CBS News, March 17, 2005.

Gonzales filed suit in the U.S. District Court for the District of Colorado against Castle Rock, Colorado, its police department, and the three individual police officers with whom she had spoken, under 42 U.S.C. §1983, claiming a federally protected property interest in enforcement of the protective order and alleging "an official policy or custom of failing to respond properly to complaints of protective order violations." A motion to dismiss the case was granted, and Gonzales appealed to the 10th Circuit Court of Appeals. That court rejected Gonzales's substantive due process claim but found a procedural due process claim. The court also affirmed the finding that the three individual officers had qualified immunity and as such could not be sued.

The U.S. Supreme Court reversed the 10th Circuit's decision, reinstating the district court's order of dismissal. The court's majority opinion by

Justice Antonin Scalia held that enforcement of the protective order was not mandatory under Colorado law. He wrote that even if there were a mandate for enforcement to exist, it would not create an individual right to enforcement that could be considered a protected entitlement, and even if there were a protected individual entitlement to enforcement of a protective order, such entitlement would have no monetary value and hence would not count as property necessary for the due process clause.

Justice John Paul Stevens wrote a dissenting opinion, in which he wrote that with respect to whether or not an arrest was mandatory under Colorado law, the court should either have deferred to the 10th Circuit Court's finding that it was or else certified the question to the Colorado Supreme Court rather than decide the issue itself. He went on to write that the law created a statutory guarantee of enforcement, which is an individual benefit and constitutes a protected property interest, rejecting the court's requirement of a monetary value and the concurrence's distinction between enforcement of the restraining order (the violator's arrest) and the benefit of enforcement (safety from the violator).

In fact, the Colorado statute (§18-6-803.6) appears quite clear. It reads: "(1) When a peace officer determines that there is probable cause to believe that a crime or offense involving domestic violence, as defined in section 18-6-800.3 (1), has been committed, the officer shall, without undue delay, arrest the person suspected of its commission pursuant to the provisions in subsection (2) of this section, if applicable, and charge the person with the appropriate crime or offense. . . . The arrested person shall be removed from the scene of the arrest and shall be taken to the peace officer's station for booking, whereupon the arrested person may be held or released in accordance with the adopted bonding schedules for the jurisdiction in which the arrest is made." Subsection (2) just pertains to the determination of primary aggressor if both parties accuse the other of domestic violence.

The National Organization for Women and others rightly attacked the court, arguing the decision reduced the utility of protective orders, effectively giving law enforcement a green light to ignore protective orders.

Denied any justice in the United States, in 2011, Jessica Lenahan took her case to the Inter-American Commission on Human Rights, a commission composed of representatives from the members of the Organization of American States (the United States is a full member by its ratification of the charter document), which found that the United States "failed to act with due diligence to protect Jessica Lenahan and her daughters, which violated the state's obligation not to discriminate and to provide for equal protection before the law." The commission also said that "the failure of the United States to adequately organize its state structure to protect (the Gonzales girls) from domestic violence was discriminatory and constituted a violation of their right to life." In its 2011 decision, the commission recommended that the government conduct an investigation into the cause, time, and place of the girls' deaths and the systemic failures of the Castle Rock police department to enforce the domestic violence restraining order. It also recommended that the government provide compensation to Lenahan and her family and adopt reforms at the federal and state levels to ensure protection from domestic violence.

Although the commission can only issue advisory opinions, the U.S. Department of State and Justice Department agreed to take steps to comply with the commission's admonition. The two cabinet departments organized a Domestic Violence, Sexual Assault, Non-Discrimination and Human Rights Roundtable in April 2014. The roundtable was to inform federal officials how human rights standards supplement existing U.S. laws and policies. However, according to rights groups, no other actions were taken. Nothing has been done to secure any justice for Jessica Lenahan, even determining who killed her children. As she declared, "For fifteen years, I have asked my government to investigate who killed my daughters, and when and where they died. I will not stop seeking answers until I see my government take concrete steps toward conducting this investigation and repairing the human rights violations that I have suffered."[8]

The ACLU's Women's Rights Project, Robert F. Kennedy Center for Justice & Human Rights, Human Rights Clinics at the University of Miami Law School and University of Chicago Law School, and Columbia Law School joined to represent Lenahan and also vowed to continue to work with the government until actionable steps toward reform in domestic violence protection and prevention are taken. In October 2014, they appeared before the Inter-American Commission and presented testimony that detailed the United States' failure to implement changes to its laws and policies that the commission had recommended three years earlier. Ironically, the month before, the United States hailed the twentieth anniversary of passage of the Violence Against Women Act. In a proclamation, the president affirmed the basic human right to be free of violence and abuse. He did not exclude Castle Rock, Colorado, in the proclamation.[9]

Although the U.S. Supreme Court has closed the door to federal suits, police are still being sued under state laws. These suits take years and are often settled only after the plaintiffs agree not to reveal the terms of the settlement. Although their potential impact is diminished, a successful suit continues to influence police arrest behavior, but sometimes not enough to make a difference.

ANOTHER COLORADO CITY SUED

Kindra Cleveland sued the police chief and several officers for ignoring her husband's abuse. The City of Brighton was accused of not properly training and supervising employees handling domestic violence situations. Kindra's affidavit paints a picture of escalating abuse by her husband, encouraged by the lack of police response when she finally began to call them for help. According to court documents, the couple married in 2006, and Cleveland's wife told investigators that initially he was "sweet, caring, and fun-loving." But abuse began in 2007 when she became pregnant. It is not uncommon for abusers to resent their partner's pregnancy, or feel threatened by competition for their partner's attention.

Court documents allege numerous instances of abuse. He allegedly bumped her with his truck while she had a baby in her arms, tackled her against a crib, causing her to drop the child, and repeatedly threw things at her. There was a hiatus in the abuse until she became pregnant again in 2009, when it started up again. Allegations include shoving his wife down the stairs, hitting her with a hammer handle, stomping on her foot so hard with his boots that she suffered a bone fracture, repeatedly telling her that if she ever called the police, he would claim it was a situation of "mutual combatives [sic]" and that the children would be taken away from her. In another episode described in the affidavit, she alleged that he "flicked" their son's head with his finger and said, "I don't even know if the . . . thing is mine."

She called Brighton police. The first time, responding officers "high-fived" Cleveland and didn't talk to her. After the second call, they told her to stay in a hotel for a couple of nights. No charges were filed. She went to the hotel, and Cleveland, according to the hotel clerk, called repeatedly, came to the front counter several times, and even looked in room windows as he searched for her. She called police the next month when he allegedly parked his truck behind her car so that she could not leave the house, but no charges were filed then either. The situation came to a head a few months later. According to court documents, her parents came by with baby bunnies for the children, which enraged Cleveland. He allegedly slammed his lawn mower into her car, told her he didn't want the rabbits, then yanked one of the animals out of his child's hand and threw it into a plastic container. That incident led to a physical confrontation. After she threatened to call 911, he allegedly called police and said his wife was about to make a false report about him.

She did ultimately call, obtained a protective order the next day, and filed for divorce. During a subsequent investigation, she alleged that Cleveland sexually assaulted her twice in 2009.

After months of trying to get the police to help her, she went directly to the Boulder County prosecutor and asked for that office to investigate. It did, and subsequently the husband was charged with fourteen counts of assault, sexual assault, stalking, and child abuse. The husband eventually pled guilty to two of the counts and received a deferred prosecution.*

NOTE

*Robles, Y., "Brighton Firefighter Sentenced, Wife Settles Civil Claim Against City," *Denver Post*, March 4, 2015.

COLORADO CITY SETTLES OUT OF COURT

Another Colorado police department was sued by an aggrieved victim years after the death of Gonzales's daughters, similarly for failing to arrest an abuser, notwithstanding the state's mandatory arrest law.

In 2013, the City settled the case out of court. An open-records request obtained by the *Denver Post* revealed that Kindra Cleveland's claim against the City and police department was settled by a $40,000 payment by Brighton's insurance company. The City declined to disclose details of the settlement, and in its response to the records request denied liability or wrongdoing by any city employees and said the settlement was done solely for economic purposes.[10]

RESEARCHERS CLAIM TO FIND THE MAGIC BULLET

Arresting batterers as a first resort, rather than a last, was also spurred on by research sponsored by the Police Foundation. The research was conducted in Milwaukee and published in 1984.[11] The researchers were interested in determining the deterrent power of arrest in general, but serendipitously, they chose to look at domestic violence to test the impact of arrests. When responding to a domestic violence call, they had Milwaukee police respond in one of three different manners on a random basis. First, they had police separate the couple and send the suspect out of the house for eight hours. Second, they had police counsel the couple to get help for their problems. Third, they had the police arrest the suspect. Researchers then followed the couples for six months. Where arrests were made, re-assaults against the victims were cut in half based on victim interviews and official records. The other two responses paled by comparison. The authors of the study were so impressed with the results, they publicly came out for laws to not only allow police to arrest without warrants, but also to make arrest the preferred policy.

Subsequent arrest research had more mixed results, but most of these researchers ignored a major problem in these studies, including the initial Milwaukee study, a problem missed by many advocates too. Arrest is supposed to be the beginning of the process to hold criminals accountable and to protect their victims. It is not designed to be the end product. That is why we have prosecutors, judges, and prisons. But in most of these studies, arrest was the end product. Once arrested in Milwaukee, for example, less than 2 percent of the suspects were ever prosecuted in court at the time of the original study! Any deterrent effect of arrest in the short run is bound to diminish when the suspect realizes that the criminal justice response is all foreplay, no follow through.

If the abuser is also committing nondomestic violence crimes that are actually prosecuted, they quickly learn even more emphatically that the domestic violence arrest is pure bluff. The latter is not theoretical. The vast majority of abusers who come to the attention of police and courts do not confine their criminal activity to domestic violence alone. It is another myth that but for battering their intimates, abusers are law-abiding, model citizens and good fathers!

Nonetheless, the Milwaukee research further mobilized advocates and state legislatures to act, convinced they had found a magic bullet, or as it turns out, a modest deterrent for lower-risk abusers. Although by no means magic, arrest has been found to have a modest deterrent impact on lower-risk abusers. Also, of course, arrest is a necessary precursor to prosecution and sentencing, which provide much greater opportunities to hold abusers accountable and protect their victims.

POLICE MORE LIKELY THAN NOT TO ARREST ABUSERS

As mentioned, lawsuits, legislative reforms, research, and advocacy combined to dramatically and significantly change police behavior across the country. Local and state police, deputy sheriffs, and other law enforcement agents began arresting batterers in great numbers. It is thought that no more than 7 to 15 percent were arrested in the 1970s and 1980s. That rose to 35 to 50 percent and even higher in some jurisdictions in the next decade. In Kansas, for example, in 1992, the domestic violence arrest rate was 37 percent. By 2010, police made arrests in 60 percent of the domestic calls. In New Jersey, less than 20,000 were arrested in 1992. That rose to 26,000 by the end of that decade. Victims facilitated the rise in arrests at the end of the last century. As more victims came to understand that their abuse was a crime, more called police. By the end of the 1990s, the reporting rates for domestic violence became equal to that of all crime.[12]

Although the heyday for domestic violence arrests was in the 1990s, they have remained relatively stable since. In 1998, Florida police arrested 64,446 persons for domestic violence, mostly for simple assaults. In 2013, the number increased to 65,107, also mostly for simple assaults. While this represents a modest increase in arrests, the state's population grew by four million in between. In Arizona, arrests for domestic violence increased from 21,500 in 2001 to over 25,000 in 2010, while the population increased from 5.3 million to 6.4 million. Though arrests peaked in 2000 in Kansas at over 15,000, they only dropped by a thousand in 2010. In Wisconsin, on the other hand, arrests increased from 17,663 in 2001 to 20,398 in 2012, largely because the arrest rate for reported incidents increased from 64.34 percent to 71 percent.[13]

Current arrest rates around the country hover around 50 percent. According to the *Columbus Dispatch*, police across Ohio, for example, responded to 75,000 domestic violence incidents in 2009. They made arrests in a little more than half the time (55 percent).[14] While Ohio law does not mandate arrest, it declares arrest to be the "preferred response." While the arrest rate was above average at 71 percent in Wisconsin in 2012, the most common charge was disorderly conduct (13,972), not misdemeanor battery or assault (6,719) as in most states. Wisconsin mandates arrest if police officers believe the offender has engaged in criminal domestic abuse. Across Tennessee, in 2011, 2012, and 2013, police responded to approximately 40,000 domestic violence cases involving spouses, 6,500 involving ex-spouses, and 109,000 involving boy/girlfriends. Most of the incidents involved simple assaults, followed by aggravated assaults. Police cleared 46.5 percent of the cases by an arrest. In 2012, across New Jersey, arrests were made in 31 percent of the 65,060 domestic violence offenses reported. Most of the reported offenses were assaults (27,602) and harassment (28,285). In 2013, Maryland's domestic violence arrest rate was 40 percent (11,098). Maryland police did not arrest in 31 percent of incidents (8,649), and what police did in the remaining 29 percent of incidents (8,038) was not reported to the state's Uniform Crime Reporting Program, administered by the state police.

Not all domestic violence cases police respond to are arrestable. Some of the incidents do not constitute crimes. As a result, even a 50 percent arrest rate still means that law enforcement is arresting a majority of abusers they find engaged in criminal acts brought to their attention. This is not to say that a majority of abusers who engage in criminal acts are arrested, as many victims do not call police. On the other hand, although a majority of abusers brought to the attention of police for domestic violence crimes are arrested, still a large proportion is not. Many cases are "exceptionally cleared" by law enforcement. For example, at the same time Tennessee reported clearing almost half the cases by an arrest, it reported that police had "exceptionally cleared" another 20 percent of the cases. Exceptionally cleared cases mean that although police found sufficient evidence for an arrest, they were prevented from doing so for reasons beyond their control. From 2011 to 2013, the Tennessee Bureau of Investigation reported that they could not clear through an arrest 123 cases because the suspect died, 4,126 because the prosecutor declined the case, nine because extradition was denied, and 146 because the suspect was a juvenile or there was no custody. But most, 24,548, were not arrested because the "victim refused to cooperate." In the latter instances, the victims told or "made it known" to the police that they would not pursue prosecution of the offender.

The odds of an arrest are, not surprisingly, higher in states with mandatory or preferred domestic violence arrest laws. In these states, arrests are made whether or not victims want them to be made. In fact, in states with such laws, law enforcement is more prone to arrest in acquaintance and stranger cases too, even though they are not required to do so. It appears in these states, police are trained or come to learn that arrest is the better alternative for any crimes of violence.

Even where police are not mandated or directed to arrest, the wishes of victims are not legally controlling. In law, the crime is not against them, even though they are the victims. The crime is against the state. If prosecuted, the case is *state v. offender*, not *victim v. offender*. Only in civil court may a crime victim be a party to the action. In criminal matters, the victim has no legal standing as anyone other than the witness to the crime, although in some states they may have additional rights such as providing a victim impact statement or allocution in court after the defendant is convicted.[15]

Some police departments do much better than others. In 2013 and 2014, Cedar Rapids, Iowa, police responded to over one thousand domestic violence cases, with an average reported arrest rate of 77 percent. After years of careful and consistent advocacy by the Family Violence Council in Lancaster (Lincoln), Nebraska, for example, local police in 2013 made arrests in 88 percent of all reported incidents. The county's prosecutors reinforced police arrest policies by prosecuting about 95 percent of those arrested for domestic assaults. When the Family Violence Council first began working with police and prosecutors twenty years ago, the county domestic violence arrest rate was exactly half, 44 percent.[16]

Unfortunately, not all law enforcement agencies have followed Lancaster's example.

BROWN DEER POLICE RETREAT WHEN ABUSER REFUSES TO BE ARRESTED

Wisconsin provides a case in point. In 2012, the entire nation was riveted on Wisconsin after Radcliffe Haughton went on a deadly rampage at a spa, shooting seven women and killing four, including his wife. Further investigation found Haughton had been running circles around the Brown Deer police for years for domestic violence. Like most mass murders in recent American history, Haughton's rampage had been preceded by domestic violence.

BROWN DEER, WISCONSIN, SUED

Just three weeks before his mass murders, police were back at Haughton's house. Brown Deer police officers had found his wife barefoot and bruised at a gas station. The officers went to the house and spotted Haughton inside. They rang the bell, but when Haughton refused to open the door, they left him alone. The police finally arrested him two days later, but not for the domestic violence. They were serving a warrant from a neighboring town where he had slashed his wife's tires outside the spa where she worked as a stylist. She had told him she was leaving him that morning.

Following that incident, Haughton's wife, Zina, got a protective order against him. Despite this, Haughton was able to buy a handgun, which he then used in the shootings. While the protective order prohibited gun possession, Haughton purchased the gun privately, not subject to federally mandated record checks thanks to Congress buckling under to the National Rifle Association.

Haughton was no stranger to the Brown Deer police. The year before, they had set up a tactical perimeter around his house, shut off area traffic, and barred neighbors from entering their homes. At that time they had also been responding to domestic violence. Zina had called police after her husband had thrown her bedding and clothes on the front lawn and poured tomato juice over her car to eat away the paint job. She ended her 911 call asking police to hurry up and send help. An officer used a bullhorn to tell Haughton, who was inside his home, that he was under arrest and to come out. Haughton didn't. Officers peering in the window saw what they thought was a long gun in his possession. The officers ordered him to drop the gun. Instead, Haughton walked away from the window. After ninety minutes, the officers retreated.*

NOTE

*Diedrich, J., "Radcliffe Haughton Sidestepped Brown Deer Police for Years," *Milwaukee Journal Sentinel*, October 22, 2012.

After the mass murder, the police chief explained that his officers did not arrest Haughton back then because the suspect was alone in the house, so there was no danger to his victim. Also, he said that the wife had told them that her husband did not have a rifle, and his officers couldn't be sure of what they saw. However, one of the officers who knew Haughton from past calls knew he was a former Marine trained in firearms and thought he probably had a gun. When Haughton appeared in the window, he pointed a long-barreled black object at his wife, who was standing next to the officer. The officer wrote in her report that she ordered Zina to get away, and the officer took cover behind a patrol car.

Despite their retreat, the officers still requested charges be filed by the county prosecutor against Haughton, including a felony charge relating to possession of the firearm their police chief later said didn't exist. The Milwaukee prosecutor did not file the felony charge, later incongruously explaining that his hands were tied because police failed to arrest the suspect. Ultimately Haughton was charged with a misdemeanor charge of disorderly conduct/domestic abuse. According to court records, that case was subsequently dismissed when neither his wife nor the police showed up in court. Turns out the officer was on vacation and had asked for a different date. The prosecutor went forward anyway, not realizing that the officer was needed to identify the defendant.

The 2011 police siege was just one of many calls at the Haughton household. The calls went back to 2001. Police had been called up to two dozen times. In 2003, after Zina was beaten, police arrested her husband, but the case was never prosecuted. Police returned in 2004, 2006, and 2008 for domestic violence, but no arrests resulted.

Ironically, Wisconsin is one of the states that mandates an arrest for domestic violence by law. Police must arrest, according to state law, if they believe the abuse is likely to continue or if there is evidence of an injury.

Subsequent to the spa shooting, a bipartisan group of legislators released a letter castigating the Brown Deer police for violating the state's mandatory arrest law and the chief for his press release blaming Zina Haughton for his department's failures to hold Haughton accountable for his domestic violence against her. The record clearly shows that Zina had been ambivalent about police intervention. After calling 911 at the gas station, for example, she then told responding police officers she had misdialed 411 and attributed her bruises to makeup, not her husband's assault. As the legislators admonished the police chief, "Your department's duty to uphold the law should not, and does not, hinge on the actions of the victim. You must stop implying that the victim was to blame for the failure of your department to make an arrest, and for the same of other victims in Brown Deer and throughout Wisconsin, you must correct your inaccurate and damaging statements."

As is often the case, the poor performance of the police was reinforced and encouraged by an equally poor performance of the county prosecutor, who subsequently declared that although the case was complicated, his impression was that the Brown Deer police performance was "very good." The district attorney, under state law, is supposed to review police incident reports where police fail to make a domestic violence arrest. However, the head prosecutor for domestic violence in the district attorney's office told the press he had never seen such a report in the three and a half years he had been in that office, from Brown Deer or any of the other police departments in Milwaukee County. A Wisconsin state senator told WTMJ radio at the time that Brown Deer police were not alone to blame. The district attorney "had something to do with them as well."[17]

A WISCONSIN POLICE DEPARTMENT AND PROSECUTOR GET IT RIGHT

As reported in the *Milwaukee Journal Sentinel*, by 2014 the Milwaukee police department and county prosecutor's office demonstrated that dangerous abusers could be held accountable even when victims were unable to do more than cry for help. The victim in the story was a twenty-three-year-old woman. She had escaped her abusive boyfriend in November 2013 by jumping out of a window after he allegedly strangled her. She ran to a neighbor to call 911. It was at least her seventeenth call to police in the last seven years.

Based on prior police reports, the captain in charge of the Sensitive Crimes Unit, which was assigned the case, had little doubt that without intervention the victim would eventually be killed by Terrell Kelly, the father of her three children. The captain's assessment was aided by a new tool the department and many others across Wisconsin had adopted, lethality assessments that made it easier to quantify the danger. The tool had been presented to every law enforcement agency across Milwaukee County at a special domestic violence training, positive fallout from the Brown Deer police conduct and the mass murder in the county two years earlier.

DETERMINED POLICE AND PROSECUTORS DO THEIR JOBS

As in Brown Deer, Kelly's girlfriend called police for immediate help but would go no further, often recanting what she had initially reported. Maybe the victim still loved her abuser and didn't want to hurt him. Maybe she relied on him for financial support to feed her children and keep a roof over their heads. Maybe she knew she and/or her children would die if she cooperated with police and prosecutors. It appears Kelly had had her under his thumb for a long time. He was twelve years older than his victim and had impregnated her when she was just fourteen years old.

In fact, Milwaukee police were first alerted to the case back when the Milwaukee County Bureau of Child Welfare reported Kelly's girlfriend's pregnancy at age fourteen. Although the victim identified the father, she said Kelly was sixteen and living in Chicago. Police were unable to track Kelly in the Chicago schools as he was really twenty-six at the time. The next year, the victim called police reporting being strangled with a belt and punched. By age seventeen, the victim had a second child by Kelly.

The victim continued to call police. Often Kelly fled the scene before police arrived. They referred cases to the county prosecutor. In 2010, Kelly was charged with three sets of domestic violence misdemeanors. All were dismissed when the victim did not appear in court. Finally, in 2011, Kelly pled guilty to disorderly conduct and was sentenced to two months in jail, allowed out for work-release.

When the victim escaped through the window, she screamed to her neighbor that Kelly was trying to kill her. He had, she said, punched her, strangled her with his hands around her neck, and threatened her life. Police arrested Kelly for strangulation, disorderly conduct, and recklessly endangering safety. They photographed the injuries received by the victim. They assembled all of their past records to impress the prosecutor of the seriousness of the case. However, a month later, the victim wrote the court recanting everything. Kelly had never strangled her with a belt, as previously charged, and had not strangled her in the latest incident. She had, she wrote, lied to police out of anger. Although the officers were confident that they knew what was going on, as a result of the U.S. Supreme Court ruling in *Crawford** limiting the admissibility of hearsay testimony, they needed the victim's testimony for the prosecutors to prove the case in court. Or they had to come up with an alternative strategy.

Police and prosecutors huddled together. They decided to go back to 2007 and focus on the victim's pregnancy when she was fourteen and Kelly was twenty-six. They would prove that Kelly was the father and charge him with sexual assault. As a child, the victim could not have legally consented to having sex with Kelly. But they needed a DNA sample from the victim, Kelly, and the children. The victim refused to cooperate. As the *Sentinel* reported, in a first for Milwaukee police and prosecutors, the district attorney authorized a search warrant to take a cheek swab from a victim.

They got the DNA and charged Kelly with second degree sexual assault.

Kelly challenged the evidence, arguing that his Fourth Amendment rights against search and seizure had been violated when police took the samples from his children. Assistant District Attorney Joshua Mathy, who prosecuted the case, successfully argued that parents couldn't vicariously assert violation of their Fourth Amendment rights through their children. Further, he argued, "This defendant has waged a long campaign of domestic violence against (the woman) in front of the kids and she nor he can be expected to participate in a criminal justice system that has thus far been unable to protect her."

A social worker testified in court on the terrible effects of the domestic violence on the now three children. One child, she testified, had taken on the role of a parent and another had become aggressive, reportedly choking classmates at school. The toddler appeared fearful of being placed on the floor, clinging to his older brother. The testimony helped educate the court of how far-reaching domestic violence is, affecting the next generation too.

Kelly blamed the victim. He alleged the victim had lied about her age back in 2007. He pointed out that the victim too had once been arrested for domestic violence. He said the victim's family had blackmailed him for money, threatening to reveal the statutory rape. When the prosecutor persisted, Kelly pled guilty to the sexual assault. The other charges were dismissed, but the judge was allowed to consider them in sentencing. The judge sentenced Kelly to ten years in prison, followed by eight years supervision.

Kelly called the sentence extreme because he hadn't engaged in "violent aggressive action," merely having sex out of ignorance. His victim still maintained that Kelly had not been abusive and his criminal conviction was based on lies.[†]

Notes

[*]Described in more detail in the section on prosecution.

[†]Luthern, A., "Police, Prosecutors Use New Tools to Help Domestic Violence Victims," *Milwaukee Journal Sentinel*, December 25, 2014.

REMAINING POLICE CHALLENGES

While police have not slid back to the abysmal arrest rates of the 1970s and 1980s, as evidenced by continuing lawsuits and Brown Deer police, there is still plenty of room for improvement, particularly involving the most dangerous abusers. These include abusers who flee the scene before police arrive and abusers who strangle or stalk their victims. These behaviors are red flags for extreme danger. Abusers who leave the scene are more dangerous than those who remain to be arrested.[18] Strangling is attempted murder, and stalking is a precursor to murder. Abusers should not be given free passes on these crimes. They are not equivalent to and should not be charged as misdemeanor assaults, harassment, menacing, trespassing, or disorderly conduct.

POLICE DON'T CHASE

One of the consistent failures of law enforcement when it comes to arresting abusers is that police don't chase. The dramatic chase on foot or by car is reserved for the movies. If abusers leave the scene before the police arrive, most are home free. Police arrest abusers who stick around, too slow or dumb to run. Many abusers do stick around, but the most dangerous don't, and that makes this police failure all the more troubling.

The percent of abusers who leave the scene runs as high as almost half in some jurisdictions. Data from twenty-five police departments from four states—Connecticut, Idaho, Tennessee, and Virginia—found that a little over 40 percent of the abusers flee the scene before police arrive.[19] While police arrested more than 80 percent of those at the scene, they arrested less than half of those who fled. In fact, the odds of an arrest for a suspect who flees were found to be almost five and a half times less than those who remained at the scene. Responding patrol officers just don't have a great deal of time to chase—the next call comes over the radio and they have to leave. Unlike detectives, their job is not to detect or pursue inconvenient misdemeanants.

The problem is that those abusers who flee are more dangerous than those who don't. They are more likely to have injured their victims.[20] They are twice as likely to reabuse their victims as those arrested at the scene. They are, not surprisingly, more likely to have greater criminal histories. One of the widely recognized risk factors for abuse lethality is "whether the offender has *avoided* being arrested for domestic violence."

Incidentally, when police do bother to search, they find their man more often than not, according to the same data. But most don't try.

There are some noteworthy exceptions that prove it can be done. In 2013, the Baltimore, Maryland, police department's Domestic Violence Warrant Squad teamed up with patrol officers to make the service of domestic violence warrants a top priority. From September 1, 2013, through August 26, 2014, there were a total of 2,003 new domestic violence warrants issued for service. The Domestic Violence Warrant Squad and patrol officers served 2,408 warrants, keeping up with the current warrants and continuing to reduce the backlog of unserved older warrants.[21]

Not only are police routinely giving up too soon, but in many cases, they also don't even get warrants for the absent suspect's arrest. (Granted, the arrest warrant may not routinely be served.) On any given day, it is estimated there are two million active arrest warrants outstanding. But if a warrant is at least issued and the suspect is stopped for something else, even a traffic violation, the computer will indicate the warrant and the suspect can then be arrested for the domestic violence. Better late than never.

Though counterintuitive, many officers may believe that if the abuser has left, the victim is safe, like the police chief claimed in Brown Deer. The opposite turns out to be true.

POLICE FAIL TO CAPTURE VICTIM CONTACT INFORMATION

While the suspect may be gone, the victim is generally available to police. A simple but critical task at that point is to obtain victim contact information to use in a follow-up investigation or if the case is eventually prosecuted.

The problem is the contact information police record at the scene is often outdated within twenty-four hours. Many victims leave the next day for safety's sake or to get on with their lives.

There is an easy answer. Police can ask the victim to supply the name and contact information for a third person who will know how to reach the victim in the future no matter where she is. Many police routinely capture this critical information. Many don't.

Across Oklahoma, for example, between 2009 and 2013, researchers tried to follow up with a thousand domestic violence victims based on phone numbers provided by Oklahoma police who had responded to the most recent domestic violence incident. Researchers were unable to contact more than 40 percent of the victims on the phone. In fact, many of the numbers were no longer in service, indicating that the victims were no longer there or had changed their numbers.[22] The failure of the police to obtain victim contact information was especially disappointing because these Oklahoma police departments were participating in a highly touted model program where the officers interviewed each victim to assess her danger and then connected victims with a domestic violence agency hotline for services. Tracking victims is even a greater challenge with cell phones because telephone numbers are no longer tied to a residence.

This too-common police oversight sabotages prosecution.

STRANGULATION IS NOT CHOKING

Often dismissed in the media and in courts as mere "choking," and consequently overlooked by police and prosecutors, strangulation is as serious as any assault with a weapon. The act requires surprisingly little effort from the abuser to inflict considerable terror, even death. It only takes eleven pounds of pressure to a victim's carotid artery for ten seconds to cause unconsciousness. Thirty-three pounds of pressure will close off the trachea. Brain death will occur in four to five minutes.

Non-lethal strangulation is, in fact, torture. Researchers call it the domestic violence equivalent of "waterboarding."[23] Like waterboarding, it leaves few marks even when it results in loss of consciousness or death. The perpetrator's dominance and authority over the life of his victim creates intense fear that can be used repeatedly, often with impunity, as in the Hardy case (see Introduction). Strangulation is part and parcel of many abusive partners' repertoire. It is also an excellent predictor of a subsequent domestic homicide.

Abusers who slap their victims can escalate to punching. Abusers who strangle can only escalate by applying greater pressure. One study showed that "the odds of becoming an attempted homicide increased by about seven-fold for women who had been strangled by their partner."[24] Victims may have no visible injuries whatsoever, yet because of underlying brain damage due to the lack of oxygen during the strangulation assault, they may have serious internal injuries or die days, even weeks later.

The lack of external injuries and the lack of medical training in regard to strangulation have led to the minimization of this type of violence, exposing victims to potential serious health consequences, further violence, and even death. Emergency room medical personnel and law enforcement officials often either disregard or do not collect evidence of strangulation. Victims, too, may be hesitant to even claim that strangulation occurred given little positive support for the claim.

If victims do report strangulation, their claims may be dismissed out of hand as "exaggerated" by an "emotionally unstable victim." Even physical symptoms may be dismissed. Hoarseness, occurring in up to 50 percent of strangulations, may be attributed to screaming during an argument, and broken blood vessels in the eyes attributed to pink eye or the victim abusing drugs.[25]

Not only has strangulation been overlooked in the medical literature, but many states still do not adequately address this violence in their criminal statutes, policies, or responses. Thus, abusers frequently end up getting a free pass for one of the most serious forms of domestic violence.

Law enforcement officials rely on physical evidence to determine if there is probable cause for an arrest. If the victim does not present with visible injuries, and if medical personnel fail to document any, law enforcement officials are unlikely to consider strangulation charges. Unfortunately, this occurs all too often. A San Diego study reported that police officers found no visible injuries in almost two-thirds of strangulation cases and only minor injuries, such as redness or scratch marks, in less than a quarter of cases. As a result, batterers who strangle their victims are not held accountable, and the criminal justice system misses one of the more accurate predictors of abuser danger. [26]

Every year more states enact specific strangulation statutes. Although these laws have promoted a great increase in strangulation arrests, most are still for misdemeanor charges that continue to undervalue the seriousness of the offense. Too many of the state statutes, like North Carolina's, allow strangulation to be ignored, as in the Hardy case, or treated the same as a simple assault. Difficult enough to prove in court, state statutes enacted by uninformed legislators make proving strangulation more difficult by creating two levels: the misdemeanor of strangulation without physical injury and the felony of strangulation with physical injury. In reality, the only easily observed physical injury resulting from strangulation is a comatose or dead body, in which case the crime is murder.

NEW YORK PROVIDES ABUSERS LOOPHOLE FOR STRANGULATIONS

New York enacted its first strangulation crime legislation in 2010. Before then, New York's misdemeanor assault law was used when possible to cover strangulation, although the courts required proof of "impairment of physical condition or substantial pain." The more serious felony assault charge required an even higher threshold of physical injury, one creating a substantial risk of death or serious and protracted disfigurement, impairment of health or protracted loss or impairment of the function of any bodily organ. As a result of these requirements and conflicting case law, as in North Carolina, strangulation was mostly prosecuted as lesser misdemeanors like menacing or harassment.

When New York finally created its strangulation statute, it established three new crimes, two of which were felonies: Criminal Obstruction of Breathing or Blood Circulation (Penal Law §121.11), a misdemeanor; and Strangulation in the Second Degree (PL §121.12) and Strangulation in the First Degree (PL §121.13), both felonies. The misdemeanor strangulation calls for a maximum sentence of one year in jail, and the felonies call for imprisonment of two to fifteen years. Almost all the arrests that followed were for the least serious strangulation charge.

Between November 11, 2010, when it went into effect and June 2012, New York police arrested more than 17,171 persons for strangulation, a little over half of them in New York City, illustrating how common strangulation by abusers is. Almost all the strangulation arrests (80 percent) were for misdemeanor strangulation. Only 212 were for the most serious felony charge. Ultimately, the more serious strangulation charges were generally lost in court.[27] The *New York Times* provided an example in its coverage of one of the first felony strangulation cases to go before a jury.

STRANGULATION STATUTE CONFOUNDS JURY

The victim testified that her boyfriend bashed her head against the bathtub, slammed her down so hard on the bed that the frame broke, and punched her all over her body. Then the woman, twenty-six, testified in the Manhattan courtroom that her broad-shouldered, much larger boyfriend "wrapped his hands around her neck" and applied pressure until "it got dark." Finally, he hurled her to the floor and kicked her in the back before lying down on the bed. The boyfriend, an MBA student, was charged with the lesser felony strangulation offense.

To convict him, the jury had to find injury, impairment, stupor, or unconsciousness consistent with the law. Police photos of the victim's injuries taken soon after the assault were projected on a courtroom screen, showing scalp and hip abrasions, a bruised eye, and contusions on her arm, breast, and back. Her neck showed red dots. The officer who responded to her 911 call testified that he had observed bruising and requested an ambulance. However, he did not write down seeing any injury to her neck, nor did the hospital emergency room team note any in its brief written report.

The first professional to flag a possible strangulation was a police officer from the Domestic Violence Unit called to the hospital. The officer saw marks on the victim's throat consistent with strangulation. She testified that when she called the suspect and ordered him to come to the station house, one of his first questions was, "Is she still breathing?" A forensic pathologist called by the prosecutor testified that the dots on her neck were petechiae—broken blood vessels suggesting strangulation. However, the defense's expert, an emergency room doctor, disagreed, telling the jury that if the victim had been strangled, her eyes would have been bloodshot. In fact, petechiae can be under the eyelid, and bruising and swelling can take as long as twenty-four to thirty-six hours after police generally photograph victims at the crime scene to show up. The victim's roommate also testified that she heard the victim telling both the police and the medical staff that she had been choked.

Nonetheless, the jury did what juries had done for the other eighteen defendants first charged with this felony in New York City. It found him not guilty of strangulation because the state failed to prove the elements of the crime beyond a reasonable doubt. The judge imposed the sentence that prosecutors typically request for the lesser charge of assault: sixty days in jail and three years probation, anger-management counseling, and a five-year protection order. The defendant served thirty-eight days before being released for good behavior.[*]

Note

[*]Besonen , J., "A New Crime, but Convictions Are Elusive," *New York Times*, February 16, 2013, downloaded October 20, 2014.

The case illustrates two big problems. First, by requiring proof of physical injury for felony strangulation charges, statutes like New York's are difficult to enforce. Second, by ordering the defendant into anger management, the judge is implicitly blaming the victim for the defendant's brutal attack by saying, in effect, that once the defendant learns not to be provoked by her, the abuse will surely stop. Of course, what the defendant really learned in that New York City courtroom was the same thing Mr. Black and Mr. Oliver learned in those North Carolina courtrooms more than a century before. Short of murdering a partner, if no permanent injuries are obvious, the parties will be left pretty much alone to forgive and forget or, more accurately, to continue to abuse and be re-victimized—even murdered.

Prosecutors fared better in Gering, Nebraska. Tragically, however, the strangulation had resulted in the death of the victim.

EXPERTS HELP JURY UNDERSTAND STRANGULATIONS

Local media reported that to prove strangulation was the cause of death on day two of the Dylan Cardeilhac first-degree murder trial, the prosecutors called an expert witness. Dr. Peter Schilke, a pathologist at Regional West Medical Center, who had performed an autopsy on Amanda Baker three days after she was strangled, testified that the cause of death was "asphyxia due to manual strangulation." He pointed to the evidence to support the charge, including hemorrhaging in Baker's face and eyes, which indicated a restriction of blood flow to the head, and in her neck. Since the hyoid bone in her neck was still intact, it was likely Cardeilhac had used something similar to the lateral vascular neck restraint to block her blood flow, rather than the bare arm to block her airway. The doctor concluded that the examination of Baker's brain tissue showed swelling, meaning the brain suffered from a lack of oxygen.

The local sheriff was also called to the stand to testify that his department didn't use the lateral vascular neck restraint anymore because of its likelihood to cause death. When used, he added, police are usually trained to release this hold as soon as the victim loses consciousness, which normally occurs in a matter of seconds. In fact, the sheriff testified that evidence showed Cardeilhac was on top of the victim for two and a half minutes, but the victim's body went limp after a minute and a half.

The defense argued that the death of Amanda Baker was not intentional. The defendant just "choked" the victim in his attempt to get away from her. After eight hours of deliberation, the Scotts Bluff District Court jury found Cardeilhac guilty of second-degree murder.[*]

Note

[*]Anderson, A., "Cardeilhac Jury Watches Strangulation Video, Learns About Choke Holds," *KOTA Territory News*, November 18, 2014.

STRANGULATION LEFT NO MARKS

Ohio prosecutors charged Lawrence Stinnett with strangling his wife in September 2014. He was subsequently indicted by a grand jury the next month. In December, the case was prosecuted before a jury. According to the local newspaper, the *Lancaster Eagle Gazette* (December 11, 2014), Stinnett's defense attorney reported that Stinnett "was accused of choking [sic] his wife, beating her head against the floor and wall and putting a knee to her chest during an altercation. . . . However, she never reported anything until over thirty-six hours later, had no marks on her, and gave inconsistent statements." The jury deliberated for less than two hours and found him not guilty. Stinnett remained in custody, however, because while cleared of the strangulation against his wife, he also faced two rape charges from where he worked before his employer fired him.*

NOTE

*Roush, S., "Man Awaits Rape Trial after Domestic Violence Clearance," *Eagle Gazette*, Lancaster, OH, December 11, 2014.

If strangulation statutes were drafted more accurately, convicting stranglers would not require a post-mortem to prove.

MAKING STRANGULATION A FELONY

Better state laws make strangulation a felony, period. In 2011, Alabama made strangulation a Class B felony, carrying a prison sentence of two to twenty years. The strangulation law (13A-6-138(2) & (3)) defines strangulation as follows: "Intentionally causing asphyxia by closure or compression of the blood vessels or air passages of the neck as a result of external pressure on the neck." The Alabama legislature also made domestic violence by strangulation, intentionally causing asphyxia by closure or compression of the blood vessels or air passages of the neck as a result of external pressure (§13A-6-139(2)), a felony.

POLICE CHASE ALLEGED FELON

Authorities informed the *Times Daily* that Joiner was angry because his wife hadn't gotten up when he thought she should have that morning. Joiner was then accused of putting his thumb in his wife's eye and pinning her to the bed while he beat her on the head. According to the victim, he threatened to "poke it out." The investigator added that Joiner grabbed the five-year-old daughter, threatening to leave with her. He said the victim then grabbed her daughter and fell to the floor, covering the girl. Joiner is accused of kicking and punching the woman in the head and face, and also kicking the daughter. The victim said she was able to pull Joiner's index finger backwards while he was strangling her and get loose.

Joiner allegedly ran off when family members at the residence dialed 911.

All the charges were misdemeanors, punishable by one year if Joiner were convicted . . . with one exception, because the Alabama legislature had made strangulation a felony. The felony charge made other differences, too. While police often do not bother to give chase to missing suspected abusers who have fled the scene after a misdemeanor, in this case, given the felony charge, police mobilized. Through the local press, they invited anyone with knowledge about Joiner to call the sheriff's department or Shoals Crime Stoppers. When they got information of where he might be, they called in the U.S. Marshals Gulf Coast Regional Fugitive Task Force, which then arrested Joiner across state lines in Tennessee![*]

Note

[*]Smith, T., "Authorities: Man Assaulted Daughter, 5, Wife," *Times Daily*, January 16, 2015.

Felonizing a domestic violence charge makes a big difference all the way up the entire criminal justice hierarchy. A case from Alabama illustrates. Timothy Joiner, thirty-one, was arrested for domestic violence in Florence, Alabama, accused of assaulting his wife and five-year-old daughter in 2015.

Because strangulation was a felony, once arrested, rather than Joiner being released on personal recognizance (a personal promise to return) or a small cash bail, the court imposed a bail of $8,000. The felony charge also got the case in the local newspaper three times following the incident. If nothing else, the three newspaper articles that followed the arrest in Tennessee put pressure on the prosecutor to proceed with the case, which he did. The case went directly to the grand jury when the defendant waived a preliminary hearing. Unlike the majority of misdemeanor domestic violence cases across Alabama, this one did not disappear.

According to the Alabama Law Enforcement Agency, in 2014, police filed reports on 31,165 misdemeanor domestic violence assaults, making arrests in 17,825 of them, constituting 57 percent. However, most of these, 56 percent, were then dropped, not prosecuted. In short, across Alabama less than a third of suspects in domestic misdemeanor assaults were prosecuted. In contrast, that same year, Alabama police filed reports on 3,351 felony domestic assaults, made arrests in 1,951 of them, and, unlike misdemeanor domestic assaults, the majority, 56 percent, were prosecuted.

It took a few years, but after Texas made strangulation a felony in 2009, punishable by two to ten years in prison, strangulation prosecutions soared. In Harris County (Houston), prosecutors filed 103 strangulation cases in

FEDERAL COURT LAYS DOWN THE LAW FOR STRANGULATION

In March 2014, Doris Rivera-Black was kidnapped at gunpoint, assaulted, and strangled by her estranged husband, Mitchell Gibson. She was a deputy sheriff at the time but on light duty because of an injury and was unarmed, which her ex knew because he had been stalking her. She had not revealed her prior abuse, fearing her colleagues would perceive her as weak. She was a soldier, but he was a civilian. A subsequent police and FBI investigation found that Gibson had whipped her with a coaxial cable, which he regularly made her get for him prior to the beatings. He would strangle her with the cable until she blacked out, and then pour boiling hot water on her stomach, groin, and leg to revive her.

Realizing that leaving him did not stop the abuse, this time she called 911. Fort Carson police responded and sent the victim to the hospital for her extensive injuries. Doris Rivera-Black was pregnant at the time. The Fort Carson police, joined by the FBI, investigated further, and a little more than a year later, Gibson pled guilty in federal court to six counts of assault, including assault resulting in serious bodily injury, assault with a dangerous weapon, and assault of a spouse by strangling and suffocation. He faced a maximum sentence of sixty years in prison, but got forty-five years in prison and three of supervised release.*

Note

*Bishop, T., "45 Year Sentence Sets Precedent for Future Domestic Violence Rulings," *Fox 21 News*, May 27, 2015.

2013, doubling the number filed the year before. Previously, strangulation carried the same penalties as a slap or a push.

When strangulation is recognized for what it is, sentences are appropriately lengthy.

Advocates applauded the rare but welcome long sentence, expressing the hope that it would set a precedent for future domestic violence sentences. Said an area hospital victim advocate, "Forty-five years is certainly not common, and so it is very exciting and empowering I think for survivors to see that outcome. I think it not only sends a message . . . to the abusers . . . but also to the victims."

MARICOPA COUNTY, ARIZONA, FIGURES OUT HOW TO DO IT

Arizona made Aggravated Assault by Strangulation (13-1204.15) a Class 4 felony in 2010. The statute does not require injury, but only intentional or knowing impeding of normal breathing or circulation of blood by applying pressure to the throat or neck manually or with an instrument. Obviously, this is crucial, as most strangulations leave no physical injuries, and few victims seek medical attention. Nonetheless, even this was not enough to get police and prosecutors on board.

In Maricopa County, Arizona, between February and August 2011, two Maricopa County police departments identified fifty domestic violence strangulation cases. Only seven were prosecuted in court. According to prosecutors, they dropped almost all the rest for lack of corroboration.

Without visible injuries, apparently prosecutors were reluctant to proceed just based on the victim's say so, if the victims were even willing to testify. This prompted the Maricopa County Attorney's Office to agree to recommendations from law enforcement and advocates to fund the addition of a medical forensic exam for all domestic violence cases with a report of strangulation for a six-month pilot period.

Starting December 1, 2011, the Maricopa County Attorney's Office (MCAO) collaborated with Scottsdale Healthcare forensic nurse examiners and law enforcement in the two police departments to provide comprehensive medical forensic examinations to victims of domestic violence. This comprises a specialized exam including high-definition photographic documentation and DNA collection to obtain sufficient evidence to proceed with a criminal case even if the victim doesn't want to testify. The high-tech cameras capture the broken vessels and veins under the skin and in the mouth and eyes even when bruises may not be visible to the naked eye.[28]

During the pilot, the two police departments identified forty-one strangulation cases. This time, police took all the victims for medical exams. Prosecutors filed sixteen cases in court. In other words, strangulation prosecutions increased from 14 to 61.5 percent. Following the six-month trial, the Maricopa County Attorney's Office supported efforts to have medical forensic exams become an integral part of the community response for all victims of domestic violence strangulation cases throughout Maricopa County, and by 2015, nearly four hundred medical forensic strangulation exams were performed as part of the strangulation protocol. It is estimated that Maricopa County police departments will forthwith handle over fifteen hundred strangulation cases a year.

In 2014, perhaps coincidently, perhaps not, the Maricopa County sheriff's office reported the lowest number of domestic violence incidents across the county in ten years and a 30 percent drop from the year before. In 2012, there were 139 domestic violence fatalities, 125 in 2013, and only 106 in 2014.[29]

IF YOU FELONIZE IT, ARRESTS WILL COME

Making strangulation a more serious offense changes police behavior. They make more arrests. According to a Washington State superior court serving Seattle, when that state led the nation in making strangulation a felony in 2007, strangulation became one of the "most common domestic violence charges brought." Since 2007, the court has heard more than one thousand strangulation cases. According to the prosecutor, "Today it is considered one of the strongest criminal justice responses to domestic violence assault."[30] When Virginia and Maine made strangulation a felony aggravated assault as opposed to a simple misdemeanor assault, arrests also soared, increasing across Virginia and up by 61 percent in Maine over two years.[31] Similarly in Travis County, Texas, in 2012, the district and county attorney offices and the police department revised the domestic assault case form to include an extra page that officers must complete if the victim has been strangled. It asks for details about how and where the victim was strangled and for any symptoms, including defecation, urination, and the bursting of small blood vessels in the eyes or skin, leaving behind tiny red spots—things most likely to lead to a strangulation conviction. By referencing a checklist, officers don't have to know off the top of their heads all the signs to look for and then write them up in a narrative. The number of strangulation cases filed in Travis County increased from the year 2012 to 2013.[32]

STALKING: THE SUM IS FAR GREATER THAN THE PARTS

Stalking laws have proven quite popular among legislators. Since California enacted its first stalking law in 1989 to protect Hollywood starlets from deluded fans, every state in the union has followed suit. Unlike in California, the laws target the far more common stalkers, those who stalk current or former intimates. Only a small minority of stalkers target strangers or imagined lovers. Mostly, husbands, ex-husbands, current or former boyfriends, and current or former cohabiting partners stalk women. Fewer men are stalked and it's more likely to be by non-intimates. Stalking often begins when a woman is still in the abusive relationship and escalates when she leaves or attempts to leave.

Stalking is no small matter, even if the individual acts that constitute it—following victims, repeated contacts, and the like—may seem trivial. The *Intimate Partner Stalking and Femicide Study*, which studied female victims who had been killed by intimate partners, found that abusers stalked 76 percent of femicide victims and 85 percent of attempted femicide victims in the year prior to the (attempted) murders.[33] One of the standard questions asked to determine likelihood of a victim's murder is: "Does he follow you, spy on you, or leave you threatening messages?"

Contrary to popular belief, of all types of stalkers, domestic violence stalkers are the "most malignant." They have the most violent criminal histories, and are the most apt to abuse stimulants or alcohol, but are rarely psychotic like stalkers portrayed on TV. They are persistent and escalate in frequency and intensity of pursuit. Over half will physically assault their victims. According to the experts, virtually all of them reoffend, and they do so more quickly than non-intimate stalkers.[34]

Abusers who stalk after their victims have obtained protective orders against them are among the worst of the worst. They typically combine their stalking with almost every other kind of abuse a victim can experience, much more than typically experienced by abused women who are not stalked after a protective order. Women who are stalked by violent partners after obtaining protective orders are four times more likely to experience physical assaults, almost ten times more likely to experience sexual assaults, and almost five times more likely to be injured than women with protective orders who are not stalked. Further, the same research indicates that those who stalk their victims after protective orders are issued most likely stalked them before the order too.[35]

STALKING PREVALENCE

The popularity of stalking laws reflects its popularity as an abuse tactic. According to a national survey, during a twelve-month period, an estimated 1.5 percent of persons age eighteen or older were victims of stalking in this country. The percentage of stalking victims was highest for individuals who were divorced or separated (3.3 percent), compared to those married, never married, or widowed.[36] About half of the victims experienced unwanted contacts at least weekly, and more than 10 percent reported it had been going on for five years or more! Cyberstalking is growing as the technology becomes more accessible and sophisticated. Almost half of stalking victims admitted to being fearful, not knowing what will happen next. More than half of the victims reported missing at least five days of work because of the stalking.

In the national survey, individuals are classified as stalking victims if they experienced at least one of the following behaviors on at least two separate occasions: receiving unwanted phone calls, unsolicited or unwanted letters, or e-mails; being following or spied upon; having the abuser show up at places without a legitimate reason; waiting at places for the victim; leaving unwanted items, presents, or flowers; and posting information or spreading rumors about the victim on the Internet, in a public place, or by word of mouth. In addition, victims must fear for their safety or that of a family member, or have experienced additional threatening behaviors that would cause a reasonable person to fear.

Stalking is involved in half of protective order violations. Violating orders shows the requisite offender intent to control and intimidate the victim despite the legal restraint placed on him by a judge. The course of conduct here may involve repeatedly following or harassing the victim and placing the victim in reasonable fear of harm. While repeated violations of protective orders constitute stalking, even the first violation of a protective order may in fact be stalking, because the original series of events that caused the victim to seek the court's protection may fit the legal definition of the crime.

Yet the connection between protective order violations and stalking violations is mostly ignored. Studies show that even when states have mandatory arrest laws for violations of protective orders, law enforcement officers do not always arrest offenders who commit these violations. One study showed that only 44 percent of protective order violations resulted in arrest and that the likelihood of arrest decreased as the number of prior incidents increased![37]

A violation of a protective order may seem isolated, even trivial, but if the officer digs deeper, the victim will typically be able to disclose previously reported or unreported violations of the same order. The "single" violation becomes part of a more serious and threatening picture—stalking. For this reason some states, such as Florida, added a provision to their stalking laws in 2004 (Fla. Stat §784.048(4)) that defines more than one violation of a protective order as felony stalking. Kansas legislators took similar action (KSA 21-3843).

Confronted with stalking, however, many police either overlook it or discount its significance.

POLICE ADVISE STALKING VICTIM TO GET PROTECTIVE ORDER IN LIEU OF ACTUALLY PROVIDING PROTECTION

On September 20, 2011, Rafael Zarate secreted an eight-inch kitchen knife into his boot and entered the restaurant where his ex-girlfriend worked in San Pablo, California. Several weeks earlier, she had ended the relationship, after which he had begun his campaign of stalking and threats.

Zarate called his ex-girlfriend repeatedly and followed her to work daily. The stalking got particularly scary and intense when it forced

Zarate's ex to hide in another restaurant's walk-in refrigerator. When she called the San Pablo police, all they did was tell her to take out a protective order. Though a prosecutor later said that the 911 call made it "pretty clear" that some crimes had occurred, officers didn't even bother to write up an incident report, apparently dismissing the stalking as trivial.

That was four days before the murder.

Later, investigators found Zarate's license plate number carefully written down and saved among his victim's things, something victims do when they fear they may be killed and want to leave a clue as to the perpetrator. In her purse, investigators also found a business card for STAND! For Families Free of Violence, a local domestic violence advocacy group. The head of that agency later admitted to the media that her agency could have done a better job for the ex-girlfriend, including better linkages with police to hold the abuser accountable.[1]*

The police department also had an opportunity to protect her, but failed, according to the prosecutor who subsequently prosecuted Zarate for the murder. As the prosecutor explained to the media, the police were not looking at domestic violence from a lethality-prevention standpoint.

Note

*Bartos, L., "Contra Costa County Aims to Stop Domestic Violence Homicides Before They Happen," *California Health Report*, February 9, 2015.

STALKING LAWS

Unfortunately, most legislatures have misdiagnosed the danger and grievously detrimental impact of intimate partner stalking just as they have strangulation. Only fifteen states classify stalking as a felony for a first offense, although thirty-four do for a second offense or when the crime involves aggravating factors. Stalking laws vary regarding the element of victim fear and emotional distress required, as well as the requisite intent of the stalker. Some specify that the victim must be frightened by the stalking, while others require only that the stalking behavior would cause a reasonable person to experience fear. The level of fear required varies too. Some state laws require prosecutors to establish fear of death or serious bodily harm, while others require only that prosecutors establish that the victim suffered emotional distress. Stalking becomes a federal crime if the abuser crosses state lines. The federal law requires a credible threat to the victim's physical safety.

While every state has criminalized stalking in their criminal codes, in practice it remains decriminalized. Police rarely arrest for stalking, substituting lesser charges. Stalkers who violate protective orders are charged with simple violations, not stalking.

Admittedly, stalking, like strangulation, can be difficult to identify and harder yet to prosecute. Almost all other domestic crimes, as most crimes, are discrete acts, not defined by patterns of behavior. Heroin addicts, for example, are not arrested for being addicts, but for possessing or selling the illegal substance at a specific point in time. In contrast, stalking, by definition, consists of multiple acts over time, each of which must be proven at trial. The Massachusetts stalking law, for example, requires "repeated" acts for an offense to be defined as stalking. That state's supreme judicial court subsequently held that "repeatedly," in fact requires at least *three* acts (MGL c 265 §43).

When police arrive on the scene, they are trained to record the facts pertaining to the specific incident that brought them there. Going back to amass prior incidents that demonstrate stalking requires further investigation and evidence gathering. It is not something most departments are going to do for a misdemeanor charge, which most state stalking statutes make the crime. Further, increasingly stalking has become electronic. As researchers found in Rhode Island, it will probably take the next generation of law enforcement officers before most police recognize electronic stalking and know how to prove it. In a Rhode Island study, for example, although the state legislature had enacted a specific cyberstalking statute in 2001, police identified only one case of cyberstalking through 2005. Combing through police incident reports, however, researchers found repeated references to e-mails and other electronic means of communication used by the suspects.[38]

The one cyberstalking complaint brought illustrates both how tricky it is to prove, but also why it is so important to pursue the charge.

As this defendant discovered, if you are intent on committing multiple offenses, it pays to do them in quick succession because prosecutors and courts tend to wrap them up and sentence the separate crimes concurrently. Three-for-one court specials save criminal justice resources, but not

RHODE ISLAND'S ONLY CYBERSTALKING ARREST THROUGH 2005

Almost immediately after the court had issued a mutual protective order against the Rhode Island victim and her former live-in boyfriend, forty-six, of six years, in October 2003, the victim told police she began receiving harassing and threatening e-mails. They came under three different addresses: "shallowman," "neilnbobnomore," and "afoollikeu." She received fifteen in all. According to the police, the e-mails were "sexually degrading" and "threatening." They also indicated that the sender was observing the victim, identifying what she was wearing the day an e-mail was sent, for example.

The police detective verified that the protective order existed and that the ex-boyfriend had been arrested by another police department a few days earlier for crank/obscene phone calls, classified as a domestic violence offense and violation of the protective order. At his arraignment, the ex-boyfriend had also been ordered to have no contact with the victim.

The detective analyzed the header information of the e-mails in question and identified the originating Internet Protocol Number. He then referenced the American Registry for Internet Numbers and determined that the number was subscribed to XXX Communications (name changed). Within the week, the detective obtained a court search warrant and got confirmation from XXX Communications that the IP address was assigned to the ex-boyfriend. The ex-boyfriend was then arraigned for cyberstalking. Bail was set at $1,000 cash with the stipulation of no contact with the victim, but because it was determined that he had violated the bail release of the pending violation of protective order charge and crank/obscene phone call, he was not released.

The detective then secured a formal witness statement from the victim. The victim indicated that in addition to the e-mails, the defendant had left messages on her voicemail. She told police the e-mails made her fear for her safety, causing her to get rides to and from work and sleep in different locations each night. She also said she received hang-up calls at work. Her boss had observed the defendant in front of the building where the victim worked and received calls from the defendant the day the victim received the hang-up calls.

The boss also told police that the suspect had worked for him prior to the victim. When shown the e-mails sent to the victim, he said the phrases were similar to those used by the defendant, including statements about oral sex. The boss also stated that he observed the defendant in front of his business and had conversations with him about his alleged embezzlement of company funds, in which the defendant asked that the company fire the victim.

The victim later told police that the defendant had told her he had acquired a .357 handgun. The boss said he owned such a gun, but it was missing from his office soon after the defendant stopped working for him. The detective secured a search warrant for the defendant's home, which turned up a computer that was seized along with a handwritten note that listed the three names used in the e-mails. The defendant's brother, who was at the house at the time of the search, said the handwriting was his father's. The father told police he had minimal use of the computer and had no part in sending e-mails to the victim or any involvement in the Hotmail account.

A record check revealed that the defendant had first been arrested for a domestic assault and two violations of protective orders in a case in 1991 not involving the current victim. Both sets of those cases were eventually dismissed.

Before being tried on the cyberstalking charge, the defendant was sentenced for the prior threatening phone call to thirty days in jail and eleven months suspended with probation. He was ordered to complete a batterer program and have no contact with the victim. Subsequently, he was sentenced to one year suspended in November 2003 for cyberstalking, concurrent with the prior phone threats case. On that same day, he was also arraigned for yet another violation of the protective order that was still outstanding. He was given another one-year suspended sentence for that case. A little more than a month later, he was arraigned for violation of a no contact order issued when he was sentenced to prison. He was given another one-year suspended sentence and ordered to complete a batterer program and have no contact with the victim. Two months later, in January 2004, he was arraigned again for violating the protective order. The following May, he was sentenced to forty-five days home confinement, 320 days suspended, and probation for one year. He was ordered to complete the batterer program again and have no contact with the victim.[*]

Note

[*]Klein, A., Salomon, A., Huntington, N., Dubois, J., and Long, D., *Statewide Study of Stalking and Its Criminal Justice Response*, U.S. Department of Justice, National Institute of Justice, NCJ 228354, May 2009.

victims. The prosecutors' and courts' tepid response to this stalker ensures this—or a new victim—future terror.

Also, keep in mind that this cyberstalking took place in 2003, when e-mail served as the primary venue. Today, with the numerous social networks now online, cyberstalkers have even more opportunity to threaten and intimidate.

In 2006, the U.S. Congress amended the Violence Against Women Act to make online threats of death and injury a federal crime. According to a Massachusetts congresswoman, between 2010 and 2013, despite 2.5 million cases of cyberstalking across the United States, the U.S. Justice Department pursued only ten of them![39]

The low arrest rate is all the more problematic because generally the victims who report stalking are the ones most victimized and threatened.[40]

UNPOPULARITY OF STALKING LAW ENFORCEMENT AND PROSECUTION

Though stalking is as popular with abusers as laws to punish it are with legislators, stalking is not so popular with police or prosecutors.

In central Florida, the police and prosecutors finally showed that together they could protect a young woman from an ex-boyfriend accused of stalking her and her mother. It took a Channel 9 WFTV news broadcast where the young woman accused authorities of ignoring her repeated pleas for assistance.

The prosecutor made the case out of the hundreds of texted threats to kill the victim and her family. Because some of the texts showed pictures of a gun, that justified a felony stalking charge, "aggravated stalking with a credible threat." The Orange County sheriff's office released a statement regarding the victim: "We understand her frustrations and hope that by making this arrest, and holding the suspect with a no bond status, this restores her sense of safety and security as this case goes through the legal system."

Unfortunately, most terrorized victims don't have TV news to get law enforcement and prosecutors to take the time to put all the pieces together when it comes to stalking. Police regularly overlook it, and rarely arrest for it even when they correctly identify it, and prosecutors don't prosecute the few who are arrested for it. Across Florida, for example, where over 108,000 abusers were arrested for various domestic violence–related crimes in 2013, only 701 were arrested for either simple or aggravated stalking. Even that is up from the year before, when the total was even less, with just 589 stalking arrests. Of the 21,654 domestic violence arrests New Jersey reported in

STALKING REQUIRES POLICE TO CONNECT THE DOTS

In the Channel 9 WFTV news broadcast, the young woman described how she and her mother had been stalked and terrorized by her ex-boyfriend, receiving hundreds of texts threatening to kill them. The ex-girlfriend had filed six separate complaints with Orange County investigators. She and her mother were granted a protective order, which law enforcement never served because they couldn't locate the abuser. The victim and her family moved, blocked his number, and deleted all of her social media accounts.

All to no avail.

The ex-boyfriend always found her using other people's phones and fake accounts. As the young woman related to Channel 9, "He always gets away. Next time he's going to shoot me. I don't understand the system. It's not set up correctly. Victims have no rights." Her ex was also caught slashing her tires by a neighbor's camera, and he had recently confronted her at a Wawa store, then followed her for miles while armed with a gun. "And, he's like, 'Roll down the window, I'm going to shoot you in the head.'" She called 911, but when an Orange County deputy arrived, her ex-boyfriend had already fled the area.

The victim declared on the TV news, "To feel that law enforcement can't do anything to help me; the only thing I feel is when I'm in a body bag, then they'll do their steps. He's winning and he knows it." Her mother added, "We have no protection, no protection. He's made it a living hell for all of us." The victims charged that the authorities had not even issued a warrant for his arrest. Reached by the reporter, the Orange County sheriff's office said it was actively investigating the case.

After the story was broadcast, a detective was assigned the case and immediately sat down with the victim. She related all the awful details of her and her family's ordeal and prior attempts to get authorities to pay attention. The very next day, the alleged stalker, the same man deputies could not find to serve the protective order, was arrested.

WFTV broadcast the follow-up in January 2015. The victim expressed "massive relief." She reported that she had not received any threatening texts since the arrest! She could drive without fear of being followed. "I feel," she said, "safe now." The judge had ordered the suspected stalker to be held without bond on five charges, including aggravated assault, false imprisonment, and aggravated stalking.*

2011, only 111 were for stalking. Reporting a 34 percent arrest rate for the crime, New Jersey police only identified 322 incidents of stalking that year. These numbers are up from 2010, when police made only one hundred stalking arrests, with an arrest rate of 31 percent. In Tennessee, police only track domestic violence among spouses and identified one hundred stalkers out of 13,250 spousal domestic violence incidents in 2012. Kentucky sheriffs and police did a bit better than most, arresting over five hundred abusers for stalking in 2008.[41]

New Mexico law enforcement reported 162 stalking cases in 2007. A health survey a few years before revealed 17,177 individuals had been stalked in the state, an average of 14.3 times. Almost half reported being injured by their stalkers, and a little under a third of the stalkers used a weapon. A third of the stalking victims reported it to police. A little over a quarter filed for a protective order, and half reported the order was violated. Only 5.5 percent of the stalking crimes resulted in an arrest, and only 5.9 percent of cases were filed in court. Charges were then dropped in 13 percent of the cases, but 51 percent of the stalkers pleaded guilty.[42]

At one point, North Dakota reported the greatest per capita arrests for stalking in the country. Even so, its rate, if applied nationally, would have resulted in only 22,805 stalking arrests for the entire nation. According to a 2009 Justice Department report of its National Crime Victim survey, 41 percent of female stalking victims reported their stalking to police. Based on survey estimates, that would have resulted in 1,036,886 reports to police. In short, there is a gigantic disconnect between stalking committed and reported and police stalking incident reports, much less arrests for stalking. When stalkers are arrested, it is for simple assault, harassment, menacing, intimidation, threats to commit a crime, protective order violation, vandalism, breaking and entering, robbery, trespassing, and disorderly conduct. These alternative charges do not reflect the true nature of the offense, and turn patterned, premeditated behavior into a single, isolated act.

Several studies in different states that have examined police domestic violence incident reports found that even where the reports documented all the elements necessary to define the crime of stalking pursuant to that state's law, it was not charged. During a study period from 2001 to 2005 in Rhode Island, police identified only 108 stalking incidents out of 33,000 domestic violence incident reports. Based on the research identification of stalking cases, 6.8 percent of the police incident reports, in fact, documented stalking, but were not so identified by police. Instead, police charged the stalkers most often with violation of protective orders or threatening phone calls, or did not charge the abuser with any crime.[43] It makes a big difference, because under state law, stalking (R.I. Gen. Laws §11-59-2) is a felony punishable by imprisonment for not more than five years, by a fine of not more than $10,000, or both. The other crimes are all misdemeanors, punishable by a fine of no more than $1,000 or by imprisonment for not more than one year, or both.

An example of a stalking case police missed shows how correctly identifying the crime is not rocket science. The police report involved three incidents.

STALKER EVADES STALKING CHARGES

On May 26, officers responded to a victim who informed them that her ex-boyfriend "called her from a bar near her house" in violation of an active restraining order. The victim had been out for the evening and, upon returning home, checked her messages and noticed on her caller ID the phone number of a local bar. When she played the messages, she heard her seemingly intoxicated ex-boyfriend asking her "who she was out with the other night and that he would find out even if she did not tell him." She reported that the message left her "very scared and nervous" because it had originated from a bar just a short distance from her home. Her fear was heightened because, she said, "he is very unstable when he drinks." She added that the suspect's mother and sister had told her that he "often becomes violent when he is drinking" and that she contacted police because she was afraid he would come to her home from the bar. Officers listened to the message and noted that the suspect, who identified himself by name, seemed "angry." After taking the victim's statement, officers noticed a taxi in front of her residence with the passenger fitting the suspect's description. The suspect stated that he "did not want any trouble . . . he was just going to see his girl." Officers confirmed with dispatch that the suspect had recently been served with the restraining order, which was still valid. The suspect was arrested and, while being transported to the station, stated "several times that he loved [the victim] and that he was just going there to talk to her."

Three days later, officers responded to a report made by the same victim for a second violation of the restraining order. This time, both she and her coworker had observed her ex-boyfriend across from her place of work. When police responded, the suspect was seated on the front steps of a church, identified himself as the ex-boyfriend of the victim, and, as police began handcuffing him, stated, "Not again." He claimed to have been walking to a bank on a neighboring street, and that passing by the victim's place of work was "the quickest way" to get there after he left his job, adding that he "had no intention of violating the restraining order." After some investigation, police ascertained that the suspect had left work two hours earlier and that the route he claimed to be taking from work to the bank did not include passing by the victim's place of work, but actually was "out of [his] way." Officers measured the suspect's distance from the victim's place of work as "20 feet away from her" and noted that the office was "entirely enclosed in glass" and was "in full view of everything in the office to parties walking outside." According to the victim, the suspect was aware that she worked from 3:00 p.m. to midnight and is frequently alone in the office. She was grateful that her coworker arrived when he did because she feared that the suspect "may have done something to her" had she been alone.

The victim explained to police that she and the suspect had been in a "serious relationship for approximately four months" that had ended about one month earlier. She obtained a restraining order after having alleged that he "threatened her and her friends and made remarks stating he would make a bomb and blow her up and he would be long gone when it happens." Officers noticed that while making this report, the victim "was nervous, shaking and afraid."

The victim's statement provided additional information about previous threats made by the suspect. She included in her statement that he was "very possessive and jealous and told me several times that he would kill me." After the relationship ended, he threatened her and her friend, and he told her she "didn't know who [she] was messing with and what he was capable of." She said that this last statement "stuck in [her] mind" and caused her to be "afraid of what he will do next."

After the suspect was in custody, police further probed about his questionable route to the bank from work. He responded, "I don't know, I thought I was in love." Police cited the stalker for violation of a protective order. The charges were dismissed by a local prosecutor. The stalker was then arrested yet again for violation of protective order, but still not for stalking.[*]

Note

[*]Klein, A., Salomon, A., Huntington, N., Dubois, J., and Long, D. *Statewide Study of Stalking and Its Criminal Justice Response*, U.S. Department of Justice, National Institute of Justice, NCJ 228354, May 2009.

Rhode Island is far from unique. Two researchers reviewed almost two thousand domestic violence complaints taken out by police in Colorado Springs, Colorado, which was known nationally for its aggressive domestic violence policing program, in 1998. The state made stalking a felony in 1992. The review found that 16.5 percent of the police reports indicated on their face that stalking was involved. However, only one of the 285 complaints with evidence of stalking resulted in the filing of a stalking charge. Instead, police charged the stalkers with harassment or a single act of violation of a protective order.[44] A couple of years after the study, the Colorado Springs police department's special domestic violence unit resolved to do better, expecting to make seventy stalking arrests that year. However, in the latest 2013 crime report issued by the Colorado Bureau of Investigation, while Colorado Springs reported 11,860 domestic violence arrests of adults, none were for stalking.

Ironically, in enacting its stalking law, the Colorado legislators included the following legislative intent:

> Because stalking involves highly inappropriate intensity, persistence, and possessiveness, it entails great unpredictability and creates great stress and fear for the victim. Stalking involves severe intrusions on the victim's personal privacy and autonomy, with an immediate and long-lasting impact on quality of life as well as risks to security and safety of the victim and persons close to the victim, even in the absence of express threats of physical harm. The general assembly hereby recognizes the seriousness posed by stalking and adopts [these] provisions . . . with the goal of encouraging and authorizing effective intervention before stalking can escalate into behavior that has even more serious consequences.[45]

Unfortunately, stalking is an easy crime for police and prosecutors to ignore. It is far less easy for victims. While the individual, specific acts that make up stalking may appear trivial in isolation, the cumulative effect is what makes stalking a serious crime. Victims can find themselves in a no-win situation. The more they call police to report stalking incidents, the more they may be dismissed as nuisances, crying wolf.

This attitude persists up through prosecution. A recent stalking prosecution study in Kentucky found that fully 62 percent of cases for misdemeanor stalking and 55 percent of cases for felony stalking were dismissed. Only 24 percent of those charged with misdemeanor and 14 percent of those charged with felony stalking charges were eventually found guilty or pleaded guilty. Meanwhile, half of the dismissed cases had occurred after the victim had obtained a protective order. Further, most of the suspects had prior significant criminal histories. Researchers found that prosecutors across the state dismissed cases regardless of the seriousness of the offense, the seriousness of the offenders' criminal record, concerns for victim safety, or even the evidence available. Instead, researchers concluded, they were guided by their own biases and/or lack of "political will."[46] Comparing stalking outcomes to assaults and violations of protective orders, researchers found that stalking charges were about twice as likely to be dismissed and much less likely to have a guilty disposition.

The aforementioned Rhode Island study showed the importance of accurately identifying stalking. When police correctly identified the crime as stalking, it significantly increased the likelihood that these chronic and dangerous abusers were held accountable, significantly decreasing further victim abuse. Police identification of stalkers was significantly associated with increased likelihood of arrest and court prosecution, compared to equivalent stalkers identified by police for non-stalking domestic violence offenses. Further, police-identified stalkers were significantly less likely to be charged with new domestic violence up to six years after police intervention. Unfortunately, the latter applied only to the lower-risk stalkers identified by police, a minority of those stalkers arrested without prior criminal histories. As the research consistently documents, very little that is being done to date deters high-risk abusers.

ARRESTING VICTIMS

Another major law enforcement domestic violence challenge remaining is the failure of some officers to identify victims from abusers. This failure results in the arrest of victims. Like Connecticut, when states first enacted mandatory and preferred arrest statutes, some law enforcement officers began arresting everyone involved, victim and abuser alike. Some arrested just the victim, because by the time they arrived on the scene the victim appeared to be the more active aggressor or the more disorderly of the parties. This is especially true in jurisdictions that regularly substitute charges of disorderly conduct or breach of the peace for assaults.

As a result, legislators went back to the drawing boards to enact "primary aggressor" laws and then "predominant aggressor" laws, instructing police to arrest the true abuser (read male, in straight couples) in most cases. These laws vary. The Washington legislature enacted one of the first such laws after its mandatory arrest law increased victim arrests. The law advised police to consider that the intent of the mandatory arrest law was to protect, not arrest, victims of domestic violence. It directs police to compare the extent of injuries suffered by both parties or the seriousness of the threats made by each party as well as the prior history of domestic violence. Other states added provisions for police to investigate whether the victim engaged in self-defense, which party was more likely to injure the other in the future, even to compare the "relative sizes and apparent strengths" of the parties. Missouri law cautioned that the primary aggressor is the more significant aggressor, not necessarily the *first* aggressor. Another state law required officers to consider the accounts of other household members and witnesses before picking which party to arrest.

While these laws are gender neutral, it does not take much to realize that these laws were based on the correct assumption that women have much more to fear from domestic violence than men.

DETERMINING THE PRIMARY AGGRESSOR

According to an essay by defense attorney Adam Banner, University of Oklahoma Sooners running back Joe Mixon was charged with a misdemeanor for "Acts Resulting in Gross Injury" after he punched a young woman who first uttered a racial epithet, pushed him, and slapped him. The female was not charged even though she committed assault and battery against Mixon prior to being knocked out by a single punch. In deciding to charge Mixon with a misdemeanor, the Cleveland County district attorney explained, "In this particular case, I felt like this statute more fit what happened because now we don't have to talk about who the initial aggressor was. Was there gross injury? And there was. And was that against public morals? And I believe that anytime you punch a girl with that much force, even when she had hit you first, that it would be against public morals."

Disregarding Banner's condescending remark about women, his statement is on point.[47]

Generally, whether states enacted these laws or not, most law enforcement officers have little trouble arresting the abuser, not the victim. With few statewide exceptions, like Connecticut where dual arrests are the rule, only limited law enforcement agencies or sheriff's offices are still consistently arresting victims, alone or with their abuser. To the extent this remains a problem, it appears to be in rural jurisdictions where a good ole boy network may protect its own, or where sheriffs fail to properly supervise their deputies. One of the largest examinations of domestic and family violence arrests across the country found very few domestic violence arrests of both parties. Further, it found that more than 80 percent of those arrested for domestic violence were male, and at least some of the females arrested may have assaulted female partners. Same sex couple abuse is at least as prevalent as heterosexual domestic violence. Where local or state domestic violence statistics show an elevated percentage of domestic violence arrests of females, it is often because intimate partner violence is conflated with other family violence and child abuse. In the multistate arrest study, for example, the rate for female perpetrators was much higher for family violence than for domestic violence cases. It is also true that police may be a bit less likely to arrest black males for abusing black females. Some suggest that police may be more apt to dismiss such abuse as normal. In urban settings, police may ignore domestic violence, given the prevalence of other criminal activity they deem more pressing.

When police do arrest females, prosecutors are less likely to charge them in court. Either prosecutors share the same radical feminist ideology that fathers' rights groups surprisingly suggest influence police behavior, or, a bit removed from the scene, they believe the police made an understandable but wrong decision when making the initial arrest.

There is one big exception across the country. Police are much more likely to arrest both parties when confronted with same sex couples. In fact, they arrest both parties a quarter of the time for both same sex female and male couples compared to less than 1 percent involving male offenders and female victims.[48]

GAY, LESBIAN, BISEXUAL, TRANSGENDER, AND QUEER DOMESTIC VIOLENCE

Police are more apt to get it wrong in responding to intimate partner violence among same sex couples. Why? The simple answer is, many don't know how to spot and handle same sex domestic violence. Abusive same sex relationships haven't been a priority in police training, and the signs for determining the primary aggressor in such relationships aren't the same as those where straight couples are involved.

While threats, overtly controlling behavior, prior assault, and other domestic violence history (within and outside of the current relationship) help identify abusers in both hetero and same sex relationships, things like size, past protective orders, witness statements, and seriousness of injuries

TWO FEMALE "OFFENDERS" LEAD TO DUAL ARREST

Brittney Griner and Glory Johnson were engaged to each other in 2015. At the time, both were professional basketball players in the WNBA, Griner for the Phoenix Mercury and Johnson for the Tulsa Shock. During the couple's engagement, in April 2015, both were arrested in Phoenix after Johnson's sister summoned the police.

In the background of the 911 call, made public on the Internet, there was yelling, while Johnson's sister told the operator that the two women were hurling plates around. Both women had visible injuries when the police arrived. Furthermore, both looked to be of similar physical size and stature—tall and powerful, as their profession demands. Police arrested both Griner and Johnson at the scene for domestic violence.

Griner ultimately owned up as the primary aggressor. She got a plea deal that compelled her to undergo domestic violence counseling in exchange for the domestic violence charges against her to be dropped upon completion. She and Johnson got married two weeks later, claiming that the violent incident was an isolated one and admitting that they needed to set a better example as public figures and role models. Griner released a statement saying that she would never turn violent against her wife again.*

Note

*Information from contemporary news reports, including the *Washington Post, NBC*, and *ABC15 News*. The latter included audio from Johnson's sister's 911 call.

may be less reliable to indicate a primary aggressor in same sex couples. In a heterosexual couple, it's usually the male who's more physically domineering, and the bruises and other physical injuries correspond. In same sex couples, size and strength don't serve as such reliable predictors for controlling behavior.

POLICE ARREST ANOTHER VICTIM

Deanna and Rita (whose names have been changed to protect their privacy) had been together for several years before Rita started showing some red flag behaviors. At first, there was nothing overtly wrong with the way Rita acted. She made a point of getting close to Deanna's friends at work (Deanna was a schoolteacher) and got a little jealous if Deanna went out with them on the weekends without her.

Eventually, this progressed to Rita turning Deanna's coworkers against her by spreading false, mean-spirited rumors about her partner, including that Deanna had been hitting her. This escalated to where none of Deanna's friends would believe in her innocence, as Rita had made a point of getting them "on her side." Rita got the police involved too, by filing false reports of Deanna's violence, which led to her arrest. Rita also took out protective orders against her, ultimately costing Deanna her job as a teacher at her local school, notwithstanding the fact that she was beloved by her students. Rita's campaign of befriending Deanna's coworkers had, after all, included her principal.

Though Rita was clearly the abuser in this relationship, stereotypes were against her victim. Rita was smaller, more feminine, and lighter-skinned than Deanna. She came from a relatively well-off family in the suburbs. Deanna had grown up in the projects, had dark skin, was larger than Rita, and appeared more "butch." She didn't look like a victim. Since Rita's abuse didn't leave any marks on Deanna, the court that granted Rita the protective order didn't have anything to go on other than Rita's story and its own bias.[*]

Note

[*]This material comes from a personal conversation with the author. Names and other details have been changed to protect those involved.

If police can tell a man from a woman and arrest the former, they will get it right almost all the time when it comes to straight couples. Obviously, this logic does not apply when it comes to same sex couples.

If Brittney Griner hadn't confessed in the Phoenix case, chances are police, prosecutors, and judges may never have been able to put a finger on any primary aggressor. The case would never have been prosecuted either, because in dual arrests, the alleged abusers are also the alleged victims. Of course, with a little bit of awareness and training, police might have identified the primary aggressor. First and foremost, they could have tried, beginning with interviewing the pair separately, in lieu of proceeding directly to a knee-jerk joint arrest.[49]

Admittedly, it is not always simple, and perpetrators do not normally confess. Many same sex victims get further victimized by the criminal justice system as a result.

Overall, domestic violence manifests in physical violence in same sex relationships less frequently than it does otherwise. According to the 2013 National Coalition of Anti-Violence Programs (NCAVP) report, *LGBTQ Intimate Partner Violence*, which includes data from NCAVP programs all over the country, only 17.3 percent of the domestic violence incidents reported to these programs involved physical violence; the rest consisted of verbal, psychological, and financial abuse. It doesn't take superior strength to damage someone's psyche or control access to their bank account.

MIS-ARRESTS IN SAME SEX RELATIONSHIPS

Johnson and Deanna in the examples cited in the previous section are far from the only domestic violence victims in same sex relationships to have gotten arrested. In 57.9 percent of same sex domestic violence incidents reported to the NCAVP in 2013 across the United States, police arrested the victim instead of the perpetrator, much worse than what the NCAVP reported in 2012 (29.7 percent). However, much of the increase may be because more same sex relationship incidents were identified as domestic violence, instead of being classified as miscellaneous violence. Still, this number explains the decrease of same sex abuser arrests from 2012, which dropped from 44 percent among LGBTQ couples to 30.2 percent.

Dual arrest has even been used as a *threat* by police responding to same sex domestic violence calls. Declining to try to figure our primary aggressors, responding police officers have been reported to warn same sex couples that if they are called again, they will arrest both parties![50]

Some same sex abusers have realized that whoever contacts police first can determine which party police will arrest. This even extended to a case where a female abuser had just shot a gun at her female partner. The abuser got to the responding officers first and explained how she had been attacked first. While the true victim sat in a jail cell, her abuser took the opportunity to use the arrest of her victim to convince the court to grant her a protective order, giving her a legally sanctioned vehicle to continue to harass and stalk her victim.[51]

POLICE BEHAVING BADLY CONFRONTED WITH SAME SEX DOMESTIC VIOLENCE

If law enforcement is called, they often don't make getting help look like a better option. A horrible example made national news back in 1991. A fourteen-year-old boy was killed by a thirty-year-old man because police, arriving at what should have been a disconcerting scene, left the two alone after the older man claimed the "young adult" as his lover. Neighbors had initially contacted the police because the fourteen-year-old was naked, bleeding, disoriented, and running around in the street. When cops arrived at the scene, the thirty-year-old insisted that the boy was actually his adult lover, and he was only drunk and getting carried away. A police officer who spoke to the adult male even said that it looked like the two had a caring relationship. Shortly after the officers left, the man brought the boy back inside his apartment, where he proceeded to strangle and kill him.

This took place in Milwaukee, Wisconsin. The boy was Konerak Sinthasomphone. The man was serial killer Jeffrey Dahmer.[52]

While this did not represent an actual instance of domestic violence, it illustrates that ignorance can be as harmful as outright bias in situations of intimate, same sex violence. While the officers in this situation seemed to be "understanding" of a gay couple having a little bit too much fun one evening, they actually proved the intensity of their bias by ignoring what others, those who called the police, saw as a clearly not right, dangerous situation. Advocates subsequently called the responding police officers in Milwaukee both homophobic and racist, as the murder victim, Sinthasomphone, was Laotian.

Police misconduct, lack of knowledge, and indifference all count among the reasons why LGBTQ victims may not reach out to law enforcement. Prejudice is often deeply ingrained in precincts that value the traditional, heteronormative image of masculinity and relationships. This perpetuates the attitude that "spats" between same sex couples are just that, "catfights" between two women or two gay men.

In 2005, an Amnesty International study found that just five of the twenty-nine police departments they looked at had specific policies for same sex domestic violence cases. Police departments in several major U.S. cities—Wilmington, Delaware; Baltimore, Maryland; Omaha, Nebraska; and Atlanta, Georgia—didn't offer any training for LGBTQ domestic violence.[53] The lack of policy has had some serious negative consequences for LGBTQ domestic violence victims. One weekend in Houston, Texas, in 2000, police refused to help Marc Kajs file a report against his abusive ex-boyfriend because "the domestic violence unit was closed." Kajs was shot and killed by his abuser later that day. That wasn't the first time Kajs had turned to police for protection against his violent ex-boyfriend. Kajs had spoken to the police multiple times about his ex stalking and threatening him. In one of these instances, police even witnessed Kajs's abuser threatening him. At 2:30 a.m., Kajs's ex-boyfriend followed him to the police station when he tried to report, and even though police officers actually saw and heard this going on in front of their workplace, they did nothing to help Kajs, leaving him instead with the man who was threatening his life. That was just days before Kajs's murder.

In an incident three years later, police in San Antonio failed to protect a lesbian woman from her gun-wielding partner. When police arrived at the victim's home, they saw obvious signs of struggle. The house was trashed, not to mention that the abuser was standing there with a gun in her hand. Though police left with the gun, they also left the couple alone together. The victim was later shot and killed by her abuser.

That same year in New York, police came to the scene of a gay man fearing that his partner would kill him. Like the San Antonio officers, they took one means of violence from the abuser (this time, the keys to the victim's apartment) and then left the scene, assuming their work there was done. The victim in this situation was killed two hours after the police left.

In addition to indifference, police officers have a history of being actively abusive to LGBTQ victims of domestic violence. Male victims may get taunted for not acting manly in the face of physical altercations. One instance noted by Amnesty International found an officer calling a gay victim a "sissy," insisting he wasn't "hurt that bad." The man had two black eyes and a fractured arm. He had to walk to the nearest hospital's emergency room because police were too busy making fun of him to take him to the hospital. Interestingly, the man's abusive boyfriend reportedly was a police officer, perhaps contributing to the victim's abuse at the hands of the responding police.

To this day, many LGBTQ survivors of domestic violence who report to the police say they experienced either "hostile" or "indifferent" attitudes from them. This "hostile" behavior spans verbal abuse, the use of slurs/biased language, and physical and sexual violence. Indifferent attitudes frequently come by way of stereotypes—like women being unable to truly abuse their partners because "women aren't violent," and men needing to "man up" and sort out issues with other men between themselves, without police intervention. It's not as if people who identify as LGBTQ are naive about police biases. In an Atlanta, Georgia, study from 2013, 59 percent of gay and bisexual men said they believed that police would be less helpful to gay domestic violence survivors than to straight, female victims.[54]

That's not to say that all police categorically fail to respond appropriately to same sex domestic violence calls. In August 2014, three Washington, D.C. police officers (all male) arrived at the scene of a serious domestic assault between female partners. The twenty-five-year-old perpetrator, Maya Shelia Moore, had stabbed the victim—her girlfriend of about two years—multiple times on the chest, neck, abdomen, and thigh. Moore had severed an artery in her girlfriend's thigh, and two of the responding officers quickly attended to the wound by making a tourniquet "out of an unknown citizen's belt," according to the affidavit. Meanwhile, the third officer apprehended Moore, who had run from the scene the moment police arrived.[55]

Moore had been arrested twice for assaulting her partner prior to the stabbing. The most recent arrest took place just two months before the stabbing, and the other happened back in September 2013. In the more recent incident, Moore hit her partner first with her fist, then with an unopened pocketknife. The arrests in both instances reveal a positive police response. The abuser was arrested instead of the victim, and the victim continued to engage with police on multiple occasions, showing that she trusted the responding officers. However, prosecution clearly proved ineffective in keeping the abuser away from her victim until this last assault, as explained in the following chapter.

TRANSGENDER PEOPLE EXPERIENCE DISPROPORTIONATE VIOLENCE

Transgender people, women in particular, are more likely to experience physical violence and discrimination due to intimate partner abuse, from both their partners and responding police officers. According to the NCAVP, in 2013 this population experienced police violence in connection with intimate partner violence at a rate 5.2 times higher than others who identified as LGBTQ. Transgender women and men report high levels of physical assault and rape by their abusive intimate partners, and a significant portion of them don't feel like they can call the police for help.

They have good reason not to call, after all. It's quite common for transgender victims to be arrested instead of their batterers. This can lead to further abuses and disrespect throughout the criminal justice system. Officers often put transgender women into men's holding cells, and legal personnel may refuse to use a trans person's preferred gender pronouns, repeatedly referring to a transgender man, for example, as "she" or "her."

A few such cases have been covered in the media. In San Antonio in the early 2000s, after a transgender woman reached out to the police to report that her boyfriend had acted violently toward her, breaking her property and a window, the responding officers took the boyfriend's word over the victim's. The boyfriend, who told police the victim was bipolar, ended up standing by while they arrested the victim and took her down to the police station. At the station, police treated the transgender woman as if she were a man, giving her forms to fill out that made her use her male name and then leaving her in a male holding cell, in spite of her multiple protests. She was held there for a couple of hours for not committing a crime.

Another transgender woman who called the police because her boyfriend was assaulting her (chasing her through their shared apartment and strangling her) was also arrested, essentially for defending herself (and for being transgender). This took place in Washington, D.C., in 2002. Responding officers failed to arrest the woman's abuser and instead arrested her for assault. The officers also made a point to refer to her with male gender pronouns after seeing her ID. Fortunately, the charges against her were ultimately dismissed—but her abusive boyfriend apparently suffered no consequences.

Police reactions, of course, vary. In 2003, police driving by ignored a Mexican transgender woman crying out for help while being severely beaten by her boyfriend on the street in Los Angeles. The victim was also homeless at the time, another factor that often garners discrimination from law enforcement. Police finally responded to the scene after being called by a bystander. In this case, they did arrest the boyfriend, but not for assault. They brought him in on drug charges because he happened to be holding.

Two years earlier, another transgender woman in Los Angeles called the police on her abusive, live-in boyfriend a number of times. Many of these times, when officers first arrived at the apartment, they were helpful, listening to the victim and preparing to take her side against her abuser's. However, their behavior markedly changed when it dawned on them that she was a trans person. Sometimes, they would noticeably discuss the victim's gender identity among themselves in her presence. Other times, they would insist that all they could do to help was remove her boyfriend from the home for one hour. In an instance where there was excessive visible damage to both the victim's home and her body, police left the scene without doing a thing.[56]

Imagine how helpful law enforcement might be when it comes to the all too prevalent "hidden" forms of abuse that trans people experience? Abusive partners of trans people often engage in psychological, emotional, and verbal abuse by suggesting, for example, that their partner is "lucky" to have them, because "who else would want to date someone who's not even a real man/woman?" This tactic serves to make victims feel at once more isolated and dependent on their abusive partners, who have manipulated them into thinking that they're the only ones who will truly support and understand their trans partners.

Not all forms of physical abuse even leave marks noticeable to law enforcement. Hiding a trans partner's hormones is one form of physical abuse that doesn't. Controlling a partner's transition, which can also mean hiding wigs, informational materials, and so forth, can be damaging in many ways. Besides toying with a person's identity, it also leaves that trans person vulnerable to increased violence in situations where they are then not able to "pass" as the gender they identify as.

When it comes to getting away from abusers, transgender survivors face another difficulty in terms of the often gendered shelter system. Domestic violence shelters meant for women may well turn away trans women, and all trans people can encounter trouble and become targets in a general shelter population. Shelters like Safe Horizon in New York seek to provide a safe space for LGBTQ people who are living on the streets or escaping from abusive relationships, for instance, but as is generally the case, the more rural you get, the harder it becomes to find safe services for trans people.

6

PROSECUTING ABUSERS

With increased arrests, the challenge of what to do with abusers passed higher up on the criminal justice food chain. While an arrest alone has a limited deterrent effect on low-risk abusers, most abusers who make it to the attention of police are not low risk. The challenge of getting prosecutors and judges on board has proven much more difficult than police. Unlike arrest, legislators cannot mandate that prosecutors prosecute abusers because the standard for arrest is lower than for prosecution. As mentioned before, the legal standard for arrest is probable cause. The standard for successful prosecution is beyond a reasonable doubt. In fact, it is considered prosecutorial misconduct to prosecute cases where there is no reasonable likelihood of obtaining a conviction.

Florida's legislature, and more recently Arkansas's, went about as far as legislatures can go. In 1991, frustrated with the lack of domestic violence prosecution, Florida's legislators directed each county prosecutor to develop special units or assign prosecutors to specialize in the prosecution of domestic violence cases. These prosecutors and their support staff were also required to receive training in domestic violence issues. As the law (741.2901) made clear:

> It is the intent of the Legislature that domestic violence be treated as a criminal act rather than a private matter. For that reason, criminal prosecution shall be the favored method of enforcing compliance with injunctions for

protection against domestic violence as both length and severity of sentence for those found to have committed the crime of domestic violence can be greater, thus providing greater protection to victims and better accountability of perpetrators. This provision shall not preclude such enforcement by the court through the use of indirect criminal contempt. The state attorney in each circuit shall adopt a pro-prosecution policy for acts of domestic violence. . . . The filing, nonfiling, or diversion of criminal charges, and the prosecution of violations of injunctions for protection against domestic violence by the state attorney, shall be determined by these specialized prosecutors over the objection of the victim, if necessary.

Finally, the legislation directed prosecutors to conduct "a thorough investigation of the defendant's history, including, but not limited to prior arrests for domestic violence, prior arrests for nondomestic charges, prior injunctions for protection against domestic and repeat violence filed listing the defendant as respondent and noting history of other victims, and prior walk-in domestic complaints filed against the defendant. This information shall be presented at first appearance, when setting bond, and when passing sentence, for consideration by the court." To safeguard the victim after arrest but before trial, the law bars release of abusers until they are brought before the court for admittance to bail. In determining bail, the court is required to consider the safety of the victim, the victim's children, and any other person who may be in danger if the defendant is released.

In 2015, Arkansas legislators enacted a new law (§12-12-108) requiring law enforcement agencies investigating a complaint or accusation of domestic violence to do so "in a manner that allows the prosecuting attorney to prosecute the offense if the prosecuting attorney has probable cause an offense was committed and achieve a guilty verdict based on evidence independent of the testimony of the victim of the offense." The law goes further to suggest that compliance with this mandate "may be achieved through the collection of evidence including without limitation: 1) witness statements, 2) properly obtained statements from the alleged offender, 3) medical records, 4) photographs or other media, 5) other physical evidence, and 6) statements from the victim that are exclusions or exceptions to the Arkansas Rules of Evidence that prohibit hearsay evidence." Whether or not this law will increase domestic violence prosecutions is not yet known.

Lawsuits have not played an equivalent role in getting prosecutors to prosecute domestic violence cases, as they did in getting police to arrest. Because prosecutors have such broad discretion, lawsuits against them have been far fewer. None has resulted in the kind of awards and notoriety as *Thurman v. Torrington* and its multimillion-dollar settlement.

There has been no seminal research leading to the declaration of domestic violence prosecution to be a "magic bullet," as arrests were once labeled. Perhaps more important, advocates and the public at large have little idea what they should expect of prosecutors because they have little idea what prosecutors really do and how they do it. As a result, some of the most inept, misogynistic prosecutors can get elected and reelected based on a few cases picked up by the media that cover up a pattern of incompetence and lack of commitment when it comes to prosecuting domestic violence perpetrators.

A STEP BACK TO CONSIDER WHAT PROSECUTORS REALLY DO

Most people think criminal prosecution is about an adversarial system, featuring a trial, a verdict of guilt or innocence, and an independent solon dressed in black making a wise, considered sentencing decision after being apprised of all the facts, the defendant's background, and the victim's status. *Law and Order* notwithstanding, for the most part, what was just described only happens when the real system breaks down. As a result of this basic misunderstanding of how prosecutors function, when prosecutors ignore domestic violence, unlike police, they are less likely to be called on it.

Successful prosecuting is not about trying cases. It is about establishing agreed-upon "going rates" so that defense counsel can convince their clients to plead guilty to the charges. The fact is, criminal cases rarely have to be proven beyond a reasonable doubt at trial before a judge or jury based on the legal evidence secured by police or prosecutors' investigation. A criminal trial occurs only when plea bargaining doesn't work out. Across the United States, criminal cases are negotiated, not tried. Persons called for jury duty usually learn this after sitting in the basement of the courthouse all day. When they are finally released, a judge comes down to tell them how valuable their service was. By just their being there, His or Her Honor explains, both prosecutors and defense attorneys were encouraged to reach deals so they didn't have to actually try or defend the case.

While abusers come from all races, backgrounds, and socioeconomic classes, those that end up in courts are disproportionately poor. Like most criminal defendants, they are likely to be represented by public defenders or court-appointed attorneys. These defense counsel are generally paid a set fee per case, regardless of how many hours they spend on it. As a result, many overburdened and underfunded public defenders meet their clients in the courthouse halls for the first time the morning of the trial. As Lenny Bruce famously commented, "In the halls of justice, the justice is in the halls." In the halls of justice, it is fair to say, the defense is transacted in the halls.

The fact is, as Judge Jed Rakoff argued recently in his perceptive essay in the *New York Review of Books*,[1] the criminal justice system in the United States today bears little relationship to what the Founding Fathers envisioned. Gone is the critical element of trial by jury, which was supposed to serve as a truth-seeking mechanism and a means of achieving fairness. The Sixth Amendment guarantee that "in all criminal prosecutions, the accused shall enjoy the right to a speedy and public trial, by an impartial jury" has been replaced by the right to avoid a trial by a speedy plea deal negotiated in secret, outside the public's and the victim's gaze.

In 2013, for example, more than 97 percent of all cases prosecuted in federal courts were resolved through plea bargains. The statistics are similar in state courts. Further, the plea bargains largely determine the sentences imposed, reducing the judges' role to approving or disapproving the deal reached. The role of defense attorneys is also diminished to that of a supplicant, trying to get the best deal for a client. Their biggest bargaining chip is not the innocence of their client, but the threat to demand a trial, which is generally not in the best interest of any of the parties—defense lawyer, prosecutor, or defendant. The interests of defense attorneys are, in fact, aligned with those of the prosecutor—not to take a case to trial. It is expensive to do so, and, more likely than not, they risk losing, damaging their win/loss record, not to mention subjecting their client to increased sanctions. Given this, they don't expend much effort examining the prosecution's case or fashioning a defense for the defendant.

As Rakoff concludes, "the power to determine the terms of the plea bargain is, as a practical matter, lodged largely in the prosecutor, with the defense counsel having little say and the judge even less." Threats of guilty sentences, much less prison time, provide prosecutors with weapons to bludgeon defendants into plea bargains. Given that the defense counsel has little knowledge of his or her client, the lawyer brings little to the table. The prosecutor, by contrast, has at least a police report, which may contain witness interviews and any other evidence obtained. While much of what is entered into the police report may not stand up under the scrutiny of cross-examination, the prosecutor also knows that such scrutiny is the exception, not the rule, and can threaten with some confidence the most draconian sentence.

Not insisting on a trial has other benefits for defendants. Judges are allowed to consider, if the defendant is ultimately convicted, the demand for a trial as a sign that the defendant is unrepentant, justifying a harsher sentence. If the defendant does not insist on a trial, the prosecutor can offer not only to reduce the sentence, but also reduce the charges.

All of this holds true for domestic violence prosecutions. It also helps explain why so many abused women are imprisoned across the country, including those whose only crime is self-defense.

Even when it comes to lesser domestic violence charges, domestic violence statutes give prosecutors a lot of cards to play. If, for example, the state statute is like Rhode Island's, which calls for a minimum jail sentence

POLICE AND PROSECUTORS ENTRAP VICTIMS

Maria Ventura met Lawrence Ham as a homeless fifteen-year-old in New York. He was twenty-eight, took her in, and hooked her on drugs. When she refused to become a prostitute, he beat her. Beatings followed on a daily basis. Maria called police, but the only times they arrested him were when they spotted a crack pipe or other drug paraphernalia on him. Ham threw her down the stairs when he discovered she was pregnant. She ran away a couple of times, but he always found her and dragged her back. The last time, he strangled her in a parking lot. She managed to grab a rock and hit him on the head. She ran away only to be arrested two days later and charged with his murder. Although just shy of her sixteenth birthday, she was close enough to be threatened with twenty-five years to life imprisonment for murder as an adult unless she pleaded guilty. Calculating the risk presented by the prosecutor, she pleaded guilty and got fifteen to twenty-five years in prison.

There's a somewhat happier postscript to this story. A marine on leave captured Ham's attack on Maria preceding his death, but unfortunately the marine was shipped out to Iraq and only presented the evidenced four years later to the district attorney. Maria was released on parole ten days later.[*]

Note

[*]Law, V., "Domestic Violence Victims in NY Prisons May Get Some Relief," *Aljazeera America*, January 1, 2015.

for a second domestic assault (ten days), the prosecutor can agree to charge the repeat defendant as a first offender to avoid the minimum mandatory sentence. If the defendant is a first offender, the prosecutor can agree to reduce the charge to a simple assault, removing the "domestic" designation that may require, like in Rhode Island, the defendant to pay for and attend a twenty-six-week batterer program.

The law of every U.S. jurisdiction leaves to the prosecutor's unfettered discretion what charges to bring, regardless of what the defendant was arrested for. Even in regard to felony charges that must be determined by a grand jury in some states, as the saying goes, a good prosecutor can get a grand jury to indict a ham sandwich. Grand juries hear only the evidence prosecutors want to present, including their own witnesses. Practically the only time grand juries don't do what prosecutors want is when the prosecutor isn't anxious to charge the defendant in the first place, like in cases where a police officer is charged with excessive force, even killing suspects.

According to Rakoff, in 2012 the average sentence for federal narcotics defendants, for example, who entered into any kind of plea bargain was five years and four months. The average sentence for defendants who went to trial was sixteen years! Further, if the defense counsel seeks to delay the assembly line of plea bargaining to explore the merits of the underlying case, she or he faces claims of providing "ineffective assistance of counsel," because the prosecutor has the power to withdraw the plea deal and pursue more serious charges and/or more severe sentences.

Defense counsel cannot go to the judge to seek a fairer sentence or reduced charges because typically the judge is not party to the negotiations. Further, in a plea bargain, the prosecutor does not have to present the evidence in court; thus there is little incentive for the prosecutor to double-check the evidence or worry about the veracity of witness testimony. This, of course, can backfire when the defense does demand a trial. The prosecutor may learn to his or her chagrin that the police, too, relied on prospective pleas and failed to gather the requisite evidence.

Finally, the prosecutor is largely immune to any oversight or penalties, even for misconduct.

The bottom line is simple: Prosecutors don't need evidence to prove their cases beyond a reasonable doubt, they just need enough to cow defendants so the defense lawyers can convince them to accept the negotiated plea. The result is that of the 2.2 million Americans now in prison, well over 2 million are there as a result of deals dictated by prosecutors.

Judges are supposed to ensure that the prosecution has the evidence to convict the defendant. But they rely on the agreement between prosecutors and defenders as verification. When it comes time for sentencing the defendant, judges get a quick reading of the police incident report to establish the facts, and then they endorse the deal already settled between the prosecutor and the defense. The U.S. Supreme Court has provided judges wide latitude, going so far as uniquely allowing American judges to accept so-called Alford pleas. These allow defendants to enter a guilty plea while maintaining their innocence!

Civil libertarians and practitioners like Rakoff point out how the power imbalance between prosecutors and defense lawyers rigs the system dramatically in favor of the former. Perpetrators of domestic violence are no less hapless than the other several million defendants who currently inhabit American prisons and jails as the result of misdemeanor and felony pleas. And yet, when it comes to domestic violence prosecution, even a rigged system hasn't resulted in consistent, successful domestic violence prosecution across the country.

Why is this?

There are two reasons, one real and one phony but often claimed by prosecutors called out for their failure to prosecute domestic violence crimes. The real reason is prosecutors have to give a damn, and many don't. The phony reason is because victims typically fail to cooperate.

Prosecutors have to care about domestic violence. That means, given that most abusers are arrested for misdemeanor assaults, prosecutors have to care about prosecuting of misdemeanors. This requires better prosecutors, those usually reserved for the superior or higher criminal courts for the higher publicity cases like big drug busts or gang violence. Assigning experienced, better-trained prosecutors for misdemeanor cases represents a seismic culture change in most prosecutors' offices.

PROSECUTORS SWEEP DOMESTIC VIOLENCE CASES OUT THE COURT DOOR

Confronted with increased caseloads as a result of increased police domestic violence arrests, prosecutors' initial response was to get rid of them as expeditiously as possible by diverting the cases out of court, dismissing them, or reducing the underlying charges to facilitate quick plea bargains.

Responding to growing domestic violence arrests in California, for example, the state legislature enacted legislation in 1979 specifically creating a domestic violence diversion program to keep these cases from court. The law encouraged judges to send abusers to batterer treatment. One of the abusers diverted to treatment for assaulting his wife was O. J. Simpson. Due to his special circumstances, he was allowed to complete his counseling program with periodic phone calls to a therapist.

Domestic violence diversion programs are straightforward on their face. If offenders agree to behave and perhaps complete a court-ordered treatment program, generally anger management or batterer intervention, their cases are never prosecuted. If they don't fulfill their end of the bargain, they are threatened with prosecution. Of course, the threat of prosecution is empty. Prosecutors, uninterested in trying abusers immediately after the crime, when victims' injuries and their determination to testify are equally fresh, are even less interested in resurrecting the case months later. Further, if abusers violate their court diversion by reabusing their victims, the prosecutor's interest will be in dealing with the new case, not prosecuting the old.

Diversion programs have many names: "deferred prosecution," "continuing cases without a finding," "pretrial probation in contemplation of dismissal," "deferred adjudication," and, in Rhode Island, even "probation." They allow prosecutors and judges to pretend they are holding abusers accountable and safeguarding victims. The bottom line of all these dispositions is the same: The case, but not the recalcitrant abuser, goes away.

Rhode Island, for example, allows defendants to actually be found guilty of domestic violence by a judge or jury, and, as long as the sentence is "probation" without a suspended sentence, the case does not count as a first offense conviction. As a result, the mandatory second offense sanction of a minimum ten-day jail sentence doesn't kick in until the third domestic violence conviction, which includes only prior convictions without probation as a disposition.

While diversion programs clear court calendars, for abusers they share a common, consistent problem. They don't work. A quarter to a third of the diverted abusers typically reabuse their victims.[2] This was a prime reason why the U.S. Civil Rights Commission came out against domestic violence diversion as early as 1984, declaring it violated victims' civil rights. The National Council of Juvenile and Family Court Judges followed suit a decade later. In California, it took O. J. Simpson to stop it . . . in theory if not practice. Outraged over the not guilty jury verdict in Simpson's murder trial, the California legislature repealed that state's domestic violence diversion law in 1995.

Still, prosecutors haven't stopped diverting domestic violence cases to this day, even in California. In 2014 the Kern County district attorney, Lisa Green, for example, proudly announced a new domestic violence initiative in her California county. After completing negotiations with the county's public defenders, she declared that abusers charged with misdemeanor domestic violence would be enrolled in a counseling program in lieu of prosecution. Ironically, the prosecutor said she thought about the diversion program "a lot" after a jury recommended a California man, Robert Dale Fuller, be sentenced to death for killing his estranged wife and her mother. Apparently the Kern prosecutor did not accept what is widely held among prosecutors who get it—domestic violence misdemeanor prosecution is homicide prevention.[3]

An earlier 2005 report by California's attorney general, unfortunately, found Green was not alone. At least one of the state's larger city attorney's offices charged with prosecuting misdemeanors regularly diverted a third of all domestic violence cases referred by police. If the defendants bothered to show (which many don't), they were provided, according to the city attorney's office, with "education, admonishments, and referrals for services."[4]

This took place in California, which repealed domestic violence diversion a decade earlier.

A dozen other states, like Connecticut, still have statutes authorizing domestic violence diversion programs. Ironically, Connecticut's diversion program was established as part of the Family Violence Prevention and Response Act passed in 1986 that made broad changes in state law following Tracey Thurman's lawsuit against Torrington. Mandatory arrest, tempered with diversion, was among two key provisions of the law. Although Connecticut has stuck with its nine-week diversion program since, insisting it works, its own data belie this. Like all domestic violence diversion, it continues to endanger victims.

The data provided by the courts to a legislative panel in 2012 illustrates The courts claimed 85 percent of diversion referrals successfully completed the diversion program. By this, the officials meant only 12 percent of those who completed the program were arrested for more domestic violence in the next year, but given the 15 percent noncompletion rate, the courts' data reveal that a quarter of those diverted either failed to complete the program or completed the program and were rearrested for domestic violence. Further, measuring success by arrest alone and limiting follow-up to twelve months dramatically under-reveal true reabuse rates, since half of victims don't report and police don't always make arrests when they do. In addition, it takes three years to reveal most abusers who will continue to be arrested for reabuse. In short, it is fair to conclude that the courts grossly exaggerated the success of their diversion programs.[5]

Even if that 25 percent failure rate represented all reabuse, this is not the kind of odds one would desire for a get-out-of-court-free card! If Connecticut had a similar "success" rate for a nine-week diversion program for bank robbers, one would suspect such a "success" to quickly mean the program's demise.

**RAY RICE'S CHARGES ERASED AFTER
COURT DIVERSION**

Ray Rice, the former Baltimore Ravens running back who was video-taped knocking his now wife unconscious in an elevator in February 2014 had all of his aggravated assault felony charges dismissed in May 2015. The prosecutor recommended dismissal because Rice had completed all terms and conditions of his diversion program, and an Atlantic City judge signed off.*

Note

*Wilson, A., "Ray Rice's Domestic Violence Charges Dismissed by New Jersey Judge," *The Baltimore Sun*, May 21, 2015.

Notwithstanding limited explicit state statutory authorization for domestic violence diversion, surveys suggest that up to half of prosecutors' offices in large jurisdictions engage in domestic violence diversion. Most even allow abusers to enter the programs directly without admitting guilt in court.

DISMISSING DOMESTIC VIOLENCE

Diverting domestic violence cases was never the main means to dump them. Most were dismissed outright. Historically, many prosecutors created specific barriers to avoid prosecuting domestic violence. Some, for example, required victims to personally file the charges against their abusers or come to the prosecutors' office to sign affidavits that they wanted to prosecute, preventing many domestic violence arrests from ending up in court. In 1984, for example, researchers noted in the Milwaukee police arrest study described earlier that less than 2 percent of those arrested for domestic violence were prosecuted in court.

Dismissing domestic violence cases is still the rule in way too many jurisdictions.

Arizona's statewide domestic violence prosecution data aren't reassuring either. In its latest posted report from 2013 reviewing all domestic violence prosecutions between 2001 and 2010, it revealed that the most common outcome of domestic violence arrests is still case dismissals. Ditto for Connecticut between 2009 and 2011, where conviction rates averaged from a low

TOWN WITHDRAWS DOMESTIC VIOLENCE FROM COUNTY PROSECUTOR FOR LOSING WARRANTS, DISMISSING 50 PERCENT OF CASES

After investigating 598 domestic violence cases, Canton, Michigan, police turned over 374 to the Wayne County prosecutor's office for warrants against the alleged perpetrators. Only eighty-six were issued. An official town investigation found that at least forty of the misdemeanor domestic violence warrants "simply disappeared" during the last two years in the prosecutor's office. The town also accused the county prosecutor of dismissing half of all domestic violence cases that reached the courts. In September 2015, the Canton police announced they had had enough, and the township board voted to have Canton's local prosecutor take over domestic violence cases. The town prosecutor, however, is restricted to misdemeanor cases with maximum penalties of just ninety-three days in jail.*

Note

*Clem, D., "Canton Domestic Violence Warrant Requests Disappeared," *Detroit Free Press*, September 23, 2015.

of 17.7 percent in Bantam to a high of only 45 percent in Bridgeport, which boasted one of the state's special domestic violence courts. In contrast, New Haven had a conviction rate over the same three years of only 25.3 percent.[6]

In the Toledo, Ohio, municipal court, researchers found in 2000 and 2001 that two-thirds of the domestic violence cases were dismissed, 23.8 percent were convicted, and 8.6 percent were unresolved, notwithstanding that more than half the abusers had a history of one or more prior domestic violence arrests. Almost all had a prior arrest for something.[7] Things were worse in a 2011 follow-up study, when prosecutors brought 1,599 domestic violence cases to the Toledo court. Only 13 percent were convicted for domestic violence, although an additional 7 percent were still pending at the time of the review. The extremely low conviction rate is all the more troubling because, like the earlier study, almost two-thirds of the abusers charged had prior domestic violence charges. A local advocate commented to WTVG-TV, "If the fire department were only putting out 13 percent of the fires . . . or if the garbage was only being picked up 13 percent of the time, the community would be outraged."[8]

Across Ohio in 2012, police filed 68,277 domestic violence incident reports. Prosecutors prosecuted 35,006 of them for domestic violence and another 6,047 after dropping the domestic violence–related charges. They did not charge 27,224 (39.9 percent). Rates varied widely by city. In Cincinnati, prosecutors went forward on all arrested cases; in Columbus, on 73.5 percent of the cases; in Cleveland, on 41.5 percent of them.[9]

The Bloomington, Indiana, Commission on the Status of Women looked at Monroe County prosecutions in 2009. While the county prosecutor boasted a 63 percent conviction rate, the prosecutor also declined to prosecute more than half the domestic violence arrests. The real conviction rate ranged from 17 percent for felony domestic violence assaults to 42 percent for misdemeanor domestic violence assaults. Further, to reach even this rate, prosecutors reduced many of the assault charges to disorderly conduct. Because they reduced the assault charges, abusers did not have to give up their firearms, and the convictions didn't count as first offenses should the abusers get caught for subsequent domestic violence assaults.

The commission highlighted the case of an abuser arrested five times for domestic violence assaults in 2009. As a result of a prior conviction, he could have been charged with five felonies under the state law that enhances sanctions for repeat abuse. Instead, he was allowed to plead guilty to two reduced charges and sentenced to twenty-four days in jail, with sixteen days credit for time served while awaiting trial. As the commission concluded, by failing to file even one felony charge for these repeated assaults, the prosecutor "defeat[ed] the purpose of legislation specifically written to assure that meaningful sentences would be meted out for repeat domestic violence offenses." As noted in the *National Bulletin on Domestic Violence Prevention*, the Indiana prosecutors "not only took the 'domestic' out of domestic violence, they also took out the 'violence.'"[10]

A review of the 126 domestic violence fatalities across Georgia in 2013 paints a harrowing portrait of domestic violence prosecution in the state. As the report concludes: "A review of the case histories reveals that calling law enforcement does not always result in increased safety, justice, or perpetrator accountability." The report writers were able to track 178 of the 235 calls victims who were later murdered made to police. Ninety resulted in the abuser's arrest while eighty-eight did not, constituting an arrest rate of 50 percent for the calls with known outcomes. Of the ninety arrests, only twenty-eight were prosecuted as charged, sixty-one were dismissed or pled down, including seventeen that were dismissed because the victim was murdered before the case could be tried![11]

In May 2015, the *Register-Mail* newspaper of Galesburg, Illinois, ran a series of special reports on domestic violence. On day five, it looked at domestic violence prosecutions in the county court. It began its story reporting on the case of a police officer accused of battering his girlfriend. It concluded, "Like most domestic violence cases—about 74 percent in Knox County—the prosecutor failed to land a domestic battery conviction." According to the newspaper, the Knox County state attorney's office had a domestic violence conviction rate of 20 percent in misdemeanor cases (maximum sentence of 364 days) and 48 percent in felony cases (maximum sentence seven to fourteen years). All but eighteen of these cases were resolved with a plea bargain. Another 151 were not charged as domestic violence, including more than a third that were reduced to lesser charges, usually disorderly conduct. Once so reduced, all but four were let go with a fine and court costs. Of the four jailed, the longest sentence was seven days.[12]

Asked about its lack of success in prosecuting domestic violence, a prosecutor explained to the newspaper that in more than a third of the cases, victims requested to end the prosecution. Further, the prosecutor explained, convictions may not be the best response. He pointed to a case where an abuser hit his girlfriend in the head with a lamp after ripping a bedroom door off its hinges to get to her. The prosecution dropped the case but only on the condition that both the abuser *and his victim* complete counseling services. The newspaper, however, found that only five of nearly five hundred cases dropped by the prosecutor were conditionally dropped (requiring anyone to do anything).

While Knox County prosecutors were busy convicting less than sixty abusers for domestic battery per year, Safe Harbor, the local domestic violence shelter and service provider, reported serving seven to eight hundred area domestic violence victims each year.

Prosecutors in other jurisdictions do a bit better.

TEXAS PROSECUTOR TRIES TO TURN AROUND COURT CULTURE OF DOMESTIC VIOLENCE DISMISSALS

Cameron County, Texas, district attorney Luis V. Saenz ended a common practice among prosecutors when he took over in 2013. As he explained, it used to be that the defense lawyer would talk to his client, the alleged abuser, and the client would take the victim to the prosecutor's office and say they wanted to file an affidavit of nonprosecution. The affidavits were sworn statements by an alleged victim expressing a desire to halt prosecution. The defense attorney would then walk into court and wave an affidavit of nonprosecution from the victim. The judge would look at the prosecutor and the prosecutor would say, "'OK, we're dismissing.' It was almost automatic." But Saenz ended the practice, declining to work for the accused anymore. While victims can still go to court and testify that they do not want the case prosecuted, the prosecutor refuses to facilitate dismissals, his way to slow down the culture of automatic dismissals of domestic violence cases. "Believe me," Saenz declared, "even within the office, and defense attorneys and also judges, I've gotten pushed back on what I want to do on these cases."*

Note

*Perez-Trevino, E., "District Attorney Stresses Pro-Victim Stance in Domestic Violence Cases," *The Herald*, August 9, 2015.

PROSECUTING DOMESTIC VIOLENCE, AVERAGE AND ABOVE AVERAGE

Across Massachusetts, the probation department reported a conviction rate of 42 percent, with only 29.4 percent of the cases dismissed and 20.2 percent diverted, and 3.3 percent were found not guilty.[13] A study of domestic violence arrests in Idaho and Virginia as well as Connecticut similarly found 44.1 percent ended in convictions. Only a little over 30 percent of the cases was dismissed. More than two-thirds had prior criminal records with more than 40 percent for crimes of violence.[14]

It is difficult to assess the extent to which prosecutors have improved since the 1970s. Many are doing a great deal better than the 2 percent rate documented in the original Milwaukee police domestic violence arrest study in 1981–1982. Two researchers reviewed eighty-five domestic violence prosecution studies from around the country between 1973 and 2006 and found an overall conviction rate of 35 percent, ranging from a low of 8.1 percent to a high of 90.1 percent. If one very large study of 123,507 Maryland prosecutions from 1993 to 2003 was removed, the average conviction rate increased to almost half, 47.7 percent. Unfortunately, the researchers found no consistent pattern to indicate that prosecutors were doing better in the more recent studies than in the older studies.[15]

In 2002, the Bureau of Justice Statistics looked at 3,750 domestic violence cases brought in a large urban county in Arizona, Georgia, Indiana, Ohio, and Tennessee as well as multiple counties in California, Florida, and Texas. It found an average prosecution rate of 56 percent, mostly for misdemeanor simple assaults. Only 9 percent were diverted, and 1 percent of the defendants were acquitted. However, in nine of the sixteen jurisdictions, prosecutors screened out cases before they reached court, dismissing 33 percent of them. In the remaining seven jurisdictions, they screened out cases after they reached court. As a result, prosecution rates based on those arrested for domestic violence ranged from a low of 17 percent to as high as 89 percent and conviction rates from 9.5 percent to 49.8 percent. Unfortunately, the report does not provide the dismissal rates for each jurisdiction, so the average prosecution and conviction rate cannot be determined.

The Bureau of Justice Statistics also looked at which cases were most likely to be prosecuted in the sixteen large urban jurisdictions. It found that cases where defendants talked to police or prosecutors were the mostly likely. Apparently these defendants incriminated themselves, because they were twice as likely to be convicted than in the 90 percent of cases where defendants kept quiet. In addition, if there was a witness, defendants were one and three-quarters more likely to be convicted. A history of prior abuse and the presence of physical evidence also boosted the likelihood of a conviction by one and a half. Injuries, use of alcohol or drugs by the suspect, presence of a child, or use of a weapon had little impact on conviction rates. The conviction rate of male suspects was 59.8 percent; for female suspects it was 40.3 percent.[16]

In its biennial report to Congress, last filed in 2012, the Office on Violence Against Women reported that prosecutors funded under its largest grant program received 163,364 cases of domestic violence, dating violence, stalking, and sexual assault; filed on three-quarters of them; and then dismissed a third. This means that less than half the cases were successfully prosecuted.

A 2012 investigation in California's Bay Area found prosecution rates as depressingly low as those found in the state's Attorney General Report almost a decade earlier. Over the last half decade, the San Francisco district attorney's office pursued just slightly more than a quarter of the cases. Across the Bay Area, seven of the eight counties did better, but not much. Court charges were filed less than half the time, except in Contra Costa County, which was tied for last with San Francisco.

The San Francisco district attorney made local headlines in 2012 for declining to drop domestic violence charges against the county sheriff even though the victim, his wife, denied any assault against her and resisted cooperating with police. However, an investigation by the city's *Public Press* found that in less publicized cases over the last five years, prosecutors dropped over 6,000 cases out of 8,600 brought by police. Across the Bay, between 2007 and 2011, prosecutors dropped 50,000 cases out of 92,000 (54 percent).

Ironically, most of the Bay Area prosecutors claim to have instituted "no drop" policies for domestic violence and "victimless prosecution." These policies mean that prosecutors pursue any case where they have sufficient evidence to convict, regardless of whether or not the victim wants to proceed. However, the *Public Press* investigation found multiple examples of cases with ample evidence that were not prosecuted. It highlighted a case with three separate incidents involving the same victim.

In January 2010, police responded to a call from a woman who reported her ex-boyfriend threw a broken vase at her, punched her, and "choked" her while threatening to kill her. Officers responded. When they tried to handcuff the suspect, he took a swing at them. Police had physical evidence, photos, and a taped interview with the victim. The district attorney's office declined to prosecute on any of the ten charges recorded by police because the victim "withdrew her complaint." Later that same year, new charges against the same suspect were dismissed in court. A few months later, the suspect was arrested for a third set of charges for injuring the same victim while violating a protective order. Prosecutors dropped these charges too, citing "lack of evidence."

The *Public Press* article ended with a subsequent case. A woman with two black eyes and a swollen cheek rang her neighbor's doorbell saying she had been assaulted by her boyfriend and didn't know what to do. The neighbor called 911, and the subsequent report filed by the responding officers indicated the boyfriend had bruises on his hands, suggesting he had struck her. The suspect's own father told police that he had witnessed the couple physically fighting the previous evening. However, the injured woman said she loved her boyfriend and did not want him to face charges. The San Francisco "no drop" prosecutor's office dropped the charge, citing "lack of evidence."[17]

TAKING "DOMESTIC" OUT OF "DOMESTIC VIOLENCE"

In addition to diverting domestic violence and dismissing charges, prosecutors routinely reduce domestic violence charges. This is a relatively recent prosecutorial practice when it comes to domestic violence, largely the unintended consequence of legislators' dissatisfaction with prosecutors. To require more aggressive sanctioning of abusers, legislators across the country have enhanced domestic violence sentences, including for repeat abuse.

The initial laws that defined domestic violence as a distinct crime made it a misdemeanor, confining it to the lower criminal courts. The crime remained a misdemeanor no matter how many times the same abuser was convicted. When it became increasingly apparent that a majority of abusers were not deterred by even repeat misdemeanor prosecutions, the majority of state legislators increased domestic violence sanctions. Many made a second or third offense a felony and gradually increased first offense sanctions. In 1996, for example, Congress prohibited abusers convicted of misdemeanor domestic violence assaults from possessing firearms. States added on fines and costs, required attendance at batterer intervention programs, and imposed other conditions and sanctions.

The increased sanctions, however, provided even more incentives for abusers to plead guilty if allowed to circumvent them. Many prosecutors have proven more than happy to accommodate. In fact, across some states, prosecutors have proven so accommodating that it is difficult to find any abuser actually prosecuted and sentenced in accordance with their state's law!

ROUTINE CHARGE REDUCTIONS SUBVERT HABITUAL OFFENDER PROSECUTION

In August, Jefferson County, Colorado, prosecutors asked that David Lee Razey, forty-six, be sentenced to thirty days in jail for harassment, not an insignificant sentence for a fairly trivial misdemeanor. However, Razey had initially been arrested for a domestic assault against his wife, after allegedly throwing her against a glass door. It was also Razey's third domestic assault arrest against her. The prior two had also been pleaded down. Further, the victim was Razey's third domestic partner he had similarly victimized. Court records document twenty-three arrests of Razey since 1987, including four for violating a succession of protective orders taken out by his victims. It was also revealed at Razey's plea hearing that in the past two months, he had skipped three drug and alcohol tests and failed a fourth that had been ordered as a condition of his bond, imposed after his latest arrest. But prosecutors did not ask for his bond to be revoked or upgrade the thirty days sentence recommendation. The judge did, however, order Razey to wear a GPS ankle monitor when the victim testified that security guards at her workplace had seen his truck in the employee parking lot. Razey denied he was stalking his estranged wife, who was in the process of divorcing him. As part of the sentence, Razey was also required to attend domestic violence classes, notwithstanding the fact that he was already attending such classes ordered in another county where he was convicted of violating a protective order. Colorado has a habitual offender law that allows three domestic violence–related misdemeanor convictions to be upgraded to a felony, if properly charged.*

NOTE

*Low, R., "Wife Says 30 Days for Domestic Violence Just Slap of Hand for Repeat Offender," *Fox 31*, Denver, CO, August 18, 2015.

While violating the spirit and intent of these laws, prosecutors are free to charge the abuser for an equivalent nondomestic violence–designated offense or charge the repeat offender as a pristine first offender, regardless of what police may have arrested him for. In California, for example, most abusers across that state are initially arrested for "willful infliction of corporal injury on an intimate partner (Penal Code §273.5)," a felony. However, prosecutors subsequently file from 70 to 90 percent of the arrests as misdemeanors. Prosecuted as a felony, abusers face from two to four years in prison. As a misdemeanor, they face only up to one year in county jail.

A report by the South Carolina Department of Public Safety examined the almost thirteen thousand domestic violence charges brought in that state from mid-2005 through mid-2006. It found that a little more than 10 percent were reduced to nondomestic violence charges, notwithstanding the fact that at the time South Carolina had the most lenient sentence for domestic violence, barring incarceration of more than thirty days regardless of the number of prior domestic violence convictions.[18]

The *Columbus Dispatch*'s investigation of domestic violence across Ohio found that thirty-five abusers in Franklin County racked up 297 domestic violence cases and 176 convictions. Yet, on average, they spent less than two weeks in jail for each conviction. One abuser punched his girlfriend, smashed a beer bottle over her head (a real one, not the fake ones that shatter at the softest touch in movies), and slammed a car door on her hand. He got seventy-seven days in jail.

The insignificant sanctions for these chronic abusers were made possible by consistent charge reductions. In a fifth of the cases, felonies were reduced; even misdemeanors were dropped to charges equivalent to traffic tickets. Thus, in two-thirds of the cases tried, the abusers got no jail time at all. In Ohio, abusers face from six to twelve months in prison for felonies. For misdemeanors, the maximum sanction is 180 days in jail.

Prosecutors do a bit better in other jurisdictions. A study of prosecution practices in three other states found that only slightly more than a quarter of domestic violence charges were amended by prosecutors.[19]

CREATING PERPETUAL FIRST OFFENDERS

The upshot of case diversion, high dismissals, and reduction of charges has been to create jail-proof "perpetual first offenders." Most abusers who get the attention of the criminal justice system aren't even first offenders to begin with. It is extremely rare that a victim calls police the first time she is assaulted or seriously abused. Most suffer repeated criminal abuse before calling police, who may not arrest after the first call. When the abuser finally reaches court, prosecutors diverting, dismissing, or reducing domestic violence charges allow the abuser to avoid a record of conviction for domestic violence. This means that the next time around, if the charges are not diverted, dismissed, or reduced, the defendant is still legally a "first" offender because he has no prior domestic violence convictions!

If America's criminal justice system treated bank robbers as they do abusers, the FDIC would have gone bankrupt decades ago shoring up robbed banks. Bank robber intervention programs would replace them as a bigger business!

Even if a domestic violence arrest really represented the abuser's first domestic violence offense, if the abuser has a prior arrest for *any* offense, he is at as high a risk to reabuse as if he had a prior arrest for domestic violence. It turns out domestic violence is, after all, a real crime and abusers real criminals. Their risk for recidivism, including reabuse, is not less because their prior arrests were for nondomestic violence offenses.[20] Ironically, feminist insistence that domestic violence derives from patriarchy,

ALMOST PATHOLOGICAL CREATIVITY IN TERRORIZING WOMEN

In October 2012, Scottye Miller was released from county jail where he had been held for less than a year after failing to abide by the terms of a previously imposed suspended sentence. The prior January, Tricia Patricelli had called 911 urging police to hurry, as Miller was chasing her in the parking lot of her apartment threatening to kill her. For that he had been charged with fourth-degree assault and harassment. In jail, Miller wrote her letters in violation of a no contact order. In the letters, he continued his death threats against her. Two weeks after his release, Miller brought three knives to her apartment and used them to stab her at least twenty times, killing her. She left behind two young daughters. Although he had been ordered as a condition of his supervised release to stay away from her, he was apparently living with her at the time. Patricelli had related that she was safe, having moved to a new address unknown to Miller.

In 2014, Miller was sentenced to fifty years in prison for the murder. While normally the state's sentencing guidelines called for a sentence of thirty to forty years, Miller got more for two aggravating factors: a prior pattern of domestic violence against multiple victims and the fact that the murder occurred upon his release for a crime against the same victim. The sentencing judge declared that Miller, a serial abuser, had "shown an almost pathological creativity in terrorizing women," characterizing his domestic violence crime history as "twisted and disturbing." The record showed he had hit, strangled, and threatened his ex-wife and then went on to beat, stalk, and ambush Patricelli while violating every court order ever issued to protect the women and their families.

In fact, the press reported fifteen prior domestic violence convictions on his record and even more arrests. Between 2002 and 2010, his domestic violence convictions included six violations of court protective orders, as well as assorted assaults, harassment, firearm violations, and tampering with a witness. The felony arrests had been reduced to misdemeanors. The convictions in cases involving Patricelli began in 2009 when he forced his way into her apartment and assaulted her in front of her two young daughters. He was charged with burglary and assault. The burglary was a felony that could have resulted in a twenty-year sentence, but he got less than a year in county jail.

After the murder, the victim's mother sued the Washington State Department of Corrections.[*]

Note

[*]Whale, R., "Grieving Mother Sues State over Daughter's 2012 Murder," *Auburn Reporter News Reporter*, December 11, 2014.

separate and apart from other criminal behavior, has inadvertently helped obfuscate abuser risk. It is an undeserving gift that state enhancement statutes have given abusers by providing a free pass for prior nondomestic violence crimes when limiting increased punishments only for repeat domestic violence convictions.

Even prior domestic violence convictions do not prevent abusers from being considered "first" offenders.

While the majority of states now enhance sentences for repeat domestic violence, many sunset these provisions after several years have passed. This

SUNSETTING PRIOR CONVICTIONS

John Davis, thirty-seven, was arrested for domestic violence in 1997, 1998, 2002, and 2008 in Utah and California involving both a former and current wife. The 2008 fourth arrest was in Utah, and, pursuant to Utah law, Davis was legally a *first* offender because the state's enhancement statute for repeat domestic violence lapses after five years. In 2015, he was arrested for stabbing his second wife to death in front of six of the seven children in the family. Davis allegedly stabbed his wife after she confronted him for hitting one of the sons for playing a video game. If this offense had not been a capital offense, he would still have legally been a *first* domestic violence offender again under Utah law. Utah legislators apparently believe, as do those of many other states, that abusers age out of their criminal behavior over several years, something unconfirmed by any research to date.[*]

Note

[*]Casey, M., and Nichols, L., "Goodyear Murder Suspect Has History of Domestic Violence," *Arizona Republic*, March 28, 2015.

not only allows but also inadvertently encourages prosecutors to treat repeat, convicted offenders as first offenders.

Even when prior domestic violence offenses aren't sunsetted, they still don't matter if prosecutors find it convenient to ignore them.

Bay City, Michigan, prosecutors filed assault charges against Ralph Bills II in March 2015 for allegedly attacking his pregnant girlfriend. If convicted, Bills faced five years imprisonment because he was charged as a third domestic violence offender under the state's enhancement statute for repeat domestic violence. However, after filing the charges in court, prosecutors dropped them and instead proceeded on other charges involving nondomestic victims.

PROSECUTOR IGNORES THIRD DOMESTIC VIOLENCE OFFENSE

Ralph Bills's pregnant girlfriend had called 911 earlier that month reporting that Bills had pushed and slapped her, and threatened suicide while brandishing a knife. The girlfriend said that when she went to leave him, Bills shoved her down, got on top of her, and tried grabbing her phone away from her. After she escaped in her car, he called her, threatening to hurt her pets she had left behind. She returned home for her dog and cats. When she grabbed the smaller cat, she told the court that he punched the bigger cat. She reported that when she left, Bills followed her, forcing the car door open, and got on top of her, trying to get her keys and phone. She bit his arm. He forced her head back by her hair and told her that he was going to kill her when he got out of prison, where he assumed he would end up, as he had other charges pending.

However, Bills didn't go to prison. Prosecutors made a deal, allowing Bills to plead no contest to two previous counts of assault and battery and one count of malicious destruction of property between $200 and $1,000, all misdemeanors, charges that arose from an earlier incident involving two men in a hospital. In explaining why the domestic violence charges were dropped, the prosecutor blamed the victim, declaring that after meeting with her and receiving several letters from her, the office felt it could not proceed with the case. According to the mother of a prior intimate partner, Bills had assaulted her daughter, strangling her and threatening to slit her throat with a knife and smashing her cell phone. He got less than a year in jail and probation in a neighboring county. She wrote *MLive*, "I cannot understand why the prosecutor would dismiss the charges with the record he has of that kind."[*]

Note

[*]Waterman, C., "Prosecution Dismisses Felony Domestic Violence Charge Against Essexville Man," *MLive*, Bay City, MI, April 1, 2015.

COLORADO HABITUAL ABUSER LAW RARELY PROSECUTED

Colorado, like Utah, has a fourth offender domestic violence enhancement statute. Unlike Utah's, it does not sunset prior convictions, but it too is mostly ignored by prosecutors.

Danny Villela perpetrated a long campaign of terror against his common-law wife and stepchildren in Boulder, Colorado, accumulating repeated misdemeanor domestic violence convictions for assault, harassment, child abuse, and violation of protective orders. According to the *Denver Post*, like the "vast majority" of Colorado's habitual domestic violence offenders, he had never been convicted under the state's enhancement statute designed to punish habitual abusers.[21] Enacted in 2000, the law authorizes prosecutors to charge fourth offenders as felons with sentences from one to three years in prison and fines from $1,000 to $100,000 and two years parole (CRS §18-6-801(7)). But since enacted, only 155 chronic abusers have been prosecuted under the law, just ten a year across the entire state. In Denver County, no abuser has ever been charged under the law.

Police and prosecutors complain that the law is difficult to enforce. In Colorado, there is no specific domestic violence assault or abuse law, so prosecutors have to research prior convictions to see if they qualify. There is not a central state criminal record file, making it difficult to even identify past convictions. A state supreme court decision requires that if the case goes to trial, juries must decide if the prior or current case prosecuted as a fourth domestic violence offense fits the definition of domestic violence.

In 2015, Villela was finally charged as a fourth offender abuser, but the charge was subsequently plea-bargained down when he agreed to plead guilty to menacing and child abuse. Still, the prosecutor asked for six years imprisonment, but without the minimum mandatory fourth offender charge, the judge didn't have to go along, and didn't. The judge imposed five years of probation, with two years in jail work release, allowing him out during the days to work. Lamented the prosecutor to the *Denver Post*, for such repeat offenders, "it's not so much a question of if there's going to be a re-offense, but when."

Boulder prosecutors have charged ninety-one serial abusers since 2000, but half, like Villela, were eventually pled down. Denver prosecutors instead ask for counseling for first and second offenders and up to a year imprisonment for more than that. They argue it is not worth it to prove fourth offender cases, especially because even if they do, the maximum penalty is only three years. Of course, prosecutors also blame victims, claiming that victims become more reluctant to cooperate given the minimum mandatory sentence required for charged fourth offenders.

Ironically, the Colorado habitual offender law can also backfire, resulting in lesser sentences for fourth offenders. If, after being convicted of three misdemeanor domestic violence offenses, the abuser is arrested for a felony domestic violence offense, many Colorado felony judges are likely to consider him a "first" felony offender. If the fourth arrest had been a misdemeanor domestic violence offense, the same offender would have been charged as a felony habitual abuser, and considered as such, not as a first felony offender. Ignored by prosecutors or judges or not, waiting until a fourth conviction to consider an abuser habitual demonstrates a high tolerance for domestic violence indeed.

PROSECUTING SAME SEX DOMESTIC VIOLENCE

There are many examples of prosecutors holding abusers in same sex couples accountable. Unfortunately, many are connected to homicides. After Moore (see chapter 5) was arrested for stabbing her partner in August 2014, she was charged with armed assault with intent to kill. The pretrial judge ordered that Moore await her trial in jail. Moore pled guilty at the trial, which took place in November 2014. She was ultimately sentenced to eight years in prison, with five years of supervised release after she gets out. In exchange for Moore's guilty plea, the charge against her was reduced from aggravated assault with intent to kill while armed to just aggravated assault while armed. The lowered charge still could have gotten her up to thirty years in prison.[22]

Angelica Hanson killed her girlfriend, Jody Lane, in 2013 in Missouri with her car. The two had been arguing, after which Hanson backed over

Lane in the vehicle, dragging her underneath for longer than could be perceived as an accident. Still, Hanson insisted she kept driving because she thought she had "hit the curb." Hanson got seven years for first-degree involuntary manslaughter. The judge who sentenced Hanson noted her previous charges, which included assault and incidents related to drug and alcohol, as part of her reason to dole out the maximum involuntary manslaughter sentence.

In another instance of same sex domestic violence that ended in homicide, Homer Washington stabbed his intimate partner, Clarence Charles, to death in Shorewood, Wisconsin. Washington, of course, was the only one who got a chance to talk to the police. He told them that he and Charles had been arguing, at which point Charles accused him of cheating and got a knife from the kitchen. Then Charles struck Washington (with his hand, not the weapon), which led to a struggle during which Charles stabbed himself in the neck and made threats, according to Washington. To protect himself, Washington said, he stabbed and then strangled his intimate partner.

When police found Charles's body, they saw he had been stabbed thirteen times in the neck, throat, and abdomen. Washington was ultimately sentenced to thirty-six years in prison, with fourteen years of extended supervision. Also worth noting in this case is the couple's age difference; Washington was twenty-one, and Charles was fifty-seven. Again, a clear-cut homicide led to a proportionally heavy sentence.[23]

In a similar case in October 2014, Jermaine Jackson killed his boyfriend, Andre Nicholas, in Baltimore. According to a statement to police from Jackson's mother, Jackson had both stabbed and strangled Nicholas during an argument. At the time, the court charged Jackson with first- and second-degree murder, first- and second-degree assault, and a couple of weapons charges. What's worth paying attention to in this case isn't the reaction of the criminal justice system, but the media. The media coverage of the homicide sheds light on how same sex domestic violence can be misperceived from the outside. Though a specifically LGBTQ news outlet in Baltimore, *Gay Life*, reported the story as one of intimate partner violence, other news outlets framed it as a homicide between two non-romantically connected men. Such coverage reinforces the isolation of domestic violence victims and misunderstanding of same sex domestic violence, keeping it hidden.[24]

Homicides, of course, present prosecutors with clear-cut victims and abusers. Prosecutors' responses are not as good when the same sex domestic violence is less lethal, showing that prosecutors and judges aren't any better at discerning same sex abusers from victims than police. As a lesbian domestic violence victim in Massachusetts reported, a judge told her and her abuser/ex-wife, "You girls need to learn to get along," adding that they had to maintain distance from each other.[25] This judge's attitude, besides being egregiously sexist and condescending, was also extremely dangerous. The survivor in this case had asked for a protective order against her ex-wife, who had made death threats and thrown rocks at her windows. It is doubtful that the same judge would have figured a patronizing verbal order would suffice in protecting a heterosexual victim.

While failing to prosecute same sex domestic violence can endanger victims, such prosecutions don't always help in same sex cases, especially when the abusers are more privileged than their victims. In 2005, for example, Los Angeles police responded to a physical fight between a Filipino man and his partner, a white man from the United States. The latter had a history of abusing his partner, as well as drugs and alcohol. Still, when police arrived at the scene, they first threatened the Filipino victim, then made good on those threats. Reportedly, the police officers accused the man of not being an American citizen and said they would call immigration on him. Further, they admonished him, "You shouldn't be hitting Americans—you're not an American." Although the police officers did not report him to immigration, they did arrest him, and prosecutors proceeded to convict him. He was sentenced to probation and attendance at the county's fifty-two-week batterer's intervention program. His abuser got off scot-free.[26]

PROSECUTORS SUFFER FROM LEARNED HELPLESSNESS

Why are so many prosecutors having so much trouble convicting abusers, especially as the system is rigged in their favor? Those who do the worst are the loudest to blame the victims for failing to cooperate. Without victims, they assert, they are helpless. In both Toledo studies, for example, prosecutors blamed lack of victim cooperation for their failures to prosecute most domestic violence cases. In filing for 65 percent of the dismissals in 2011, the prosecutor recorded that the victim failed to appear. A local Court-Watch program, incidentally, found the prosecutor's numbers off, finding that half the victims came to court.

Be that as it may, it is a fact that many victims are understandably not thrilled about publicly testifying against their current or former partners. There are many reasons. Some don't want to have to relive the experience. It can be embarrassing, even re-traumatizing. And many are afraid because they have been threatened with retaliation. The victim of NFL player Hardy absented herself when it came time to retry him for what he had already been convicted of in a lower court. She had previously testified that she feared even going to the police because Hardy said he would kill her if she "took food out of his family's mouth."

Expecting a victim to come to court, especially if she is still subject to abuse and without any assurance of a positive outcome, is expecting too much. This is especially true because many domestic violence victims have seen few positive results in previous encounters with law enforcement and the legal system. Many are reabused while the trial is pending. Those who have taken out protective orders have found that not only don't their abusers take the orders seriously, but neither do some police and judges when it comes to enforcing them.

In addition, in 2004, the U.S. Supreme Court admittedly made it more difficult. In *Crawford v. Washington*, 541 U.S. 36 (2004), the court reformulated the standard for determining when the admission of hearsay statements in criminal cases is permitted under the Confrontation Clause of the Sixth Amendment. The court held that cross-examination is required to admit prior testimonial statements of witnesses even if they had since become unavailable. Before this case, police officers were routinely able to testify what victims told them at the scene as long as the victims' words were said in the heat of the moment, called "excited utterances." It was held that such utterances were not testimonial, but reflected what the victim perceived as true. They were not designed to support subsequent court prosecution and therefore constituted credible hearsay. After *Crawford*, it became more difficult to get such hearsay testimony admitted at trial. The live testimony of victims is required so that the defense can confront and cross-examine them.

While all this is true, it is also true that prosecutors' claims of helplessness are exaggerated. Too many prosecutors suffer from learned helplessness. They have "learned" they can't prosecute domestic violence without the victim's testimony. They have learned victims will fail to show up in court. These assumptions become self-fulfilling prophesies because those same prosecutors don't reach out to victims. They don't work with police to develop alternative evidence. They don't try to prosecute without the victim.

Further, because most domestic violence charges are misdemeanors, prosecutors have less to threaten defendants with when it comes to plea bargaining. The average maximum sentence for misdemeanors is a year or less in a local jail. Given good time, overcrowding, and parole, this may mean considerably less time is actually served. As a result, most batterers who agree to forego trial end up, at most, in probation caseloads, not jail cells. Although even a day in jail would be traumatic for the average law-abiding citizen, most abusers are not strangers when it comes to lock-ups and courtrooms.

One of the few longitudinal statewide studies of abusers sentenced to probation, with or without suspended sentences, for example, documented that 70 percent of the abusers had a prior criminal career for domestic violence and nondomestic violence crimes of at least four years, and almost half had criminal careers of at least ten years. On average, they had seven prior arrests that were prosecuted in the state's courts. That study was in Rhode Island.[27] A study of more than 66,000 abusers with cases filed between 2004 and 2006 across the state of Washington similarly found that more than two-thirds had prior criminal histories.[28] With such criminal backgrounds, even threats of maximum misdemeanor sentences might not tempt abusers to accept anything but minimal, giveaway dispositions.

Given prosecutors' fear of prosecuting without victims, abusers know their salvation lies in getting their victim to recant, disappear, or refuse to testify in court. This gives abusers great motivation to romance, manipulate, threaten or intimidate, even murder their victims before trial. It also explains why even abusers held in jail awaiting trial regularly risk getting caught calling their victims from jail, trying to get them not to testify at upcoming trials. Given lack of other evidence, either as a result of police failure to investigate or the real absence of any evidence other than the victim's testimony, defendants or their lawyers know they can call the prosecution's bluff. In fact, in explaining its low domestic violence conviction rate, San Francisco prosecutors blame the city's public defenders for refusing to plea-bargain domestic violence cases.

But, and this is a big but, for every prosecutor who says he or she can't go forward without the victim, another proves that it can be done.

"CAN DO" PROSECUTORS DO

Rather than blame victims for their failure to prosecute domestic violence, other prosecutors have initiated actions to facilitate victim witnesses. For example, in 2014, the Davidson (Nashville) County district attorney Glenn Funk established a Domestic Violence Prosecution Support Team in 2014 to assist victims and his office's prosecution of domestic violence. The team sends armed escorts out to ferry victims to and from court. In court, they secure victims in a private waiting room so the victims don't have to mingle in the halls or waiting room next to their abusers. They accompany victims into the courtroom. The added security offered by the prosecutor

PROSECUTOR FINDS HE CAN GO FORWARD WITHOUT THE VICTIM

Back in 2013, Rodericus Williams, forty-eight, had been bonded out of court for a charge of assaulting his girlfriend and violation of a protective order she had secured against him. He was arrested again when he struck his fifty-two-year-old girlfriend in the face and pulled her hair while she was driving in South Memphis where they lived. As a result of the pending charges at that time, the new assault charge was elevated to a felony with a possible sentence of fifteen years imprisonment. An hour after that assault, after police left, Williams returned to their residence and again punched his girlfriend in the face more than a half dozen times. The woman grabbed a knife, but ended up cutting herself in the struggle.

Williams had by then amassed six prior felonies and two domestic violence convictions that were charged as misdemeanors. He had been arrested six times since 2011 for alleged assaults against the same girlfriend, though most of those cases were dismissed because, according to the Shelby County prosecutor, the victim failed to show up for court.

The felony assault charges were initially dismissed in the lower court because the victim again did not show up, but this time, the prosecutors from the district attorney's Intimate Partner/Domestic Violence Prosecution Unit took the case before a grand jury for indictment and proceeded. The special unit worked closely with the County Family Safety Center, which provides services and assistance to victims and their families. On January 29, 2015, a jury found Rodericus Williams guilty of assaulting his girlfriend.

Unfortunately, the unit in that office only handles felonies.*

NOTE

*"Man with History of Domestic Violence Convicted of Assaulting Girlfriend," WHBQ, Memphis, TN, January 29, 2015.

has increased the number of victims coming to court to testify. The same prosecutor has even (finally!) begun to enforce state law that prohibits convicted or court-restrained abusers from possessing firearms. The prosecutor proudly announced his office's first gun removal from a convicted abuser, a 9mm handgun, in May 2015.[29]

Prosecutors are anything but helpless when it comes to prosecuting domestic violence, especially where prosecutors have established specialized domestic violence prosecution units as in the example above. This is not new. After adopting "no drop" policies in the 1990s for domestic violence cases, conviction rates reached 96 percent in San Diego, California; 85 percent in Omaha, Nebraska; 78 percent in Klamath Falls, Oregon; and 55 percent in Everett, Washington. The last rate was lower because the prosecutor allowed 22 percent of the cases to be diverted. Still, the dismissal rate in Everett dropped from 79 to 29 percent. In Klamath Falls, it dropped from 47 to 14 percent.[30] Other jurisdictions have shown similar successes. In Queens Borough of New York City, for example, prosecutors increased convictions from 24 to 60 percent.[31] When Cook County (Chicago) prosecutors established its specialized unit, it obtained a 71 percent conviction rate, compared to a 50 percent rate obtained by the rest of the office for domestic violence cases.[32] Similarly, in Milwaukee, a specialized unit increased felony convictions by five times.[33]

In 2009, post-*Crawford*, a new prosecutor in Bristol County, Massachusetts, decided to reverse that office's low conviction rate for domestic violence, previously blamed on uncooperative victims. Prosecutors spent more time with victims, helping them secure services and support. They began collecting records of accused abusers' phone calls from the local jail to their victims that could be used as additional evidence of their abuse or explain why victims failed to appear in court or recanted. Before the new prosecution program, the county dismissed 120 cases a month. Within a month of the new effort, that dropped to seventy-five. Within a few more months, it dropped further to just sixteen. Of the thirty-two cases that involved what were determined to be the most high-risk abusers, only two were dismissed, and most of the offenders were convicted and imprisoned.[34]

In Lancaster County, Nebraska, in 2014, prosecutors went forward in 95 percent of the domestic violence arrests. They obtained convictions in 63 percent of the cases. In another 9 percent of the cases, defendants were sent to pretrial diversion programs. Judges sentenced more than three-fourths of offenders to jail or probation. This compares to 1996 when three-quarters of Lancaster abusers sentenced were given only minimum fines commensurate with minor traffic assessments.[35]

Other prosecutors have increased convictions by videotaping defendants after arrest. In Brooklyn, New York, videotaping defendants made the largest difference in the misdemeanor courts. Prosecutors had ample evidence in their felony domestic violence prosecutions for a 95 percent conviction rate with or without the videos, but in the lower courts, the videotapes significantly increased convictions over cases without it—59 percent compared to 50 percent in Integrated Domestic Violence Courts and 37.1 percent compared to 31.5 percent in criminal courts.[36]

Prosecutors have proven equally successful prosecuting felony domestic violence as well as misdemeanor. In the 1990s, Brooklyn, New York, established a domestic violence court exclusively for all defendants indicted for a felony domestic violence charge. A subsequent study of the court documented low dismissal and high conviction rates. Prosecutors dropped only between 5 and 10 percent of cases after indictment. They obtained convictions in 94 percent of the cases prosecuted, mostly (88 percent) as a result of pleas. Only 6 percent went to trial. Four percent of cases were dismissed, and 2 percent were acquitted after trial. Most of the defendants were charged with assaults or order violations or robbery/burglary, with another 9 percent for possession or use of firearms. Although the cases all began as felonies, at disposition, 34 percent were reduced to misdemeanors.[37]

Across Minnesota, prosecutors are finding that body cameras worn by patrol officers are increasing abusers' enthusiasm for plea negotiations. Initially assigned to increase transparency and keep police officers in line, the departments have found the videos are capturing compelling evidence in domestic violence incidents. For example, in April 2015, the Columbia Heights police recorded a woman whispering onto the camera. She had been strangled and was spitting blood as she whispered. The camera also captured an enraged suspect continuing to threaten to beat her until she could not be recognized. However, minutes after their arrival and after the situation cooled, the victim refused to be photographed or give a statement. Thanks to the camera evidence, however, police charged the assailant with felony strangulation, confident the case could be won in court. According to the county prosecutor, their confidence is not misplaced; once defendants are shown the videos, they are anxious to keep them away from judges or juries.[38]

Although it is easy to find unique prosecution programs given an entire country to choose from, statewide studies make the same point. Some prosecutors manage and others don't, even in adjacent jurisdictions with similar demographics, police departments, victims, and abusers. As far back as the 1990s, for example, the *Boston Globe* examined 15,000 violations of protective order prosecutions across Massachusetts, prosecuted by the state's eleven district attorney offices. In Massachusetts, police file misdemeanor charges directly in court, so there is almost no prosecution screening pretrial. The *Globe* found an average conviction rate of 60 percent, but more interesting, it documented that in adjoining counties with similar demographics, one dismissed 33 percent of its cases while the other dismissed 60 percent! Not surprisingly, the latter provided victims with affidavits to sign indicating they did not want the case to be prosecuted.

Five years later, another newspaper, the *State*, examined 4,351 felony domestic violence cases across South Carolina. On average, prosecutors and judges dropped 54 percent of the cases. Uniformly, the prosecutors interviewed attributed the high drop rates to lack of victim cooperation. However, as found in Massachusetts, the drop rate ranged from a high of 78 percent to a low of 31 percent in adjoining counties. The district with the lowest drop rate was one of the few that had a specialized domestic violence prosecution unit.

Interestingly, after the *State* ran its exposé of poor prosecution performances, the South Carolina attorney general promulgated a directive, ordering prosecutors to pursue all domestic violence cases where "there is evidence available, direct or circumstantial." Further, he threatened to take over local domestic violence prosecutions. The *State* reported that the month after the attorney general's threats, the statewide dismissal rate fell to just 29 percent! Obviously, it was not the victims who changed their behaviors as a result of the attorney general's threats.

Again two years later, the Raleigh, North Carolina, *News and Observer* conducted its investigation, reviewing 238,000 misdemeanor domestic violence cases across that state. It found an average conviction rate of 47 percent, ranging from a low of 21 percent to a high of 57 percent. In one of the counties with the lowest conviction rate, the sheriff told the newspaper that he instructed officers not to complete domestic violence incident reports if the victim was not visibly wounded or did not want to press charges. The sheriff explained that the district attorney would not prosecute such cases. Interviewed, the district attorney, in turn, blamed local judges and juries that, he said, would not convict without direct victim testimony, making domestic violence cases a "waste of time."[39]

In addition to blaming victims, prosecutors blame police for failing to provide them with sufficient evidence to prosecute the cases or for arresting the wrong persons. Although most law enforcement agencies do not often make dual arrests, any police failure to discriminate between victim and offender generally means these cases cannot (and should not) be prosecuted. When both parties are arrested, neither can credibly testify against the other because they both are charged. In explaining the high dismissal rate in Arizona, a brief published by Arizona State University's Morrison Institute for Public Policy on Domestic Violence reported that dual arrests were one of the explanations for the state's low conviction rate.[40] In Connecticut, as in Arizona, prosecutors can legitimately point to an unusually high dual arrest rate accounting for thousands of dismissals.

But dual arrests and arrests of the wrong party are the exception, not the rule. More typically, prosecutors blame law enforcement's failure to investigate cases and supply them with sufficient evidence to prosecute the cases. Often the only thing prosecutors are provided with are victim statements taken by police at the scenes. Because most abusers are arrested for misdemeanors, no detectives are assigned. Any evidence obtained must be obtained by the responding patrol officers at the scene. As a result, little evidence is provided prosecutors. Across Rhode Island, for example, police were found to secure physical evidence in less than 10 percent of the domestic violence incidents and interviewed additional witnesses in less than a quarter of the incidents. In Ohio, police were found to provide prosecutors with 911 tapes, medical records, or eyewitness testimony in less than 10 percent of the cases. In North Carolina, patrol officers were found to provide prosecutors with photos of victim injuries or damaged property in less than 15 percent of the cases, although a smaller specialized domestic violence unit in the same police department was able to more than double that rate. The study of prosecution in large urban jurisdictions found that half the incidents were witnessed by a third party, but 22 percent of those witnesses were children. Physical evidence such as photos, tapes of the 911 calls, and forensic evidence was available in 68 percent of the cases, mostly photos and 911 tapes. Victim statements were obtained in 50 percent of the cases and defendant statements in 10 percent of the cases.[41]

Nevertheless, although counterintuitive, research has yet to demonstrate that physical evidence has an independent, positive relationship to convictions! Like all criminal cases, domestic violence cases are not tried, they are negotiated. After all, prosecutors need only enough evidence to convince abusers to plead, not to convict them in court.

Successful prosecution of domestic violence is not rocket science. It does, however, require prosecutors not to shoot themselves in the foot.

FAILING TO STOP ABUSERS AFTER ARREST

Prosecutors can effectively cripple their efforts before their domestic violence prosecutions ever reach trial. Allowed to be free and unsupervised after arrest, abusers do what prosecutors often fail to do. They make a beeline to their victims. Whether with roses or blows, they help the prosecutor justify the subsequent dismissal by making the victim "uncooperative." It's not malice on the part of prosecutors, but mainly misunderstanding. In most of their criminal cases, prosecutors only have to worry about whether or not the defendant shows up for trial. Imposition of even token bail usually suffices. When most defendants are charged with crimes or even accused of assaulting a stranger, police, prosecutors, and courts can concentrate on scheduling and preparing for a subsequent trial. They don't have to worry about a vulnerable victim being manipulated, threatened, intimidated, or even killed pending trial.

None of this applies to domestic violence. Prosecutors cannot proceed as they would in most other criminal cases, but many do. As revealed in the California review, some prosecutor offices don't even bother to show up in court at arraignment when bail and/or release conditions are set, or not set, by the judge. Without specific efforts to safeguard victims and stop abusers from doing what they did to get arrested in the first place, prosecutors lose the key and often the only evidence police have provided them, the victim.

Relying on the threat of an impending trial to keep abusers in line before trial is not enough. Even jailing some abusers before trial is sometimes not enough.

MILWAUKEE DISCOVERS ABUSER TENACITY

Milwaukee prosecutors realized this in 2001 after a victim revealed to them that her abuser had repeatedly contacted her from jail and had his buddies stalk and intimidate her at her home and at work. A prosecutor checked the jail phone recordings. It was even worse than the victim knew. The phone recordings revealed that the jailed abuser had solicited three friends to murder the victim. The new crime alone, solicitation to commit murder, provided prosecutors the means to get an additional sentence of twenty years imprisonment.

The case helped make Milwaukee prosecutors aware of the heightened vulnerability victims face when cases are pending against their intimate attackers. Instead of being cowed by jail, much less impending trials, many abusers redouble their campaign of abuse against their victims. This can take the form of increased threats and intimidation, or promises of reform and enduring love. Some even take the opportunity to marry their victims during this time as evidence of their true love. Remember Ray Rice, the NFL football player who married his girlfriend shortly after he knocked her unconscious in the elevator in 2014? The fact that the abusers' lawyers let them know that wives cannot be compelled to testify against their husbands may also play a role in spurring marriage proposals.

Unfortunately, most abusers have time and freedom to get to their victims one way or the other before trial without prosecution and court intervention. Even misdemeanor trials can take six months to a year to be tried. Further, abusers routinely fail to show for trial dates; some because they fear conviction, others as a tactic to frustrate and further harass their victims who may be missing work to testify. Not surprisingly, the abusers who fail to show for trial dates are among those most likely to continue to reabuse. Technically, failure to appear, called a "court default," is a new crime, but it is a crime routinely ignored by prosecutors and courts. At most, the court orders a default warrant that is only served when the defendant is arrested for another offense and the police officer checks the computer to discover the warrant. When the defendant is brought to court on the old and new charges, at most the court may impose nominal court costs against the defendant. However, at that point, there are bigger issues than an old default for the court to worry about.

Most abusers are not held in jail pending trial. Judges may order abusers to stay away or have no contact with their victims during this period, but for many abusers, the judge's words are no more compelling than the laws they are already charged with violating.

In Milwaukee, at least, prosecutors understood the threat posed by arrested abusers. They instituted a specific protocol to protect victims with the help of the Milwaukee police. Prosecutors regularly review jail recordings of all abuser phone calls for evidence of new crimes and victim harassment or intimidation. To their surprise, especially because the inmates are informed that their jail phone calls are recorded (except for calls to lawyers if the lawyers supply the jail with their office numbers), more often than not, prosecutors find what they are looking for. They routinely add charges as a result, ranging from bribery to intimidation. Further, with the evidence on tape, prosecutors can proceed without victim testimony. In addition, the enlightened Milwaukee prosecutors target repeat abusers, including those with dismissed abuse charges, figuring that many of the dismissals could be attributed to successful abuse, as opposed to abuser innocence. They also wisely target abusers with records of court defaults. Victim/witness liaisons in their office keep in contact with victims and inform prosecutors if victims suddenly change their mind about testifying. Often this is a sign that the abuser has gotten to them. If victims report their abusers have violated conditions of pretrial release, police are sent to bring the abusers back to court immediately. Even if the violations do not constitute new crimes, prosecutors ask that the abusers' pretrial release be revoked and they be jailed pending trial for the violation. Before 2003, the Milwaukee police domestic violence unit focused exclusively on felony cases. Beginning that year, the unit expanded to go after abuser misdemeanants, and the court even began to monitor its own pretrial release conditions! The Court Pretrial Monitoring Unit began informing police of reported violations.[42]

In short, Milwaukee police, prosecutors, and courts joined to do what most people would assume is always done, enforcing the law and protecting vulnerable victims of identified abusers.

What message does it send victims when the jail provides inmates phones for their abusers to contact them in violation of court orders, much less to harass and threaten them? And worse, what do victims think when nothing is done about it? What Milwaukee pioneered in 2001 is still the exception, not the rule, unfortunately.

The majority of arrested abusers who reabuse do so relatively quickly. Studies in both Massachusetts and Brooklyn, which included those arrested for domestic violence misdemeanors in the former and felonies in the latter, document that the majority of defendants rearrested for new abuse were arrested while their initial abuse cases were still pending in court.[43] Nor do abusers obey court orders to stay away from their victims in the interim. In the latter study, violation of no contact orders were the most common domestic violence–related rearrest pending trial. How disheartening must it be for victims to realize that the police and courts can't even protect them after their abuser has finally been arrested.

PROTECTING VICTIMS CAN'T WAIT UNTIL TRIAL

The following case reported in South Jersey in January 2014 is all too common. Wilbor Doss, fifty-four, was arrested for simple assault and possession of a weapon for an unlawful purpose. Police had been dispatched to his home, where they arrested him. He was booked at the station house, given a court date, and released. According to police, once released, he went directly back to where he had been arrested and continued his abuse of his intimate partner. This time he was arrested for simple assault, possession of a weapon for an unlawful purpose, and terroristic threats. The second time around, he was not released but held in lieu of $40,000 bail.[44]

Meanwhile, in Milford, Connecticut, the prosecutor and court got it right, but it took three, not two tries. Christopher Millhouse, thirty-seven, was arrested for violating a protective order. He was released pending trial. Less than a week later, he was arrested for a domestic assault against a different victim—accused of strangulation, forcefully throwing the victim into a bathroom fixture, and damaging her cell phone. He was released again. Less than a week later, he was arrested back where the first arrest had occurred less than two weeks before, this time for burglary, home invasion, unlawful restraint, assault, interfering with an emergency call, and criminal mischief. This time, he was held in lieu of a $1.1 million bond. Although the authorities eventually came to understand the necessity to protect victims before trial, it is safe to assume that the two victims were probably not overly impressed with the commitment of the Connecticut criminal justice system to protect them.[45]

Presently, only a handful of states even require a cooling-off period, holding alleged abusers for six to twelve hours before releasing them on bond or personal recognizance (their promise to return as directed). In 2015, New Jersey's legislature debated joining their ranks. The legislators discussed holding certain alleged abusers for twelve hours when law enforcement identified specific risk factors such as threats to kill their victims, having caused serious injuries, or the use of deadly weapons. At the time of writing, legislation was still pending.

MAINE BAIL COMMISSIONER GETS IT RIGHT

The old maxim is correct: The best way to predict the future is look at the past. That's what bail commissioners should do in determining whether or not defendants should be released. Although defendants are presumed innocent until found guilty, they cannot be presumed nonviolent until found guilty. A bail commissioner in rural Aroostook, Maine, got it right.

As exemplified in this case, it takes no more effort to make a routine right decision as a routine wrong one, even when dealing with domestic violence.

BAIL DENIED FOR MISDEMEANOR DOMESTIC VIOLENCE

Kartner Bell, thirty-three, was brought before the bail commissioner for domestic assault, trespassing, criminal mischief, and threats. Not at the scene when deputies arrived, Bell was arrested the next day hiding in a bathroom. While his attempts to avoid arrest didn't prove his guilt, they did suggest that Bell might not be anxious to show up for trial, a reason to deny bail. In addition, his flight indicated heightened danger for the victim. The commissioner denied him bail, holding Bell until court, scheduled several days later. In short, the commissioner refused to play Russian roulette with the safety of the victim at stake, especially with the odds obviously stacked against her.[*]

Note

[*]Lynds, J., "Mars Hill Man Arrested, Denied Bail for Alleged Domestic Violence," *Bangor Daily News*, March 13, 2015.

SOME LEGISLATURES TIGHTEN BAIL CONDITIONS FOR DOMESTIC VIOLENCE

Some states have made it easier than others to hold defendants before trial. Some prohibit release, at least, until the case reaches a judge at arraignment, generally the defendant's first appearance in court. Others require defendants to be held for a "cooling-off" period for hours, or even a few days. Louisiana legislators went further than most, for a while.

Before Gwen Salley, thirty-nine, could divorce her estranged husband, he was charged with false imprisonment, unlawful possession of a dangerous weapon, and aggravated assault with a firearm against her. He was released the next day. Just a few days later, he kidnapped her, shot her, and then killed himself, all while he was on bail for the prior domestic violence incident. The case spurred the Louisiana legislature to pass "Gwen's Law" in 2014, requiring domestic violence felony defendants to be held five days before the judge is allowed to release them. The defendant can then still be held without bail if found to be dangerous. The law requires an investigation and a risk assessment to be conducted before the hearing, including analysis of prior criminal record, substance abuse, gun ownership, employment status, prior threats with a dangerous weapon, and threats to kill or commit suicide. The victim has the right to testify at the bail hearing. If granted bail, the suspect can be required to wear an electronic monitoring device. As one prosecutor testified, Gwen's Law gives victims a chance to beg for their lives. The legislation only applied to felony cases.

In 2015, after complaints from the courts that the law was bogging down busy urban courts with perfunctory hearings, the legislature gutted Gwen's Law, requiring only that judges notify prosecutors when they release abusers without a hearing. The new law also repealed the uniform risk assessments judges must use, allowing jurisdictions to develop their own. At least, as supporters of the new law pointed out, it will allow judges to immediately release defendants when police make mutual arrests and there is no one home as a result to care for the children.

In 2015, the New Jersey senate passed a bill (at the time of writing, still pending in the legislature) to impose more stringent bail restrictions for anyone charged with violating a protective order. Existing New Jersey law allows courts to release alleged violators on bail after they post 10 percent of the amount in cash. The senate bill only allows bail in the form of full cash, a surety bond, or a bail bond secured by real property situated in the state with an unencumbered equity equal to the amount of bail plus $20,000. According to a sponsor, the bill is needed because judges typically are allowing alleged violators to be released after posting just $50.

RIGHT HAND MUST COORDINATE WITH LEFT HAND

A problem endemic to the criminal justice system is getting the various agencies that make it up to actually work like a system. Mostly, they do their own thing. This is understandable given that they operate under different mandates by different agencies in different branches of government, guided by different legal standards. What is not as understandable is often the right hand doesn't have a clue what the left hand is doing. The agencies don't share vital information or make sure all parties have access to even basic information, including what has been ordered to protect a vulnerable victim.

Earlier, the work of Arizona's Pima County sheriff's domestic violence unit's effort to enforce protective orders was highlighted. Local media documented the challenge that agency faces to enforce protective orders or no contact orders imposed as a condition of bail after a domestic violence perpetrator is arrested.[46] Trying to get all parts of the criminal justice system to work together is like using a Band-Aid instead of stitches to heal a gaping wound, according to the head of the sheriff's domestic violence unit. One example, he explained, is the documents that list a defendant's release conditions set by the bail commissioner or judge. They tell whether or not a no contact order is in place. Although these are computerized in a court database, police don't have access to that. Instead, they have to sort by hand through a batch given to them on a daily basis. Further, the court forms dumped on their desks do not differentiate domestic violence from other types of crimes, so deputies must sort through new files every day to find the ones that involve domestic violence with special protective conditions. Once identified, the sheriff's department has to enter them into its own computer so they will then be accessible to area law enforcement to enforce.

One would think that in 2015, all jurisdictions would have figured out how to share such crucial data digitally when victims' very lives are at stake. One would be mostly wrong in Arizona and elsewhere across the country.

PROTECTING VICTIMS BEFORE TRIAL, SECOND TIME AROUND

Joshua Harrison, twenty-four, of Casa Grande, Arizona, was arrested by Pinal County deputies after allegedly strangling and assaulting his girlfriend on a Saturday in January 2015. According to the sheriff's office, Harrison punched her in the face and strangled her "until she felt her eyes would bug out." She managed to get away momentarily by kicking him in the groin and locking herself in another room. Harrison denied the assault, pointing to his own injuries, but deputies found the swelling and redness on his hands were consistent with having punched someone. Harrison was charged with aggravated assault, threatening and intimidating, criminal damage, and disorderly conduct. He was released by a bail commissioner at the police station and ordered to have no contact with the victim.

Meanwhile, detectives drove the victim to a domestic violence shelter. While they were en route, Harrison called the detective's cell, claiming to be the victim's brother, and asked her to drop the charges against him. The detectives immediately did the right thing, making up for the earlier release of the suspect despite his obvious danger to the victim. They returned to the suspect's home and arrested him. Harrison was rebooked into the Pinal County Jail for violating the conditions of his release. This time, he was held on a $5,000 secured bond.

Sheriff Babeu condemned the original release of Harrison, telling the media that he couldn't understand why the first incident wasn't enough to make it much tougher for Joshua Harrison to be free to hunt down the woman. The sheriff continued, "We're sick and tired of judges releasing violent offenders, criminals, back into our community."[*]

NOTE

[*]Stout, S., "Domestic Violence Suspect Arrested Twice in Two Days," KPHO, January 6, 2015; Smith, C., "Beating. Strangulation. Released without bond?" KGUN9-TV, Florence, AZ, January 6, 2015.

Arizona bail is actually set when the court is not in session by commissioners who have the power of judges but even less accountability to the public.

As a recent case in Nashville illustrates, arrest and the prospects of a trial and possible sentence do not deter high-risk abusers intent on harming their victims. It also shows that the laws designed to safeguard domestic violence victims are only as solid as the officials charged with enforcing them.

NO LAWYER, NO BUDDIES ON THE BENCH, NO CAMPAIGN MONEY, NO PEACE FOR VICTIMS

A Nashville woman thought she had twelve hours to escape. David Chase had been arrested for assaulting her. Under Tennessee law, domestic violence arrestees can be held twelve hours to "cool off" before being released. The magistrate on night duty had ordered Chase held. Not only was Chase an obvious threat to the victim, but he was also very drunk. Even so, the victim started packing her bags to vacate the residence before the abuser was released. Meanwhile, Judge Casey Moreland got a call at home that Sunday morning. It was from Chase's lawyer, who assured the judge that a mistake had been made. The victim had lied, and she and the accused weren't even dating partners, covered by the law. The judge ordered Chase's immediate release.

Chase returned to the house and, according to police, resumed his assault on the victim. She managed to get away and called 911 for a second time within hours. Police found blood on the walls and the victim's belongings scattered in the hallway. They subsequently arrested Chase again, charging him with aggravated assault by strangulation, vandalism, and interference with a 911 call. Chase appeared before another magistrate. This time Judge Moreland did not have to intercede because the magistrate waived the cooling-off period, imposing a cash bail that Chase paid and walked free. The police chief later complained to the local press that if the twelve hours are going to be waived, at least the police should be told so they could warn the victims. The prosecutor joined in expressing his dismay.

Subsequently, still another judge had an opportunity to hold Chase, but didn't. Chase was brought back to court for drunk driving. Prosecutors moved to have his bond release rescinded because of the latest domestic violence charges. Judge Amanda McClendon refused but ordered the defendant to stay home on weekends, be tested for drugs and alcohol, and wear a GPS monitor. He was also admonished once again to stay away from the victim of the two pending domestic assaults.[*]

Wasn't it supposedly Einstein that said the definition of insanity was doing the same thing again and again and expecting different results?

NOTE

[*]Daniels III, F., "Judge Casey Moreland Offers a Lesson," *The Tennessean*, July 22, 2015; Gonzalez, T., "Judge Casey Moreland Reprimanded by State Judicial Board," *The Tennessean*, October 24, 2014. Subsequently, Chase's ex-girlfriend recanted and the charges were dropped, although it later came out that the dismissal was conditioned on Chase dropping a suit he had brought against the Metro police department for civil rights violation. Williams, P., "Explosive Allegations Emerge from David Chase Case, $2 Million Requested to Make Case 'Go Away,'" WTVF, Nashville, Tennessee.

A newspaper investigation into the defendant's numerous releases without a cooling-off period pointed out that David Chase may have received special consideration because he is executive vice president of D.F. Chase Inc., one of the largest construction firms in Tennessee.[47] The police chief ascribed Judge Casey Moreland's initial release of Chase as a deplorable example of a "good ole boy" culture in the courts. The reason Chase's lawyer had Moreland's home number and the temerity to call the judge at home on a Sunday is that they were buddies. The lawyer and his wife both contributed the maximum to Moreland's last election campaign.

Reacting to the case, state lawmakers announced their intent to make the twelve-hour hold for arrested abusers mandatory, removing judicial and magistrate discretion. The county Republican Party called for Moreland to step down from the bench, as did the Metro Council. The General Sessions Bench created a new rule that only three General Sessions judges designated to handle domestic violence cases could waive twelve-hour holds in the future and only after a hearing with all parties present, including the victim. *The Tennessean*, the local newspaper, called for Moreland's removal from the bench "to ensure the safety of innocent victims in the Davidson County justice system." The judge was later reprimanded for "detrimentally affect[ing] the integrity of the Judiciary."

An individual judge's malfeasance or even innocent mistake makes an easy target for the press and politicians. The judge, however, was not exceptional. A citywide study found that Nashville's night court magistrates and judges waived the twelve-hour cooling-off period 40 percent of the time.

Keeping victims safe after an arrest is paramount. Keeping abusers away from their victims pretrial also increases the likelihood that victims will testify at trial. Once that agreement is nailed down, the chances of the victim then actually having to testify is reduced. The defendant will plead guilty. Prosecutors can also press for speedy trial dates to lessen the period of pretrial victim vulnerability as well as loss of freedom for the accused.

The imposition of high or no bails not only protects victims before trial, but it also convinces defendants of the seriousness of the charges. San Diego city prosecutors at one point had the highest conviction rates in the county. They were able to decrease time to trial to thirty-two days, with half the abusers admitting guilt at their first court appearance, called the arraignment. They were able to do so because the judges agreed to impose a $1,000 cash bail for each domestic violence charge. As a result, most of the abusers were held pretrial. Pleading guilty got them *out* of jail.[48] The standard disposition for abusers under California law is a three-year probationary term. Although the chronic abusers will fail that probation (if enforced) and eventually end up being imprisoned, most abusers are not good at weighing long-term versus short-term consequences of their decisions. The desire to get out of jail now trumps the future risk posed by a probationary sentence.

Of course, if prosecutors routinely reduce domestic violence charges from felonies to misdemeanors and domestic violence–specific crimes to disorderly conduct, they cannot then justify asking judges to impose high bails.

There is an old axiom in prosecution: Defendants who come to court in handcuffs, leave in handcuffs. An analysis of criminal court cases in New York City, for example, found that when abusers were held before trial, their conviction rate was 84 percent compared to 27 percent for those released before trial. The researchers found "very few additional factors were likely to influence the convictions."[49] By not asking that abusers be held pretrial, the prosecutor is delivering a message to the court, the defendant, and the victim: The case is not serious and the defendant poses no risk to his victim.

Competent domestic violence prosecutors also reach out and communicate with victims before trial. Surprisingly, many prosecutors don't, even when victims are their only evidence. An Ohio court study found that the majority of the domestic violence victims never received any information from prosecutors before trial, including notification of the court date! Most never received as much as a phone call.

They key for successful domestic violence prosecution is extending the same commitment to misdemeanor cases as is afforded felony prosecutions. Typically in prosecutors' offices, the attorneys who are assigned misdemeanor prosecutions are not as experienced as their peers assigned felony prosecutions. They have less support staff, including investigators to help them collect evidence not obtained by the officers at the scene. As the lowest prosecutor in the hierarchy, they are paid less too. One of the first dedicated domestic violence prosecutors in the country in the 1980s was assigned to Massachusetts's Quincy Court, a lower criminal court that handled only misdemeanors and reduced felonies. She did a remarkable job doing what erstwhile had been ignored or thought impossible. As a result, after several years the district attorney offered her a raise, but, consistent with office policy, coupled the raise with a transfer to superior court where felonies are prosecuted. Committed to protecting domestic violence victims (she herself had been abused by her husband), she refused to "move up" in the hierarchy to the superior court. The smart district attorney, William Delahunt (later a Massachusetts congressman, elected, in part, as a champion of domestic violence victims), gave her the raise anyway, much to the consternation of the felony prosecutors who felt slighted by a misdemeanor prosecutor getting equivalent salary. The fact that she was one of the only women prosecutors at the time probably compounded the gripes from the network of more-tenured male prosecutors.

In California, the task force appointed by the attorney general seeking to find out why prosecutors were failing to follow state law in prosecuting misdemeanor domestic violence defendants discovered that the number one reason was inexperienced prosecutors. The report concluded, "District Attorneys' assign their least experienced prosecutors to handle misdemeanor cases, which are typically easier to prosecute than felonies. Unfortunately, most District Attorneys in the (study) counties (seven of ten) include domestic violence misdemeanors in these attorneys' caseloads, even though such cases present some of the most difficult challenges that any prosecutor will face, particularly at trial."

The task force also pointed out a lack of resources for prosecutors assigned to misdemeanor domestic violence cases. It observed, "When law enforcement refers a domestic violence case to the prosecution for criminal filing, the referral often consists only of the first responder's report." Several of the district attorneys admitted that it was their office policy to reject these cases for prosecution, rather than supplement the investigation with their staff, talk to the victims themselves, or ask the police to do a better job. Finally, the task force found that the misdemeanor prosecutors regularly failed to reach out to community-based advocates for assistance, relying instead on their own office "advocates," who often did little more than send written notices of trial dates to victims. Inexperienced prosecutors may find it particularly difficult to integrate their office advocates, whose goals are to hold defendants accountable, with community-based advocates, whose goals are to support the victims' wishes.[50]

Most county prosecutor offices prosecute both felonies and misdemeanors. In some big cities in some states, however, prosecution may be divided such that one office prosecutes only misdemeanors. It is no surprise that it was a city attorney, Casey Gwinn, and his staff in San Diego, charged with misdemeanor prosecution, that is credited with pioneering "victimless" prosecution. His was among the first office of prosecutors to prosecute domestic violence cases even if the victim refused to testify. Ironically, his first such case was against a local judge. When it came time for trial, the alleged victim, the judge's girlfriend, was conveniently vacationing in Mexico, unavailable to testify. Gwinn persevered anyway . . . and lost. But his office remained committed, and before Gwinn left the office, it boasted a 96 percent conviction rate. In fact, Gwinn discovered it was easier to prosecute domestic violence cases before a jury without the victim, or better yet, with a recanting victim.

PROSECUTING WITHOUT THE VICTIM

Prosecuting domestic violence without victims requires, of course, alternative evidence. There are generally six types of evidence, both collected at the scene of a domestic violence incident and supplemented through other means, which are regularly used to successfully prosecute abusers. The six types of evidence are a 911 phone call recording, photographs, physical evidence, medical evaluation forms, expert testimony, and statements made by the accused.

The 911 phone call represents the first time that a victim can relate what happened and is usually made to secure help, not influence subsequent court prosecution. As a result, it can provide most compelling evidence. A 911 recording featuring a frightened victim pleading for help after being attacked may help jurors understand the true terror of the crime.

If the victim is available, her live testimony is also required. When she's not, tapes can serve to show that the victim has absented herself because of threats from the accused. Tapes of calls made from jail by the accused may constitute evidence of such threats. These tapes can also be used to contradict victims that have recanted or watered down their testimony since the incident.

Photographs and physical evidence are also essential elements of victimless prosecution. These may include photographs of the victim, the room where the domestic violence occurred, and the suspect. Pictures of overturned furniture, a smashed cell phone on the floor, and/or blood may show a judge and the jury how dangerous or frightening the assault was. Physical evidence collected at the scene of a domestic violence incident helps too. Similar to photographs, physical evidence like ripped clothing helps to establish the context of the assault. A combination of various photographs and physical evidence is ideal for an evidence-based prosecution.

Medical evaluation forms are another essential piece of evidence. Statements a victim provides medical personnel and social workers relating what occurred to explain her medical symptoms are considered non-testimonial or business records, and thus are admissible in court. Furthermore, medical personnel documenting injuries may provide an alternative picture to what the judge and jury see months later when the victim in court appears healthy and bruise free. Finally, expert testimony of things that are not common knowledge, including medical or psychological issues, may help illustrate the dynamics of domestic violence. An expert witness, like a social worker or psychologist, can explain why the victim didn't leave her abuser months or even years earlier.

Defendant statements made at the scene or later may also provide effective evidence. Often in denying more serious abuse, defendants will admit to what they consider lesser abuse. "I didn't hit her, just pushed her."

Although all six types of evidence are not always available, a combination of just a few of those discussed will generally prove sufficient to convict an abuser before a judge or jury, much less convince him to plead if offered a deal.

Not only is alternative evidence often available, but prosecution may also be more successful if the victim does not show at trial. Juries and judges can have trouble sympathizing with victims who do not conform to what they envision victims looking or acting like. If victims are belligerent or angry, appear vindictive, or admit to having been drinking or using drugs at the time of their assault, they may be disbelieved, especially if the abuser is cool, calm, collected, and even charming. The stereotype of abusers having Dr. Jekyll, Mr. Hyde split personalities has a large grain of truth to it. Successful abusers are good at manipulation. Many, after all, had practice, having had to romance and charm their victims before coming to control and abuse them.

Juries may start off dubious and victim blaming because they don't understand why the victim stayed with her abuser and let herself be abused. Women jurors especially, if the victim is a woman, may be in denial that they could ever be in such a position, so they reason that she must have brought it on herself. Good prosecutors know how to question jury pools to get the all-too-common victim blamers off their juries.

On the other hand, recanting victims give good prosecutors a chance to educate juries on how abusers exercise coercive control over their victims. Such prosecutors make it easier for the jury to understand the threats and manipulation that make the victim change her story. Through their gentle cross-examination of the recanting victim, they show her dependence on her abuser and the obvious contradictions in her testimony.

The prosecution of Terrell Kelly in Milwaukee, Wisconsin, described in chapter 5, is just one example of successful prosecution despite victim recantation. The case of Jeffrey Rutkunas and his girlfriend in Philadelphia, Pennsylvania, may be more typical.

INJURED VICTIM PAYS FOR ABUSER'S DEFENSE IN COURT

Jeffrey Rutkunas, twenty-nine, put his girlfriend in the hospital for a couple of weeks. Her injuries were so severe that doctors had to remove her ruptured spleen.

After Rutkunas's girlfriend's beating, she had called 911, telling the dispatcher that an unknown man had attacked her. When police arrived at the scene, Rutkunas had fled. When police interviewed the victim in the hospital, she reluctantly admitted that her boyfriend had assaulted her, because she didn't want to get an innocent person in trouble. She signed a statement she made to police saying that she had argued with her boyfriend, objecting to his drug use, before he beat her up. Later, police found Rutkunas and arrested him. He sported a new tattoo on his side—the girlfriend's name. He later told her he got it to demonstrate his love. She recanted her statement to police, this time blaming the assault on three women in Philadelphia. She gave money to her boyfriend's attorney to help with his defense.[*]

NOTE

[*]A. Klein, "Determined Prosecutor Pursues Justice," *National Bulletin on Domestic Violence Prevention* 16(6), June 2010.

The average prosecutor, even if they understood something about domestic violence and its entrapment and traumatization of its victims, would have probably given up when the victim recanted and even started paying for Rutkunas's defense especially as the defendant demanded an expensive jury trial. But not Robin Twombly, the Pennsylvania prosecutor. She pressed on. The defense lawyer told the jury that the girlfriend's initial statement to police at the hospital was manipulated by them when the victim was delirious with pain. He also pointed out to the jury that the girlfriend was helping pay for his defense costs because she knew the defendant was innocent.

Twombly, however, was ready. She showed how it was the defendant, not the police, who had manipulated the victim. She played tapes of some of the seven hundred calls Rutkunas had made from jail to her. He knew the calls were being taped, but he told her repeatedly not to cooperate with police, professing his undying love. In one of the calls, the girlfriend brought up that he had beaten her, but he assured her, "Baby, that's all over."

Twombly showed the jury photos of the many injuries. She had nurses and police testify about what they saw and heard from the victim. In her closing argument, the prosecutor explained that the case was not about the defendant's love, but his "control, manipulation, violence, and intimidation." She admonished the jury not to allow themselves to become victims of the defendant's manipulation too. She also explained that victims do not bring charges and cannot drop them either.

The jury found Rutkunas guilty. As he left the courtroom in handcuffs, he and his girlfriend professed their love for each other.

But, as emphasized previously, trials are the rare exception, not the rule. Even when prosecutors adopt "no drop" policies, aggressively pursue domestic violence cases, and consistently recommend jail sentences, demands for trial only increase for a short period of time and then decrease again as the new "going rate" for domestic violence becomes part of the courthouse culture. A study found, for example, that in San Diego, with one of the lowest case dismissal rates in the country, abusers demand trials in only 2 percent of all cases. Other courts that copied San Diego found only 10 to 13 percent of abusers demanded trials, and only initially after no drop prosecution was instituted.[51]

While prosecutors who only handle misdemeanor prosecutions are more apt to take domestic violence (and all misdemeanors) more seriously, the trade-off is that maximum sentences afforded misdemeanors are fairly trivial, especially for repeat abusers and abusers who regularly receive more severe sentences for their nondomestic violence offenses. Ironically, the creation of specialized domestic violence courts, which have proliferated around the country, has inadvertently contributed to the trivialization of domestic violence crimes, as most have been established in misdemeanor courts. As a result, prosecutors are encouraged to try domestic violence cases as misdemeanors so that these specialty courts can maintain jurisdiction. They do so because the domestic violence court judges know what domestic violence is all about, which may not be true of judges in felony courts accustomed to "high value" drug offenses or even domestic violence murders.

However, a trade-off too great can defeat the purpose of the prosecution.

7

SENTENCING ABUSERS

Despite the large proportion of domestic violence cases that are diverted, dismissed, or reduced, thousands of abusers do end up appearing in American courts each and every day for domestic violence. Here is where the courts can make it clear, once and for all, that domestic violence constitutes an intolerable crime. Despite the injuries, the terror, and the suffering of their immediate victims—and their children, who may carry the cycle of violence into the next generation as abusers and victims—most abusers will walk out of court with but the gentlest of slaps, a few months of batterer program education or anger management with or without probation supervision, and brief jail sentences at most.

Prosecutors and judges have wide discretion in most cases. Although more than half the states require jail sentences of varying lengths for second, third, or fourth offenders, unless the abusers are actually charged as such, neither prosecutors nor judges are bound by these laws. Judges are free to ratify sentence recommendations that treat the most hardened chronic abuser as a pristine first offender. As a result, the vast majority of abusers who appear before them are charged as "first" offenders, generally for simple assaults or violations of protective orders, which results in the "perpetual first offenders" discussed earlier. Maximum jail sentences range from just sixty days in North Carolina to two and a half years in Massachusetts, with most at one year. But these sentences are then mostly suspended, with little time actually served.

A few states have presumptive or mandatory sentences for abusers, beginning with the first offense. California has the most rigorous mandatory sentences for first offenders. However, in what is described as a fairly widespread practice, prosecutors enter and judges approve guilty plea agreements with domestic violence misdemeanants that, contrary to state law, do not meet the requirements of the minimum domestic violence sentence. Defendants are allowed to plead guilty to nondomestic violence crimes, such as assault or trespass without a domestic violence designation. At least one prosecutor reported that his office opposed such pleas, but judges approved them anyhow.

The agreements, according to a California Attorney General Task Force, violate the spirit if not the letter of the law. The law reads: [If] a person is granted probation for a crime in which the victim is a person defined in Section 6211 of the Family Code, the terms of probation shall include . . . [a] minimum period of probation of 36 months . . . [and] successful completion of a batterer's program . . . for a period of not less than one year." The statute does not specify that the crime has to be charged as a domestic violence crime as long as the victim of the crime is one of the people listed in the Family Code, which includes spouses, former spouses, cohabitants, former cohabitants, and persons with a dating or engagement relationship.

However, as across the country, California courts are fairly lawless places. One state district attorney revealed, for example, that almost half those initially arrested for domestic violence received probationary sentences of zero to two years, and only slightly more than half were required to attend the batterer program. A third were excused from any program, and a little over 10 percent were ordered to attend a short anger management or counseling program. A judge from another county agreed that in his county 40 percent of batterers placed on probation were not required to complete a batterer program, in contradiction of state law.[1]

Rhode Island law also mandates that any convicted abuser who is not jailed must complete a state-certified batterer program, with or without probation. Perhaps because its mandated batterer program is half the length of California's, most prosecutors and judges actually comply with this law. What Rhode Island prosecutors and judges don't do is follow the law mandating ten-day sentences for second domestic violence convictions and a year for third convictions.[2]

A smattering of sentencing data available from disparate states across the country provide a picture of how courts are disposing of the minority of cases that do end up before them still charged as domestic violence. It reveals a mixed picture.

In the sixteen large urban counties studied in 2002, 80 percent of the convicted abusers received some jail time, but only half of those prosecuted for felonies (19 percent) received a year or more. Twenty percent received a probationary sentence without any jail or prison time.[3]

In 2012 across Wisconsin, nearly half the domestic violence sentences had some financial condition such as an order of restitution to the victim, court costs, fines, or forfeitures. The second most common sentence imposed as part of 22 percent of all domestic violence sentences was behavioral, including no contact orders and firearm prohibitions or requirements that defendants undergo substance abuse counseling. The third most common sentence in 18 percent of the sentences was a period of confinement. Probation was imposed in only 11 percent of the sentences. Less than 1 percent of the sentences were deferred.[4]

Across the border in Minnesota, domestic violence felony convictions and imprisonments have increased dramatically over the last decade. The number of domestic violence felony convictions increased from 229 in 2003 to nearly 1,500 in 2013. Most were for felony assault (835), followed by felony no contact order violations (661). In 2013, 315 offenders were imprisoned with an average sentence of two years, compared to just 44 in 2003.[5] In addition to increased police and prosecutor training, several new laws explain the rise. In 2006, for example, the legislature qualified more repeat domestic violence offenses to be charged as felonies. The list of repeat qualifying prior misdemeanor offenses was expanded, as was the time period for prior offenses, to ten years. The law also included any prior domestic violence offense, not just prior offenses against the same victim. In 2007, legislators created a criminal domestic violence no contact order issued by a judge against a defendant in a pending criminal case, the violation of which is a felony. By 2011, judges were issuing nearly eleven thousand of these orders a year.

From July 2010 through June 2011, 878 domestic assault charges made it to Vermont courts. Of these, seven hundred were misdemeanors and 178 felonies. A little less than half the misdemeanants were given probationary sentences, a quarter were diverted, and 32 percent were jailed. Almost half the jail sentences were split—jail followed by probation. Two percent were fined. The majority of the felony abusers (62 percent) were incarcerated, another 20 percent were given split sentences, and 11 percent received probationary sentences. Six percent were diverted. The vast majority of cases were resolved by pleas with only 3 percent of the misdemeanor cases and 11 percent of the felony cases tried.[6]

The Arizona prosecution data discussed earlier also reveal that for those found or who pled guilty, most (85.2 percent) were placed on probation with or without jail sentences, and 11.7 percent were given suspended sentences. Overall, a little over half (51.5 percent) were sentenced to some jail, and 2.4 percent were sentenced to prison. Less than half, 43.1 percent, were fined. For the far fewer abusers who pled or were convicted of a felony domestic violence charge, most were sent to prison (44 percent) or jail (21.7 percent). Many also were sentenced to probation (67.5 percent), with 21.7 percent given a suspended sentence.

Across the state of Washington, researchers reviewed more than sixty-six thousand domestic violence cases between 2004 and 2006. If a defendant was arrested for multiple offenses, it looked at the most serious. Most of the sixty-six thousand charges were misdemeanors (87 percent), and over two-thirds stemmed from a domestic violence assault, followed by harassment (15 percent). More than three-quarters of the defendants were male with an average age of 32.7 years. Two-thirds had prior arrests for nondomestic violence charges and 29 percent for prior domestic violence charges. Dispositions could only be found in 41 percent of the cases. Of these, more than three-quarters (76.9 percent) were fined, almost three-quarters (72.5 percent) were give some jail time, and half were placed on probation with or without jail time (49.5 percent). In terms of treatment, a quarter (26.7 percent) were ordered into a batterer program, 8.8 percent into alcohol or drug treatment, 7.3 percent into anger management, and 5.1 percent into mental health treatment/counseling. In addition, almost all (96.2 percent) were given proscriptions like no contact with victims, no further violations, and no firearms.

It should be noted that these dispositions applied to only 41 percent of the cases. The cases with no dispositions included those dismissed, diverted, dropped, reduced to nondomestic violence charges, and so on. Consequently, although 72.5 percent of the abusers were jailed, this represented only 29.7 percent of the total cases initially charged.[7]

As is all too common, the dispositions were largely in violation of the spirit if not the letter of Washington State law that requires all persons convicted of domestic violence to complete a twelve-month Domestic Violence Perpetrator Treatment, certified by the state. Anger management programs do not qualify. Under the same law, misdemeanors carry a maximum sentence of ninety days in jail and a fine of $1,000, gross misdemeanors up to one year in jail and a fine up to $5,000. Felonies range from five years to life in prison.

The Brooklyn felony domestic violence court sent about a third of its abusers to prison, most up to four years. Another 10 percent were sent to jail up to one year, and 21 percent were sentenced to jail and probation. Thirteen percent were sentenced to probation without jail, and 23 percent were given conditional discharges. For those sentenced to probation, with or without jail, or conditional discharges, 42 percent were sentenced to batterer intervention, and 30 percent to substance abuse treatment.[8]

An analysis of state felony courts in fifteen large urban counties that collectively prosecuted almost 1,000 felony domestic violence physical and sexual assaults found on average that those convicted of felony domestic sexual assaults were sentenced to six years in prison or jail, with 15 percent getting sentences of more than ten years. The average sentence for those convicted of felony domestic aggravated assaults was two and a quarter years. At the time of their trials, a quarter of these defendants had active criminal justice status, including 15.5 percent who were already on probation, 4.6 percent who were on pretrial release for another crime or crimes, and 3 percent who were already on parole. Most, 93 percent, pled guilty, and most were released before trial although the defendants were armed in two-thirds of the cases.[9]

SENTENCING PARITY IS PARAMOUNT

It turns out that successful prosecution of abusers isn't enough to stop most of them, even when they're found guilty and sentenced to jail. It all depends on how domestic violence sentences compare to the abuser's nondomestic violence sentences. It is probably not surprising that an abuser who just got out of state prison after several years for third offense check larceny will not be very impressed with a subsequent thirty-day sentence for the third assault against his intimate partner.

When it comes to criminal sentencing, each jurisdiction, even each court, establishes the "going rate" for specific offenses. If the "going rate" for most domestic violence offenses is less than that for other offenses, abusers are significantly more likely to reabuse. If the "going rate" is more for domestic violence, they are significantly less likely to reabuse. It is all relative. It may not matter so much what the sentence is for domestic violence. The research suggests that what matters is how it compares.

This is particularly crucial because most abusers who come to the attention of police and courts are not first offenders who confine their crimes to their partners. Most are repeatedly in court for a variety of offenses. While their domestic violence offenses are more likely than not to be misdemeanor crimes against persons, their nondomestic violence crimes are for crimes involving property, public order, major motor vehicles, or drugs. Generally, crimes against persons are considered more serious. Yet, in many jurisdictions, even abusers before the court for repeat abuse are sentenced less severely for their domestic violence crimes than their non-domestic violence crimes.

In one of the few studies focused on comparative sentencing, researchers looked at a thousand abusers sentenced across Rhode Island over the last several decades. Across each abuser's criminal careers, researchers found that their nondomestic violence cases were more likely to be prosecuted than their domestic violence cases. Once prosecuted, the majority of abusers were sentenced more severely for their nondomestic violence offenses, even though those cases were mostly for assorted nonviolent misdemeanors. In those cases where abusers were prosecuted and sentenced more severely for their domestic violence crimes than their nondomestic violence crimes, they were significantly more likely to have shorter, less intense abuse careers. And vice versa.[10]

Sentencing disparity between domestic violence crimes and nondomestic violence crimes is all the more telling when prosecution patterns are examined since the mid-1990s. While overall arrests for all crimes remained flat, incarceration exploded as prosecutors increasingly pressed felony charges for property, non-marijuana drug, and mostly nondomestic violence crimes. According to John Pfaff, Fordham University School of Law, prosecutors filed more charges per arrest in the 1990s and 2000s than ever before. They particularly went after defendants with prior criminal records, mostly generated by the explosion of drug arrests from the 1980s and 1990s. This also increased racial disparities in prisons, as black people are much more likely to be arrested for drugs even though they are not more likely to use or sell them, according to The Sentencing Project. Black defendants also generally received longer sentences than their white counterparts for the same drug crimes, according to the U.S. Sentencing Commission in 2012.[11]

The discrepancy between domestic violence and nondomestic violence crime sentencing is perhaps no more apparent than in Michigan.

MICHIGAN JUDGE ESTABLISHES SPECIAL COURT TO RESCUE THIRD-TIME ABUSERS FROM JAIL

One of the more extreme contemporary examples of prosecutors and judges' commitment to a two-track sentence structure for domestic violence and nondomestic violence crimes can be found in Lansing, Michigan. In 2014, the judge there announced the creation of a new dedicated domestic violence court for *third* offender domestic violence *felonies* who otherwise face up to five years imprisonment. The new "Domestic Violence Swift and Sure Sanctions" pilot court, according to the presiding justice, "[g]ives [abusers] an opportunity with some special funding to have paid-for treatment, testing, accountability." To enter the court program, the offenders must volunteer to enter a one- to two-year program overseen by the court to deal with anger management, drugs or alcohol, and "anything that causes violence." If the abuser completes the program, charges against them go away. The director of the local domestic violence shelter is supportive because, as she tells the media, victims want to see their loved ones change. If abusers do reoffend, promises the judge, they will be sent to jail. The presiding judge claims that research shows abusers can change profoundly if kept in treatment for three to twelve months.

In commenting on this court in the *National Bulletin on Domestic Violence Prevention*, the editor mused that the research "must be the same research that shows that dinosaurs and man roamed the earth together 6,000 years ago."[12] Even the shock troops in the War Against Women, the most extreme of the fathers' rights hate groups, are not publicly calling for extended amnesty for repeat felony abusers! Still, the fact that a Michigan judge in 2014 created a special court to ensure repeat abusers aren't imprisoned suggests how far we *haven't* come since 1874.

Even without the creation of special domestic violence courts to liberate third offenders, laws that increase sanctions of these abusers are rarely enforced. In 2015, the governor of Iowa filed legislation to increase sanctions for third-time domestic violence offenders. At that time, third offenders could be charged as felons, punishable by at least one-year prison sentences and up to five. The governor wanted to increase the maximum imprisonment to fifteen years with a minimum sentence of three years in prison. Those who reported the governor's proposal noted that only 162 abusers had been imprisoned as third-time domestic violence offenders in 2014 out of more than 2,660 convicted for domestic assault, suggesting that Iowa prosecutors and judges rarely enforce the existing law.[13] The last year the state reported its domestic and family violence statistics was 2009. That year, law enforcement reported approximately 7,000 mostly domestic, not family, violence incidents, most involving minor injuries and "personal weapons" (shod feet, fists). Most of these incidents involved intimate partners, including 52 percent non-married intimate partners and 26 percent spouses.

In Minnesota, even if all third offender abusers were sentenced to the maximum, the maximum sentence for a third offense domestic assault is twenty-four months. Domestic assault by strangulation or suffocation is punishable by up to thirty-six months in prison. Knowingly violating a protective order within ten years of a qualified domestic violence–related offense conviction is punishable by up to sixty months imprisonment. If the same Minnesotan, however, steals a car worth $5,000 or more, the offense is punishable by up to 120 months of imprisonment.

SUPERVISING ABUSERS IN THE COMMUNITY

So what happens to the many abusers sentenced to probation?

Probation was invented by a Massachusetts shoe cobbler and temperance proponent, John Augustus. He rescued defendants who would have otherwise been sentenced to jail for third offense public drunkenness in 1840. Their release was conditional on their good behavior in the community and sobriety. Little has changed except that probation officers are no longer volunteers and the sentence is no longer exclusively predicated on treatment. Probationary sentences offer prosecutors, defense counsel, defendants, and judges an ideal outcome, meeting their collective needs. Prosecutors and defense counsel both claim a win. The former notches a conviction, the latter avoids jail for his or her client. The client gets to remain in the community, and the judge can dispose of the case quickly and pass any problems on to the probation department. Left out of the equation is much consideration for the victim and her children. Probation is offender, not victim, focused.

Persons on probation must stay out of trouble and comply with specific conditions imposed by the court. These conditions can include participation in various treatment programs, payment of restitution to victims, performance of community service, and the like. For abusers, as detailed above, conditions often include attendance at batterer intervention or anger management programs, substance abuse treatment, and the same behavior restrictions courts regularly include in protective orders. Convicted abusers lose their right to buy or possess firearms or ammunition.

Probation officers have several basic tools at their disposal. They can require the probationer to report to them periodically or they can contact the probationer at his home or work. They can require the probationer to prove attendance at treatment programs. If the probationer has been ordered to remain drug and alcohol free, the officer can require him to pee in a cup periodically to test for violations. They can search probationers' homes and vehicles, in most states without a warrant, to check for prohibited possession of firearms or contraband. If the probationer violates any of his conditions, the probation officer can charge the probationer with a probation violation and return him to court for a revocation hearing.

Unlike trials, revocation hearings are informal affairs, needed to be proven only on the civil standard—preponderance of the evidence. Illegal evidence, hearsay, and other evidence that is barred at criminal trials are generally admissible in probation revocations. The revocation is not about criminal guilt or innocence, but whether or not the defendant violated his sentence. It is difficult for either the probation officer or the prosecution assigned these hearings to lose, even though probationers are provided free attorneys if they are indigent or may hire their own otherwise. Revocations, in short, are efficient ways to incarcerate offenders. About a third of persons in prisons and jails are recycled offenders revoked from community corrections, probation, or parole.[14] The tremendous jail and prison overcrowding that began toward the end of the last century and continues today was not so much the result of new criminals entering these institutions but the recycling of ex-inmates who failed field urine tests for drugs while under parole or probation supervision.

Probation has come to serve two critical functions with regard to domestic violence if—and this is a big if—the department has the resources and commitment to do its job supervising offenders and has an understanding of domestic violence. First, probation departments can correct unwarranted and unsafe sentences typically imposed by the courts. Second, probation departments can provide an early warning system for vulnerable victims. Without resources or commitment, however, probationary sentences are just a holding action until the next offense. Unfortunately, most probation departments across the country fit into this latter category.

This is a shame because probation done right has the potential to assist in victim protection. By tightly monitoring and strictly enforcing probationary conditions, probation officers give abusers plenty of opportunities to return to court for violation hearings, holding them accountable and keeping them away from their victims. In the Brooklyn domestic violence felony court, for example, a third of the defendants released on probation, with or without preceding jail terms, were returned for probation violations. The Washington study documented much higher violation rates. Only 40 percent of the defendants sentenced for domestic violence complied with their conditions. Less than two-thirds complied with their court-ordered anger management, only 38 percent complied with the batterer program, 39 percent with drug and alcohol treatment, and 32 percent with probation visitations.

The key is how probation officers react to these violations. They can ignore them or bring them back to court for further sanctioning. Like prosecution, it depends not on the probationers but the probation officers. Rhode Island's Department of Corrections established a specialized domestic violence supervision unit for half the small state. (It didn't have the resources to cover the entire state.) Subsequent data revealed that domestic violence probation officers whose caseloads consisted only of abusers brought 44 percent back to court for revocation. However, the regular probation officers with mixed caseloads brought back only 24.7 percent of their abusers for revocation. The nature of abusers sentenced to probation was the same between the two caseloads. Researchers concluded the variance in revocation rate was one of the chief factors in a lower reabuse rate for the specialized supervised cases.[15]

Similarly, an evaluation of Milwaukee's demonstration domestic violence court attributed lower reabuse rates to the high revocation rate of that court's probation department. More than a quarter of the Milwaukee abuser caseload were returned to court for violations. Reabuse was reduced in half after the specialized domestic violence court was established because, the researchers concluded, so many of the probationers were incarcerated as a result of revocation. As they concluded, "The increase in revocation and the resulting incarceration suggests that the lower domestic violence arrest rates may have been attained primarily through early detection and incarceration of probationers who continued their pattern of domestic violence or otherwise failed to comply with conditions of probation." Most of the Milwaukee abusers were brought back to court before they reabused their victims for violations like failure to attend their batterer programs. The same evaluation looked at two other demonstration domestic violence courts with much lower revocation rates and found no reduction in rearrests for domestic violence.[16]

Across Rhode Island, like Milwaukee, probation did what prosecutors and courts dismally failed to do, get high-risk offenders into jail cells for at least as long as they were generally sentenced for the nondomestic violence crimes they committed. Unfortunately, in Rhode Island, incarceration parity for domestic violence versus nondomestic violence crimes committed by abusers came too late to stop victims from being reabused. Almost all the violations that resulted in the abusers being incarcerated were for new domestic violence offenses. In short, while probation ensured the abusers were eventually sentenced, it did so too late to prevent further assaults of probationers' victims.

Unfortunately, in many states and local jurisdictions, misdemeanants on probation are not supervised at all. Officers are reserved to serve those convicted of felonies only, notwithstanding the fact that abusers on probation for misdemeanors may be more dangerous. Abuser danger cannot be determined by the presenting offense alone. New York City, for example, has tens of thousands of convicted abusers on probation, but only hundreds ever actually see a probation officer. New York City probation does not do windows and does not do misdemeanors! Even where misdemeanor probation supervision exists, the officers may restrict their caseloads to what they consider higher-risk probationers. This tends to exclude trivial offenses like disorderly conduct, notwithstanding that most of the abusers so convicted were probably initially arrested for an assault or even unidentified stalking and represent a real danger to their victims. Unlike the lethality assessments police are using more and more to identify the most dangerous abusers, probation departments employ risk instruments for recidivism, or the likelihood of reoffending. What these instruments ignore is that a 10 percent risk for lethality should be taken much more seriously than a 90 percent risk for repeat shoplifting.

In the absence of supervision, many courts rely on a batterer or other treatment program to deal with convicted abusers. This is not a winning formula. Domestic violence is not an addiction, nor a disease that can be "cured" with the right medication or treatment regimen. If it can be unlearned, it takes more than weekly sessions for six months, especially if the abuser is allowed to continue the behavior that brought him to the treatment programs at home.

BATTERING IS NOT A CURABLE DISEASE, AN ADDICTION, OR A MENTAL AFFLICTION

The nation's most popular batterer intervention program, which has become a national model, was established in Duluth, Minnesota. Its origins reveal both the great success as well as the great failures of these programs. In the 1970s, when Duluth women's groups began to focus on domestic violence, they asked why police weren't arresting men who battered their wives or girlfriends. As different components of the criminal justice system are wont to do, the police pointed the finger at the prosecutors. The women were told that it was useless to arrest because prosecutors wouldn't prosecute these cases. Indeed, one of the first batterer programs in the Northeast, EMERGE, was located in a prosecutor's office and used as a diversion program for domestic violence. This kept these bothersome cases out of court where it was widely believed they did not belong.

As told by one of the founders of Duluth's Domestic Abuse Intervention Project (DAIP), the Duluth advocates then moved on to the prosecutors. The prosecutors, in turn, pointed the finger at the judges. Why prosecute, they asked, when the judges won't hear these cases? Approached, the judges agreed that they would gladly hear these cases but only if they had some program where they could send the defendants. In the 1970s, jail and probation were out of the question. Domestic violence was not yet considered even close to being a real crime.

The advocates listened to the judges. They recruited a local anger management instructor and began classes for court-referred batterers. If you build it, they will come. Or at least, in America, judges hungry for dispositional alternatives will send defendants. And they did. Everything proceeded smoothly until one evening before the anger management classes were set to commence, the advocates got a call from the instructor's partner. When told that their instructor had assaulted her, they immediately fired him. Ellen Pence, one of the founders, took over the class.

As she recounted later at the unveiling of the Model Code in Chicago, Pence sat there all evening and listened as the men took turns telling stories of how their partners had provoked them mercilessly until the abusers blew up, popped their corks, couldn't take it anymore, and so on before, lamentably, they were forced to strike out.

Ellen and others from around the country went back to the drawing board to come up with a better program for men who batter, one that put the responsibility on the batterers, not their victims' "bad behavior." They came up with the now famous "power and control wheel," which illustrates that the physical assaults bringing these batterers to the attention of Duluth police officers and courts are part of a pattern of abusive behavior designed to give batterers power and control over their partners. The abuse could be financial, emotional, verbal, exercises of male privilege, and so on in addition to physical.

Apparently, the judges were as happy to send batterers to this as they were the former anger management program. The important thing was they had a place to put these defendants. Begun in 1980, by 1990 its creators had developed a curriculum package with detailed lesson plans for twenty-seven weekly, two-hour sessions, beginning with three orientation sessions. The next twenty-four sessions were divided into eight three-lesson units. Each unit repeats the same cycle, beginning with the men comparing examples of abusive behaviors and matching non-abusive, egalitarian be-

haviors, and followed by an analysis of each man's use of those abusive behaviors. Then they learned and practiced applying the egalitarian behaviors
in a relationship. Videos were used to demonstrate the abusive behaviors,
and role playing to reinforce positive behavioral responses.

Analysts described the program as "feminist cognitive-behavioral"—
"feminist" because it defines battering as "oppression of women" and advocates equality between the sexes. The "cognitive-behavioral" came from its
focuses on helping men change their beliefs about men's rights to chastise
their female intimates, and helping them practice new interpersonal skills
to support the changes in their beliefs.[17]

The Duluth program was readily replicable, and it was replicated all
across the nation. While in Duluth the program was designed to be part of
a larger coordinated criminal justice approach to hold batterers accountable, most jurisdictions replicated the batterer classes but not the coordinated criminal justice response to hold participants accountable. Program
completion came to be an end in itself, not a means to safeguard women. As
one Vermont judge exclaimed to the author, "I don't care how many times
the abuser is brought forward for abusing her, I am going to see that he
completes the batterer program!"

To safeguard the fidelity of batterer programs, advocates convinced
most states to adopt standards for program certification, lest traditional
victim-blaming mental health or family relations counselors encroached.
The standards require programs to focus on victim safety and batterer accountability by addressing battering in the context of the power and control
wheel rather than as a loss of control or poor impulse control. They banned
couple's counseling, anger management programs, and psychotherapy.
Establishment of state standards helped propel replication of the Duluth
program, which grew exponentially across the country.

The batterer intervention programs were very successful. They achieved
their original aim, encouraging the criminal justice system to do something
with batterers brought to police attention. They provided a place for batterers, and something for the courts to do without substantially interfering
with their regular processing of "real" criminal cases. After all, ordering
select defendants into treatment was not new territory for courts. Judges
and probation officers had been ordering and monitoring substance abuse
in court-ordered treatment since John August invented probation to reform
drunkards.

Battering, however, is neither a treatable addiction nor a mental illness.
To this extent, batterer programs are unprecedented. If the chamber of
commerce, for example, developed a bank robbery intervention program to

teach bank robbers the value of capitalism and skills to obtain employment, it is doubtful that courts would have as readily embraced the program as an alternative to jail and traditional court sanctions. However, batterer programs were warmly embraced. They were heralded as a win-win situation for courts and battered women. In the beginning, too, researchers agreed. But there was a problem with the research and the programs themselves.

The early research found that those abusers who complete the programs were less likely to reabuse than those who did not. But it also turns out that abusers who typically complete batterer programs are lower risk than those who do not. Their reduced risk has little to do with the "doses" of treatment received. They are able to complete the program, any program, because they are better educated, more likely employed, have more stakes in social conformity, more resources, and less criminal histories than the non-completers. In short, those who complete the batterer intervention program (BIP) are less dangerous to begin with. In fact, for most, the initial arrest or their partner's exit or threats to leave is enough to stop them.

The more rigorous the research got, the less well the programs were found to perform. All came to agree that there is a hard core of abusers who prove to be immune to BIPs as well as the underlying arrest and prosecution or any actions taken by their partners. This hard core of abusers will reabuse regardless, if not their initial partner, a new partner. The only disagreement is how large this hard core is. Studies vary, but between a quarter to more than half of all abusers reabuse despite batterer intervention. Further, the studies that followed these abusers, completers and non-completers alike, found that within ten years, reabuse is the rule, not the exception. One of the pioneering longitudinal studies, for example, documented that while only a minority of arrested abusers reabused within two years, the majority reabused if followed for ten years.[18]

Any "treatment effect" of the batterer programs is small—certainly not enough to bet a victim's safety on. A review of multiple studies found an overall "treatment effect" of about 5 percent.[19] Worse, many victims will stay with their abusive partners because they believe the programs will cure them, even if advised, as good programs do, that this is by no means guaranteed. Hope, after all, springs eternal. As is now well understood, one of the risk factors for becoming an intimate violence perpetrator is growing up seeing it modeled by a parent. Given such deep roots, how would we reasonably expect two hours a week for twenty-six weeks, even fifty-two weeks, to irrevocably change a batterer?

The enthusiastic and enduring embrace of programs by most courts and state legislators despite their limited value is not without precedent.

Spurred on by Mothers Against Drunk Driving in the 1970s, courts enthusiastically latched on to Alcohol Safety Action Programs, a drunk driving educational program, to deal with the increased number of persons arrested for drunk driving. The programs were promoted at the time by the U.S. Department of Transportation. Subsequent research found the programs to be based on a misdiagnosis of drunk drivers, and the programs were found, in fact, to make them no less dangerous.[20] Notwithstanding these findings, to this day, state legislatures and the courts have made these programs a rite for drunk drivers the first time around. The programs have proven indispensable because, like batterer programs, they provide courts a place to put these numerous defendants. They facilitate plea bargaining for prosecutors and defense counsel, clear criminal calendars, and let the criminal justice system concentrate on what it perceives to be "real" criminals—felons—including the repeat drunk drivers who will go on to kill other drivers or pedestrians. The standard court-ordered drunk driving programs do everything they are supposed to do, except stop arrested drunk drivers from doing it again.

At least attending batterer programs reminds abusers that there are some consequences for their crimes. For this reason, such programs may offer a suppression effect.[21] This is limited, though, since many courts substitute shorter anger management classes for batterer programs, reducing these programs' impact. As limited as the batterer programs may be in terms of protecting victims, anger management classes have been found to be even worse. Like the drunk driving programs that misdiagnose drunk driving as a driving, not a drunkenness problem, anger management programs are based on a wholesale misdiagnosis of batterers.

Abusers may have anger control issues, but they do not batter select victims because they selectively lose control. They batter to gain or maintain their control over these victims. The battering is purposeful, instrumental violence, not accidental or situational. One of the largest investigations of court-ordered anger management programs documented that unlike the same state's batterer programs, those who failed to complete the anger management program did no worse than those who completed it! In other words, there was no treatment or suppression effect whatsoever. Many judges prefer them, however, because they are shorter so more abusers complete them, and the court doesn't have to worry about revocation hearings.[22]

Despite their failing as treatment programs, batterer programs serve an extremely useful function if enforced. They serve as dynamic risk indicators. Program failure is a bright red flag that the abuser is going to reabuse and do it sooner rather than later. If probation and courts take heed, they can prevent reabuse by cracking down on the abuser as soon as he fails to enroll or complete the batterer program. They key is to act quickly and decisively. Fortunately, advance notice for revocations is limited to a few days, so action can be almost immediate. There is no right to bail pending the hearing, because the probationer has already been found guilty or admitted to guilt before being placed on probation.

The fact is that few higher-risk batterers complete court-assigned batterer programs. The stats from Vermont are typical. In 2011, 438 batterers were ordered into batterer programs, and only 216 completed—a failure rate of half. Unfortunately, most courts miss this opportunity to protect victims from these program failures. Instead, they merely order the abusers to re-enroll and try again, a recipe for reabuse.

8

UNFINISHED BUSINESS

The best functioning criminal justice system—one where police arrest and amply investigate domestic violence crimes, prosecutors prosecute them to the fullest extent of the law, and judges impose appropriately serious sentences—still faces some fundamental challenges. The first is disarming batterers. The second is getting courts and related child/family welfare agencies to understand that domestic violence trumps family preservation. The third is increasing the attention span of the criminal justice system.

KEEPING ABUSERS ARMED AND LETHAL

Disarming abusers does not just protect their victims. It also protects children, in-laws, employers, bystanders, and responding police officers. In the last twelve years, 6,410 women were murdered across the United States by their intimate partners using a firearm. To put this in perspective, that is more than the total number of U.S. troops killed in action in Iraq and Afghanistan during this period. The failure to keep firearms from abusers makes American women eleven times more likely to be murdered with guns than women in any other high-income country around the world.[1] Abusers' easy access to firearms also contributes to mass shootings across the United States. The majority of mass shootings are committed by abusers targeting intimate partners or family members.[2] While only 13 percent of U.S. gun murder victims are women, women constitute the majority of mass shooting victims. After analyzing all mass murders of four or more persons between 2009 and mid-2015, one study found that the shooter targeted either an intimate partner (42 percent) or family member (15 percent); 64 percent of the victims were women and children.

As illustrated by Haughton's murders, described earlier, if domestic violence and violence against women were taken more seriously, more mass murders would be prevented. In another example that took place in December 2014, Ismaaiyl Brinsley shot his ex-girlfriend, Shaneka Thompson, in the stomach. Not national news, just typical violence against a woman. Later that same day, however, Ismaaiyl murdered two New York police officers, Wenjian Liu and Rafael Ramos. International headlines followed. Before Cho Seung-Hui murdered more than thirty students at Virginia Tech in 2007, police had investigated him for stalking female classmates. Elliot Rodger killed six people in Isla Vista, California, leaving behind anti-women tirades online. Previously, he had attempted to injure a woman at a party. Although the media focused on his Islamic beliefs, Man Haron Monis, killed in Sydney, Australia, in 2014 after holding seventeen people hostage, was facing charges at the time relating to the murder of his ex-wife. He also had a history of sexual assaults with multiple women, none of which had anything to do with Islam.

Yet in all these cases, on both sides of the globe, authorities failed to identify domestic or other violence against women as red flags. In doing so, they neglected a basic fact. Men who have no regard for their female partners (or women in general) represent a danger to all women and men alike. Even abusers' pets are not safe, as demonstrated by the number of states adding pets to protective orders. Even the minority of abusers who aren't violent beyond their partner are still a danger to their next partner, and the partner after that. A study of Massachusetts's protective order files, for example, found that a quarter of men with protective orders taken out against them went on over the next six years to have new orders taken out against them by as many as eight different victims.[3]

The majority of women killed by their intimate partners are shot, as high as 70 percent in Kentucky and Montana. The presence of a firearm in the household with an abuser makes it six times more likely a woman will be murdered by her abuser. Women who have been previously threatened or assaulted with a firearm or other weapon are twenty times more likely to be murdered by their abusers.[4]

In short, to safeguard abused women, get the guns.

Gun advocates argue that disarming batterers is a pyrrhic victory at best. Abusers will just use another weapon or strangle their victims with their bare hands. Some may, but probably not most. David Adams interviewed more than a dozen men in a Massachusetts maximum-security prison, all there for murdering their intimate partners. Adams found that each man had "a moment of time and window of opportunity . . . to kill." They told Adams that they couldn't stop thinking about their partners the day before their murders. They couldn't sleep, couldn't eat. They were obsessed. If they had access to a gun, they seized the moment. If they didn't, the moment passed. Generally, their obsession was triggered by indications that their partners were going to leave them. According to Adams, with the passage of time after separation, these moments of opportunity become more rare and the victim safer. Confiscating a gun from someone who is prone to these impulsive acts of retribution is incredibly important. It's the difference between life and death.[5]

Although not all domestic violence murders are impulsive, firearms make it more likely that victims will die. And they're not the only ones in danger.

LOOPHOLES KEEP LETHAL ABUSERS ARMED

David Conley had been in prison for five years for domestic violence before committing mass murder in 2015. That August, he shot and killed a former partner, her husband, and six of their children in Houston. Despite the prior prison sentence, Conley was able to evade federal and state gun prohibitions for convicted domestic violence offenders because he bought the gun online from an unlicensed seller. Thanks to NRA lobbying efforts, such sales proceed without record checks.

The murders, which qualified as a mass shooting, could have been prevented on another front. The prosecutor on Conley's earlier domestic violence case had agreed to plead down from a twenty-five-year sentence to the five years he ultimately served. This was in spite of Conley's prior felony convictions and repeated, serious domestic violence. If Conley had been sentenced to twenty-five years, the 2015 shootings would have never happened.[*]

Note

[*] "Police: Changed Locks Led Suspect to Break In, Kill 8," *USA Today*, August 9, 2015; "Recent History of Mass Shootings in the United States," *The Oregonian*, October 2, 2015.

Abusers also use firearms to threaten and intimidate intimate partners. When a firearm is kept in the home of an abuser, nearly two-thirds of victims report that it is used by the abuser to scare, threaten, or harm them.[6] Batterers often make shows of taking out their firearms and carefully disassembling and cleaning them in front of their partners. Threatening partners with firearms is a key lethality risk factor. As a victim related to the *Huffington Post*, on the "worst night of her life," she was beaten unconscious by her husband and then forced to sit beside him as he loaded and unloaded his gun, threatening to kill her. She was sure she was going to die that night. "Having a loaded gun pointed at your head is not something that you ever forget." Terrified, it took her five months to file for a protective order. She finally did and it was granted. Luckily, she lived in Michigan, which prohibits court-restrained abusers from possessing firearms. Unluckily, once she got her order, the court and police did nothing to actually remove the firearms her husband possessed.[7]

To protect victims, states and Congress have enacted a plethora of laws that purport to prohibit court-restrained or convicted abusers from possessing or buying firearms. Thanks to aggressive lobbying by the NRA, as well as lack of oversight, concern, and competence, there are so many loopholes that batterers have little trouble arming themselves. The laws themselves are incomplete and their enforcement lackadaisical, built around a national registry of prohibited persons that was stillborn from the start.

There are two federal statutes barring abusers from possessing firearms, one for persons convicted of a misdemeanor domestic assault (convicted felons are already barred) and one for persons with protective orders against them. The first only applies to persons convicted of use or attempted use of physical force or threatened use of a deadly weapon. The second covers only final orders after notice was given and a hearing held. Both fail to cover current or former boyfriends and girlfriends who do not cohabit or have children in common. Most of the nonfatal abuse in the United States is committed by current or former boyfriends, not current or former spouses.

Nonetheless, between March 1994 and the end of December 2012, 2.4 million persons were kept from (legally) purchasing firearms as a result of federal firearm record checks. In that last year, 192,000 were denied. The largest percentage denied by the FBI (43 percent) was for having felony convictions, but 10 percent was denied because of domestic violence misdemeanor convictions and/or protective orders. Of those denied by state and local officials, 28.1 percent was for domestic violence.[8]

Across four Wisconsin counties in 2010 and 2011, over a one-month period, courts issued 199 protective orders for domestic violence and thirteen for child abuse, both of which prohibit firearm possession pursuant to state law. According to the petitioners, forty-one, or 20 percent of the abusers, possessed firearms. Judges ordered almost all of them to be surrendered. According to a study, fifteen were given to local sheriffs, fifteen to third parties, five were sold, and what happened to the rest was not specified.[9]

State laws vary widely. About two-thirds have laws barring court-restrained abusers from possessing firearms, but fewer, a little over a dozen, have them for convicted abusers. Many go beyond the federal law and include a broader class of victims and offenses. California law, for example, prohibits the owning of firearms by anyone convicted of assault, battery, or stalking. However, only a handful of states actually require authorities to go out and remove firearms from prohibited abusers. Even then, strings are often attached. In Oklahoma, for example, police are only allowed to seize firearms used in the incident, and only if the abuser was arrested.

Even where state or federal laws apply, the national system, devised by the FBI and allowed by Congress, is not adequate. When an individual goes to buy a firearm, the licensed dealer checks with the National Instant Criminal Background Check System (NICS) that searches the FBI's databases—National Crime Information Center (NCIC)-Protective Order File (POF)—before selling the firearm. The NCIC-POF includes the names of all persons who are prohibited from possessing firearms, including those with final protective orders against them or those guilty of misdemeanor domestic assaults, as well as all felons and other prohibited categories of persons. The check is made within at least three days, but mostly happens within seconds. The NICS was mandated by the Brady Handgun Violence Prevention Act (Brady Law) of 1993 and launched by the FBI in 1998. Some states have their own in-state systems; most (twenty-nine) rely on the NCIC-POF exclusively to determine whether or not someone may purchase a firearm.

In reality, the system has many loopholes and gaps.

First, background checks are not required for transfers between private parties. This represents a large gap, because up to 40 percent of gun sales are made through private parties. Further, more than 85 percent of the crime-involved firearms that the Bureau of Alcohol, Tobacco, Firearms and Explosives (ATF) is asked to trace by law enforcement were in the possession of someone other than their first retail purchaser when those crimes were committed. All these firearms have gone through at least one private party transfer.[10]

Second, if the background check is not completed within three days, the dealer can sell the firearm regardless. While most checks are completed within seconds, several thousand each year are missed. If after the three days the FBI determines that the firearm should not have been sold, it notifies the ATF to retrieve it. Unfortunately, it turns out the checks that take more than three days are eight times more likely to be for persons prohibited from purchasing firearms. In 2012, this meant that 3,722 persons prohibited by law to possess firearms were sold them. Most of these new firearm owners had active protective orders against them or had prior felony or misdemeanor domestic violence convictions.[11]

Third, the FBI files and many state files are woefully incomplete. Only thirty-seven states maintain a central file of protective orders, and only nineteen share their files with the FBI. As of 2010, only 90,000 records of abusers with misdemeanor domestic violence convictions were on file, a gross undercount.[12] As of December 2013, only thirty-six states bothered to submit domestic violence misdemeanor convictions to the FBI, and of these most submitted twenty or fewer records. As a result, almost all the FBI domestic violence conviction files come from just three states: Connecticut, New Hampshire, and New Mexico. In short, the FBI domestic violence files that totaled almost 150,000 as of July 2014 were about 2.75 million short.[13]

ARIZONA JUDGES HELP KEEP COURT-RESTRAINED ABUSERS ARMED AND DANGEROUS

An Arizona study released in 2015 documented that 62 percent of domestic violence murder victims over five years in the state were killed with firearms, 45 percent higher than the national average. One reason so many abusers were dangerous and armed was due to the state's failure to enter 40 percent of its protective order files into the FBI files used for gun checks. In 2013, for example, almost 30,000 orders were issued in Arizona, but only 18,000 made it into the federal screening system. Even if all the orders were entered into the system, they would only prevent new purchases. While federal law prohibits those with protective orders to possess firearms, Arizona state law leaves firearm prohibitions up to judges when they issue protective orders. Among the seven victims who had active protective orders when they were shot and killed, only one included a judicial order prohibiting the abuser from possessing a firearm.[14]

STATE FIREARM LAWS VARY WIDELY

Some state laws copy the federal laws, while others exceed them, prohibiting firearms, for example, for temporary as well as final protective orders and covering ex-intimates. Most do neither. Only twenty-three states and the District of Columbia prohibit persons with domestic violence protective orders from owning or buying firearms. Just fifteen require firearms to be turned in when an order is issued. In other states, judges may but are not required to make an order whether or not abusers can possess firearms.

Kentucky's legislature, indicating an abysmal misunderstanding of domestic violence victimization, took a different tact in 2014. Rather than disarm unstable abusers, it authorized domestic violence victims to get concealed gun permits the day after they get a protective order. The law was prompted by an abuser who shot his estranged wife after she secured a protective order against him. He bought the gun the day before he shot and crippled her and then shot and killed himself. Apparently Kentucky lawmakers watch too much TV where the good guy always gets the drop on the bad.

ARMING STALKERS

Both federal and state gun laws fail to disarm the most dangerous abusers, stalkers. Only nine states disarm convicted stalkers, notwithstanding the fact that stalking is a red flag for lethality and almost all abusers who murder their partners stalk them first. This means thousands of convicted stalkers each year are permitted to own and buy new firearms.

In major cities, three-quarters of women murdered by their intimate partners, and even more who survived such attempts, were stalked the year before.[15] Yet few federal or state laws attempt to disarm these stalkers, not even after they are convicted of stalking or get protective orders taken out against them for stalking. A review of conviction records in twenty states showed that there are at least 11,986 individuals across the country who have been convicted of misdemeanor-level stalking but are still permitted to possess guns under federal law. It is likely that there are tens of thousands of additional convicted stalkers who are able to buy guns.

Examples are plentiful. In Ocean Springs, Mississippi, Amanda Salas was shot and killed by an ex-boyfriend in March 2014 following weeks of escalating stalking, during which she had obtained an emergency protective order. In a 2012 case in Louisville, Kentucky, Michelle Hahn was killed with one shot to the head at point-blank range in a Walmart parking lot by a man she had briefly dated. He had a seventeen-year history of stalking women.[16]

Of course, judges don't need explicit statutory authority to disarm stalkers. But even when they are given explicit statutory authority to disarm abusers, most don't.

RHODE ISLAND JUDGES PROTECT FIREARMS OF COURT-RESTRAINED ABUSERS

A review of protective orders issued over two years in Rhode Island disclosed that judges rarely order abusers to disarm, even when victims tell them that their abusers made gun-related threats. Between 2012 and 2014, 1,609 protective orders were granted. Judges ordered abusers to turn in their guns in only 5 percent of them, though firearms were mentioned in 23 percent of the cases. In one case that the report highlighted, a woman said her abuser threatened to "blow my head off," made her lie on the floor of his apartment with a gun to her head, and "said he could put a bullet in my head and leave me there." The judge granted the protective order, but didn't require the man to surrender his firearms.

Despite federal law prohibiting court-restrained abusers from possessing firearms, Rhode Island gives judges discretion. A spokesperson for the state judiciary complained that a victim asserting there are guns in the household isn't sufficient evidence for their existence. When confronted with the fact that some courts have much higher gun removal rates than others, she retorted that each case must be judged on its individual merit. At the time of the study, there was legislation pending to make firearm surrender mandatory for court-restrained abusers, removing judicial discretion. It wasn't expected to pass.

As with most criminal justice responses to domestic violence, the breakdown of judicial orders found some judges able to do the right thing. Judges in Washington District Court removed 52.9 percent of the firearms, while those in Providence District Court removed only 4.6 percent. The state's family courts did the worst, removing from 2.1 percent to 6.2 percent.[17]

Isn't it time for federal agents to swoop down and arrest these Rhode Island judges for aiding and abetting court-restrained abusers in violating federal law by knowingly allowing them to illegally possess firearms?

When jurisdictions work at it, they can do better. What occurred over the last few years in Dallas and Oregon demonstrates that the barriers are not insurmountable. They simply require the will to surmount.

DALLAS POLICE, JUDGES TOO SHY TO SEIZE FIREARMS

A *Dallas Morning News* investigation found that county officials weren't enforcing state and federal firearm prohibition laws for convicted or court-restrained abusers either. The *News* exposé highlighted the case of a man

HONOR SYSTEM RELIED UPON TO DISARM DANGEROUS BATTERERS

When Nate Holden's wife filed for a protective order against her estranged husband in Wake County, North Carolina, she described how his abusive tactics had affected her entire family. After leaving Holden and moving in with her parents, she endured multiple incidents of Holden coming to her parents' home. Her father had called the cops on Holden, and her brother had reported Holden threatening that he would shoot and kill the three children he shared with his estranged wife and then himself. Holden had also beaten his son with a broom.

During this period, Holden obtained firearm permits, one in 2004 and another in 2007. When Holden's wife secured her protective order, she informed the court that Holden had a pistol. The court ordered that Holden was not to possess any firearms.

The next day, deputies served Holden with the order and asked to collect his pistol. He told the officers he had no gun, so they left empty-handed. Shortly after, Holden shot his wife in the face, also shooting and killing her parents in front of the couple's children with the gun he had told police he didn't possess. As the sheriff later admitted to the *Eastern Wake News*, his deputies are instructed to take an abuser's word regarding whether or not he has a firearm.*

Note

*McDonald, T., and Hankerson, M., "NC Domestic Violence Order Doesn't Allow Police to Search Accused for Guns," *The News and Observer*, May 6, 2014.

who police say killed his pregnant girlfriend and shot a cop in 2013 while the former had a protective order against him. Confronted by the *News*, Dallas County officials blamed the law itself for its failure to specifically delineate who is responsible for its enforcement.

Ironically, led by the mayor with much fanfare, Dallas had launched a major public campaign against domestic violence the year before in reaction to a scandalous breakdown of domestic violence enforcement by the city's police. The campaign was big on PR, but not on gun removal. As a result of the newspaper exposé and led by Judge Roberto Cañas, who handled family violence misdemeanors, the city and county eventually did take action. The city formed a task force of police, shelters, and the district attorney's office to work to shorten the time between when a domestic violence incident occurs and when the case is resolved in the court system. Given the county's seventeen different felony courts and thirteen independently operating misdemeanor courts, this was no easy task.

Judge Cañas announced some reforms that could be made quickly, such as judges asking defendants if they had guns. As the *News* reported, courts elsewhere require abusers to sign an affidavit about whether they have guns. Judge Cañas also overcame a major barrier by figuring out where to put confiscated firearms. He arranged with a private shooting range to store the firearms until the orders expired. Dallas abusers now have forty-eight hours to turn over their firearms and then must come back to court to prove their compliance. A lack of storage receipt constitutes a red flag for non-compliance. The private range charges a one-time fee to reclaim firearms once the protective order has been removed. If not reclaimed, the guns become property of the range, an added incentive for the range's agreement to the arrangement with the court. Texas advocates have expressed enthusiasm for the program.[18]

Around the time the *News* wrote its exposé, Dallas County topped Harris County for most domestic violence murders per capita in Texas, with twenty female victims in 2013. In 2013, 119 women were killed across Texas by current or former partners. Most (58 percent) were shot; most (82 percent) were killed by current husbands or boyfriends; most (75 percent) died in their homes. In addition, seventeen witnesses and bystanders were also killed. The number of female domestic violence fatalities across Texas increased to 132 in 2014, but Dallas domestic violence fatalities (ten) that year no longer exceeded those of Harris County (twenty-three), according to the Texas Council on Family Violence.

Oregon also struggled to figure out how to enforce its firearm surrender law for abusers, even though it was enacted twenty years ago. In 2012, a Portland commissioner became increasingly alarmed reading about murders committed by court-restrained batterers. As he told the *Oregonian*, between 2003 and 2010, a little more than two hundred Oregonians were killed as a result of domestic violence, most of them from gunshot wounds. Prompted by his and others' criticism over lax enforcement of these laws, police, judges, county and city officials, and prosecutors formed a task force and met for a year to come up with new court-reporting requirements and to select sites where court-restrained batterers could turn in their firearms.

The state adopted the task force's model protocols to different degrees in different counties. Some require abusers to return to court to certify compliance with firearm surrender orders. However, in the state's most populous county, Multnomah County, which includes Portland, judges rejected this requirement because they said they were too busy to schedule additional hearings. Instead, they now give abusers two days to turn in their firearms after the judge issues an order against them. The abuser must make an appointment to surrender their firearms at one of three sites in the city, or they can transfer their firearm to a friend or relative who must pass an Oregon State Police background check and sign a notarized affidavit. After three days, the abusers must file an affidavit with the court for a receipt for their surrendered gun or a notarized signature of the person who was given the firearm. If the abuser is in jail when the order is issued, he has three days after release to file the affidavit.

The judges promise to forward lists of abusers who do not file their affidavits to the prosecutors, who have agreed to send a law enforcement officer after the abuser, or at least send the abuser a letter and hope for the best.

The chief judge admitted the system they began in June 2013 is "not perfect," but it's so much better than what preceded it. The newspaper reported that since the new protocol went into effect in another county, within the first six months, seventy-two court-restrained batterers were found to possess firearms. Of these, forty-nine complied with the surrender order, while five were referred to prosecutors for contempt hearings. The newspaper did not say what happened with the remaining eighteen.[19]

Of course, giving an abuser three days to turn in his firearms makes victims more vulnerable when they're at their greatest risk, since they have finally acted to separate from their abuser.

GUN LAWS WORK WHEN ENFORCED

States with gun laws disarming court-restrained abusers work when enforced. Deaths are significantly reduced.[20] The reverse is also true.

Nevada allows dangerous abusers and stalkers easy access to firearms, and victims pay the price. Forty percent of the women murdered in Nevada are killed by intimate partners, and half of those murders are committed with guns. Gun murders of women in Nevada are 38 percent higher than the national average, while gun murders of men are 3 percent lower than the national average! Among other failures, Nevada allows gun purchases without background checks that would screen out dangerous abusers.

DON'T ASK, NEVADA SELLS GUNS TO ALL

Kevin Gipson was both a convicted felon and an abuser, both of which should have prevented him from buying firearms. However, the state did not require a background check when he purchased his .25 caliber handgun privately. Gipson used the gun to murder Brittney Lavoll, his ex-girlfriend, who had separated from him with their children. Gipson tracked her down by calling her coworker, then hid behind some bushes outside the restaurant where she worked. When she arrived for work, he shot her in the head. This was in 2010. Two years later, Jeffrey Rodriquez, another convicted felon and registered sex offender, was similarly able to keep a prohibited firearm that he used to shoot and kill his wife in Reno. Like a lot of batterers, he started the day of the murder by accusing his wife of having an affair. When she left for work, Rodriquez followed her in his car, ran her off the highway, shot her in the chest, and then fired at two people who tried to intervene. The couple had two young children. Between 2003 and 2012, 185 Nevada women were murdered by their intimate partners.[*]

Note

[*]McCabe, F., "Man Sentenced to Prison for Killing Ex-Girlfriend," *Las Vegas Review-Journal*, February 24, 2012.

SAN MATEO GETS IT RIGHT

Beginning in 2006, with supplemental funding available, San Mateo County established a pilot program to disarm court-restrained batterers. The supplemental funding ran out in 2010, but the county continued the program because, according to the sheriff, it was responsible for the elimination of domestic violence homicides the prior three years.

The program is straightforward. Once the court grants a protective order, sheriff's deputies contact the victims for information on firearms the restrained abuser may have. They also check the various law enforcement databases that track gun purchases and licenses. They then head out to serve the order and collect the firearms. Officially the abusers have another day to turn them in, but the deputies ask for them immediately. The deputies have search warrants just in case the abuser denies having firearms or refuses to turn them over. In 2013, the sheriff collected 324 firearms from eighty-one court-restrained abusers, representing about 10 percent of all court-restrained abusers that year.

The program was featured in the *New York Times*. The article described a typical case in which a woman files for a protective order as a result of escalating abuse. She checks the box on the petition indicating the abuser has firearms. In her affidavit, she also mentions that he had used a firearm to threaten her. When deputies check, a database confirms that the abuser has both a handgun and an assault rifle. The deputies visit the victim, who tells how the abuser has threatened suicide, sending her a picture of himself holding the rifle to his head. The deputies get a search warrant and stake out the abuser's house. When he leaves the house to walk the dog, they serve him with the protective order. They then search the house and find not two firearms but five handguns and two AR-15 assault rifles.[21]

MIAMI DOMESTIC VIOLENCE COURT FIGURED IT OUT

The Miami-Dade County domestic violence court, created in 1992, has also figured out how to enforce firearm prohibitions. The feds cited the court's program as exemplary, writing it up in a manual still available to judges and law enforcement across the country.[22] The court, staffed by seven full-time and eight part-time judges, handles approximately nine thousand protective order petitions a year. In addition to judges, the court has case managers, a bailiff, an intake staff, the Miami-Dade County sheriff's department liaison, and two court clerks. It has four locations in the county to make the protective order process more accessible for victims and law enforcement personnel. High-risk victims in immediate need of protective orders can access the system by calling a hotline that is staffed around the clock.

Former chief administrative judge Amy Karan made it a personal mission to get guns out of the hands of batterers. She realized that court personnel, like those of most bureaucracies, revolve around forms. She directed the preparation of several forms to facilitate the complex flow of information regarding firearm possession and surrender. Designed to document each system interaction that related to an abuser and his firearm, the forms help ensure that an abuser is disarmed as required by law and that he remains so for as long as required by court order or statute. When law enforcement officers serve temporary (*ex parte*) protective orders, they also provide notice that respondents must surrender firearms and/or ammunition to their local police department. Officers inform respondents (the abusers) that they must bring the receipts to court as proof of the relinquishment. The majority of respondents willingly surrender firearms before the final protective order hearing.

Two databases document the existence of protective orders. Court clerks enter orders issued by the court into a court-based system. The Miami-Dade County sheriff's department, which is responsible for serving protective orders, enters the orders into the National Crime Information Center-Protection Order File and the Florida Crime Information Center, which provide officers with twenty-four-hour access to orders.

The surrender of firearms is mandatory as soon as the judge issues a temporary protective order. If the abuser appears at the hearing, the judge requires the respondent to fill out and sign a sworn statement, printed on orange paper and available in English, Spanish, and Creole, as to whether or not he possesses firearms. The judge makes an "on record" inquiry of each respondent regarding the content of the firearm form. In many cases, this will be as simple as verbally verifying that the respondent does not now and has not in the past six months possessed a firearm and/or ammunition. In other cases, it may be necessary to clarify the current status and location of a weapon—for example, when and to whom it was sold and whether supporting documentation for the transfer has been provided. If, after a full inquiry, the judge is satisfied that the respondent does not currently possess a firearm and has complied with all surrender requirements, the court requires no further action. On the other hand, if the judge determines that the respondent still possesses a weapon, the court completes the order to surrender firearms and delivers it to the respondent at the conclusion of the hearing. The court's case manager monitors the respondent's compliance in providing proof of surrender. Case managers or probation in some of the four domestic violence courts maintain a firearm surrender logbook. If a respondent does not comply, the case manager notifies the judge, and the judge directs the matter to be set for hearing. Respondents may transfer their firearms to a third party. However, if they do so, they are required to fill out forms spelling out the transfer. Although some judges may be reluctant to allow such transfers, if allowed, respondents are responsible for bringing the third parties to the court so that the judge can inform them of their legal obligations regarding storage of the firearm and notify them that they may not allow the respondent to have access to the firearm.

Interestingly, according to officials, most of the firearms turned over to law enforcement in Miami-Dade County are never reclaimed. The theory is that the conditions for return deter many abusers. To reclaim firearms, a respondent must prove that he legally owned them before the protective order was issued. This condition alone serves as a significant barrier to reclamation for some respondents. A respondent must further prove that he qualifies for its return and attests to the following: He has not been found guilty of a felony or misdemeanor domestic violence assault; there is no protective order in effect in Florida or in any other state against him; no forfeiture action is pending in another court; he has never been adjudicated mentally defective or been committed to a mental institution; and there is no other legal impediment to his owning or possessing a firearm.

If a firearm can be legally returned, victims are notified.[23]

PHOENIX PROBATION OFFICERS, JUDGES NOT TOO SHY TO DISARM ABUSERS

Many abusers end up on probation supervision for domestic violence, barred by federal law, and in some states, state law, from possessing firearms. In such cases, it becomes the responsibility of probation to enforce firearm prohibitions. A few do, including the Maricopa County (Phoenix) probation department. The department has a specialized probation team, which aggressively goes after abusers' guns.

Although Arizona police confiscate firearms when they arrest abusers, probation officers still find plenty of work to do. The following cases from the files of the Maricopa probation department show just how much.[24]

SEEK AND YOU SHALL FIND

A probation officer suspected that his probationer's violent boyfriend, also on probation, was at her house and stashing a firearm there. As was customary, officers from the Mesa Police Domestic Violence Emergency Response Team accompanied several probation officers to the home. Upon arrival, a probation officer knocked on the door. Although the probationer was at home, the knock initially went unanswered. The officer called her on the phone, and she said she had just gotten out of the shower, subsequently letting them in. The probation officer asked her if anyone else was in the house. She repeatedly answered in the negative. The Mesa officers secured the premises, declaring it was safe for the probation officers to search for weapons. One of the probation officers went to the bedroom, lifted the mattress, and observed three long guns and a hatchet. He also observed a foot sticking out of the bed. The officer summoned the Mesa police officers, who drew their weapons and ordered the suspect to exit the bed. He was taken into custody without incident and was later identified as the male probationer in question. A search of the male probationer's knapsack revealed an X26 Taser gun as well as drugs. Later it was discovered that the Taser gun had been stolen from a neighboring town's police department.

The Mesa police would not have been able to secure a search warrant without probable cause, but by teaming up with the probation department, they could enter the premises without a warrant, as probation officers need not obtain warrants to search a probationer's home or person.

A PROBATION OFFICER WORKS OVERTIME

Maricopa probation officers alerted the Tempe police when responding to a call from the victim of a domestic assault after her partner had been sentenced to probation. Together, the probation officers and the police searched two storage lockers identified by the victim. The victim provided a key. The police officers brought along the department's explosive-sniffing dog, who immediately indicated a "hit" upon approaching the locker. The locker was double-locked, and the key provided by the victim did not fit either lock. The manager of the storage company told the officers that he had provided special locks by request of the probationer.

The officers returned the next day with ATF agents and a locksmith to drill open the locker. They did not find any explosives, but discovered that what the victim had reported as explosives were actually "sleeves" of ammunition, each containing ten boxes of .308 ammunition. ATF agents estimated that there were twenty-five hundred rounds. They also found a twelve-gauge shotgun, a semiautomatic pistol, and a video titled *The Ultimate Sniper*. ATF agents seized the weapons and led charges against the defendant. The probation officer accompanying the agents came from the department's Warrant Squad. He was also deputized as a U.S. marshal and, by agreement, the ATF paid for his overtime.

A CHILD SAVES HIS MOTHER

A probation officer left her card with her probationer's family members after conducting a home visit, which included the oldest of the probationer's three children, an eight-year-old son. She indicated they should feel free to call her. One evening, one did. Although no one spoke to her when she answered, she heard in the background sounds of a loud argument. She recognized the voices of her probationer and his victim, the mother of the children. The officer contacted local police and asked them to meet her at the residence. At the scene, they stopped a domestic assault in progress. A search uncovered a loaded handgun. The probationer was arrested and later incarcerated for a probation violation. As it turns out, the eight-year-old had called and left the phone off the hook to reveal the crime in progress.

OVER THE LIMIT

The sister of a domestic violence victim called the abuser's probation officer, concerned over her sister's safety. She reported that her sister had told her that the probationer kept loaded guns in the house. She also reported that both her sister and the probationer were currently intoxicated, and she feared for her sister's life. A team of probation officers, joined by Phoenix police officers, went to the house. As they approached, they observed the victim sitting outside on the driveway, intoxicated and obviously distraught. She stated that the probationer had assaulted her that evening. The probation officer went to the front door, which was open, and observed the probationer putting on his pants. He was extremely intoxicated. The probation officer handcuffed the probationer to ensure that no further incidents would occur.

A subsequent search yielded a semiautomatic Browning 40-caliber handgun and a .357 magnum handgun. The Phoenix officers impounded the firearms and ammunition and arrested the probationer for illegal possession of firearms. The probation violations were added to the paperwork, and the Phoenix police transported the defendant to the police station for booking. Later the defendant was given a breathalyzer test that registered .333, more than four times the legal limit. He was subsequently imprisoned.

The Office on Violence Against Women also hailed the Maricopa department's program as a model.[25]

NEW JERSEY COURT UPHOLDS JUDGE UPHOLDING COMMON SENSE

Although many are reluctant to act, the law generally gives judges broad discretion in disarming dangerous abusers. For instance, New Jersey law requires a law enforcement officer responding to a domestic violence complaint where the officer believes that domestic violence has occurred to question people on the scene about the presence of firearms. If the officer learns that firearms are present, the officer is mandated to seize the firearms if they pose a risk to the victim. In addition, the officer is supposed to also seize any state-issued firearm purchaser identification card or permit to purchase a handgun. The local prosecutor then has forty-five days to request that the court prohibit the firearms from being returned to the alleged batterer, after which time the firearms will be returned.

New Jersey police were called to the scene of a domestic violence crime by an abuser who had been arrested twice. This was the fourth time they had been called about this abuser, and his Beretta 9mm handgun, which he stored at his mother's house, had been temporarily seized twice. This time, a local judge ordered the gun's permanent forfeiture when the man was brought before him for the latest domestic violence arrest. Subsequently, the prosecutor dropped the prosecution because, the prosecutor declared, the wife did not want to go forward. The husband demanded the return of his Beretta.

The State of New Jersey petitioned that the handgun should not be returned, citing state law that prohibits firearm possession if it "would not be in the interest of the public health, safety, or welfare." The defendant's wife, however, supported her husband, stating that the handgun should be returned because he had not threatened her with it. The husband admitted that on each of the four occasions the police had been called, the couple's behavior was "childish," and that he knew the conduct would result in the seizure of his handgun. The judge expressed concern at the number of domestic disputes related to the defendant's drinking as well as the defendant's access to the handgun even when it was at his mother's house. The judge ruled that the defendant was disqualified to possess firearms. His possession of a firearm permit card would not be in the interest of public health, safety, or welfare because, among other things, the defendant presented a threat to his wife under these circumstances. The judge gave the defendant sixty days to sell his firearm to a licensed dealer before it would be forfeited. The judge also revoked the defendant's firearm permit card and barred him from obtaining a new card or possessing a firearm without further order of the court.

The defendant appealed. The appellate court ruled that even if the domestic violence "complaint has been dismissed at the request of the complainant and the prosecutor determines that there is insufficient probable cause to indict," the court is not required to order the return of the firearm or authorization papers if it determines the owner is "subject to any of the disabilities set forth (state law)." Thus, "the Legislature intended that courts not return guns to a defendant in a domestic violence action, even after the dismissal of the complaint, if the court finds that the defendant poses a threat to public health, safety, or welfare."

The appellate court found that the history of the defendant's interactions with his wife supported the finding that return of his handgun would not be in the interest of public health, safety, or welfare. The state's supreme court, it ruled, had warned that "a court should not return weapons to a defendant who is a threat to the public health, safety, or welfare. The contrary result—the return of weapons to a defendant who is a threat to the public—would be an invitation to a tragedy."[26]

FEDS FAIL

One of the biggest barriers to enforcement of gun prohibitions is U.S. Attorneys, appointed by the president, charged with prosecuting federal laws. Their collective record at enforcing federal firearm prohibitions is hardly robust, to say the least. In 2012, all ninety-three U.S. Attorneys together filed less than fifty domestic violence firearms cases in federal courts. Since the majority of states don't bar convicted abusers from possessing firearms, their failure endangers some of the most vulnerable victims.[27]

U.S. Attorneys are also responsible for prosecuting serious crimes on Indian reservations, although the latest reauthorization of the Violence Against Women Act increased some tribes' authority to prosecute nontribal members for sentences up to two years. The failure of U.S. Attorneys to enforce abuser federal firearms violations significantly contributes to the scandalously high rate of domestic violence and sexual assaults against Indian women.

ABUSERS JUST DON'T MAKE GOOD DADS

As challenging and sometimes dangerous as it is for victims to extricate themselves from abusive marriages and intimate relationships, it is ten times more difficult for domestic violence victims if there are children involved. If the children are not biologically the abusers', it is that much more dangerous. Having children that are not the abusers increases the likelihood of victim abuse, including lethal abuse. Having children with the abuser invariably means that in addition to having to contend with the abuser, the mother will have to contend with a court system that is intent on preserving the family even if it means endangering most of its members.

Though many judges regularly endanger victims and their children this way, not all go as far as a California judge did in 2013. We know about this judge because his actions were appealed. Otherwise, except for the parties directly involved, no one would be the wiser. But in this case, the judge's actions spurred the legislature to enact legislation limiting the judicial discretion that allowed him, like so many custody judges, to blithely ignore domestic violence.

The California judge acted in favor of an abusive father seeking custody and visitation, notwithstanding the fact that during the proceedings, the father was tried and convicted of raping his wife, the mother of their child.

"FOR GOOD OF THE FAMILY," JUDGE SIDES WITH RAPIST DAD

Crystal and Shawn were married in 1996. During the early years of their marriage, Shawn was arrested for three counts of battery against his wife. He was sentenced to two days in jail and three years of probation and was ordered to complete a fifty-two-week batterer program. Later, the couple had two sons, born in 2002 and 2005. Crystal worked, while Shawn stayed home to care for their sons. After the birth of the sons, the abuse got worse, according to Crystal. In 2008, Shawn strangled her in front of the children. A week later, she returned from work and was attacked by Shawn in the children's bedroom where the boys were sleeping. Shawn proceeded to sexually assault her. He also threatened to carve something on her head and dump her body. Three days later, he strangled her when she came home from work and threatened to sodomize her, which he then did. This time, the boys were upstairs.

Later that night, Crystal ran out of the house, called 911, and hid until the police came. They arrested Shawn. Crystal was brought to the hospital. The next day, Crystal was granted a protective order for herself and her children. At trial, she explained that she had resisted calling the police before because Shawn had vowed to kill her if she left him or called the police. Shawn was prosecuted for three felony counts of forcible spousal rape, sodomy, and oral copulation. A split jury verdict landed Shawn in prison for a six-year sentence.

During the pendency of the criminal case, the protective order remained in effect, keeping Shawn away from his wife and children. Crystal filed for divorce. Shawn filed a request to allow visitation with his children. At the time, he was out on bail. The court ordered both Crystal and Shawn to attend custody mediation. Crystal did not attend. The next month, Shawn filed another motion seeking visitation and joint custody. This time, Crystal attended the mediation, and the mediator recommended that the court continue to order no contact for Shawn until the criminal case was resolved.

San Diego Superior Court judge Gregory Pollack then heard the custody case. He appointed an outside expert to evaluate the parties and talk to the children. The evaluator concluded that Shawn presented a high risk to the mother as well as to the children and should not be given custody or visitation until he had intensive therapy. He also noted that both boys did not want to see their father. The older boy had witnessed some of the assaults and said he had tried to stop his father when he was strangling his mother. He also said that his father had hit him too, and "left awesome marks." The younger boy, who was five at the time, explained that his father had hit his mother. He had not seen it, but he heard her scream. He told the expert that his father should stay in jail forever because "that is where he needs to be."

Judge Pollack extended Crystal's protective order for Crystal but not the children. He explained to Crystal, "The reason I'm denying it, is dad's wrongful behavior was directed against you. It was not directed against the children." He added that Shawn's involvement in therapy would allow him to successfully reunite with his children, which, he stated, would be in their best interest as well as Shawn's best interest. He then lectured Crystal that she should not badmouth Shawn in front of the kids. Further, he said he believed the children's statements to the court expert seemed like they were just repeating the mother. Although he didn't blame the mother for being angry with her rapist, he reasoned that she said things to the kids consistent with her anger. In addition, the judge said that he had talked to an expert who said children would regret later on if ties with a parent were broken and probably resent their mother for it.

Next the judge characterized Shawn as "a little bit more towards the mean side" than the "warm and fuzzy Ward Cleaver side." But, he questioned, "Do you say that just because dad's mean that he loses his kids? No." The judge was obviously upset that the mother had worked, leaving her children. He explained, "And I just can't square that with her going off to work every day as a stockbroker leaving her kids with someone she truly believes is a monster. Now, does she now feel he's a monster? Sure. Because of what he did to her."

The judge ordered that the father could communicate with his children from prison. When released, he directed that Shawn should be immediately reunited with his children before completing any domestic violence classes or therapy. He should have a reunification therapist who is "very pro-reunification." The judge explained that the children suffered from "parental alienation syndrome," a junk pseudo-science adopted by fathers' rights groups to explain why children are frightened by abusive fathers who they witness assaulting their mothers. The judge also ordered the victim to pay spousal support to her abusive husband of $1,000 per month (temporarily stayed while Shawn was in prison) and $47,000 of his attorney fees.

In regard to Pollack's rulings, Crystal appealed, and eventually the court of appeals at least reversed the part of the order concerning immediate reunification upon release from prison. It found that Pollack had "failed to fully acknowledge the magnitude of the domestic violence," resulting in his blaming the victim for the "troubled relationship" between Shawn and his children. The appellate court also actually looked up the outside expert Pollack had cited in his decision and found the judge had failed to appreciate the exception to her support for joint parenting. The court quoted her writings: "Children who are realistically estranged from one of their parents as a consequence of that parent's history of family violence, abuse, or neglect *need to be clearly distinguished* from alienated children. (Kelly and Johnson, *The*

Alienated Child: A Reformulation of Parental Alienation Syndrome
(2001) 39 Fam. Ct. Rev. 249, 253, *italics added.*)"*

Note

In re Marriage of Crystal and Shawn H., 2013 WL 2940952 (Cal. App.
4th Dist. 2013).

Unfortunately, the same junk science applied in this case supporting "parental alienation syndrome" can be found in numerous custody rulings and even state statutes that explicitly encourage custody with the "friendly parent," the parent most agreeable to sharing parenting with the other party. Such a playing field is slanted against the abused parent, who has come to understand a simple fact most custody judges seem to be unable to grasp: Batterers do not make good parents, even if their physical assaults are limited to their partners. That is a big "if," because the overlap between intimate partner violence and child abuse is much more likely than not.

California legislators were so outraged by Judge Gregory Pollack's order in Crystal's case that they quickly enacted a new law prohibiting California judges from ordering attorney fee awards to be paid out of the injured spouse's separate assets. They also further limited judicial discretion in cases where a spouse convicted of a violent sexual felony against the other spouse would otherwise receive spousal support. Although California did already have a statutory presumption against awarding spousal support to a spouse convicted of domestic violence, it had not proven sufficient to effectively shield victims from having to pay spousal support and attorney's fees to their convicted ex-husbands. The new categorical exception to this judicial discretion is designed to once and for all prevent the re-victimization of injured spouses who would otherwise be required to provide financially for their abusers. Judge Pollack's orders went further than most, but were not unique for many custody judges.

PUTTING THE BEST INTEREST OF ABUSERS ABOVE CHILDREN AND THEIR ABUSED MOMS

Although by the end of the twentieth century, judges sitting in criminal courts showed some understanding of domestic violence and were letting these prosecutions go forward, their peers sitting in civil courts have proven uniformly oblivious to domestic violence in making decisions about custody and visitation. Louisiana's legislature was the first to try to get judges to pay attention to domestic violence. In 1992, it amended its custody code, making a legislative finding:

> The legislature . . . finds that the problems of family violence do not necessarily cease when the victimized family is legally separated or divorced. In fact, the violence often escalates, and child custody and visitation become the new forum for the continuation of the abuse. Because current laws relative to child custody and visitation are based on an assumption that even divorcing parents are in relatively equal positions of power and that such parents act in the children's best interests, these laws often work against the protection of the children and the abused spouses in families with a history of family violence. Consequently, laws designed to act in the children's best interest may actually effect a contrary result due to the unique dynamics of family violence.[28]

Almost every state in the union followed Louisiana's lead and enacted legislation directing judges to stop ignoring domestic violence when considering what was in the best interests of the child regarding decisions about custody and visitation rulings. About half of the state legislatures went further, enacting a custodial presumption against awarding child custody to perpetrators of domestic violence.

Colorado enacted a version of the latter. It declared: "It shall not be in the best interests of the child to award joint custody over the objection of the other party or the guardian *ad litem* of the child, unless the court finds that the parties are able to make shared decisions about their child without physical confrontation and in a place and manner which is not a danger to the abused spouse or the child (Colo. Rev. Stats. § 14-10-124)." It wasn't enough.

COLORADO ACTS TO REIN IN JUDGES AGAIN

A string of outlandish custody decisions in Colorado, similar to the California case sited earlier, prompted that state's legislature to try again to rein in judges and their custody decisions involving domestic violence. In 2013, Colorado's legislature enacted a landmark child custody law, attempting, once and for all, to dramatically reverse how the courts deal with domestic violence. According to the *Domestic Violence Report*,[29] one of the cases that spurred the legislators to intervene involved a woman named Julia, a survivor of years of abuse by her husband.

AN ABUSIVE HUSBAND MAKES FOR
AN ABUSIVE FATHER

Julia finally left her abusive husband when her son, at age six, revealed that the father had physically abused him too. She sought a protective order to keep the father away from both of them. She then moved to divorce her abuser, and the custody courts got involved. First, the court ignored evidence from teachers and others who had filed multiple reports to Child Protective Services on the father's abuse of the son in favor of a report by a child and family investigator and reintegration therapist that declared Julia was making it all up. The court not only awarded the father unsupervised parenting time, but also awarded him joint legal custody.

More years of devastating abuse followed, so bad that at one point the son jumped out of his bedroom window to escape his father. He ran to a gas station and frantically called his mother for help. The mother tried again to stop the visitation with the father, but the court ordered it to resume. By the time the son was sixteen, the father was finally arrested and convicted of punching and strangling him. The court then modified its order to limit the father's parenting time and awarded Julia sole decision-making authority.

Julia's story of unsuccessfully battling custody courts and many similar stories from victims mobilized the state coalition against domestic violence. In 2011, the coalition formed a task force to end the state judges' reign of errors. The number one issue the task force identified was the courts' failures to safeguard the abused parent and child. The task force found that the law allowed judges, given their biases, to exercise too much discretion that led to cases like Julia's, putting family preservation over family safety. Continuing to ask abused victims to negotiate with their batterers, the task force concluded, was never going to result in anything good. The coalition decided that state law had to make it clear that the primary concern should be safety of the children and the abused parent. Once their safety was assured, then and only then should the court be concerned with custody, and those decisions should be based on the parenting plan that would give the child the best chance to reach his or her full potential as well as reflect the child's preferences as much as possible.

The task force also found that judges still had not come to recognize the extent of domestic violence in the cases before them or the fact that abusers often seek custody as a tactic to harass, control, and threaten their partners. So the task force came up with a number of recommendations, some of which made it into legislation that subsequently amended the state custody statute. The amendments made safety the primary concern in domestic relations cases involving children when the court finds intimate partner violence. The amendments do this by declaring it a right for children to be safe and live in homes free of domestic violence as well as child abuse, directing courts to make findings about domestic violence before deciding on custody (i.e., facts before verdict!), and prohibiting courts from holding a parent's protective actions to prevent the child from witnessing or being a victim of domestic violence or child abuse against that parent. The latter is intended to mitigate the harm of "friendly parent" provisions used by judges to promote children's relationships with the parent who is more likely to promote contact with the other parent. The law declares flatly that co-parenting should not be the court's goal following a marriage breakup.

Whether the new law will work better than the last wave of legal reforms designed to get judges to take domestic violence seriously in custody cases is as yet unknown.

FATHERS WHO BEAT THEIR CHILDREN'S MOTHERS AREN'T GOOD PARENTS

John Jonchuck was accused of throwing his five-year-old daughter, Phoebe, from a bridge into Tampa Bay in 2015. At the time, he had sole custody of his daughter. After the child's death, it came out, not surprisingly, that Jonchuck had a history of domestic violence. A subsequent report on Phoebe's death revealed that John Jonchuck's background included a number of arrests for domestic violence, battery, and stalking involving Phoebe's mother, his own mother, and two other women. In June 2013, after his last arrest for a domestic violence incident against Phoebe's mother, he and his daughter had moved out. Two weeks later, the Hillsborough County sheriff's office conducted a child-protective investigation to determine if his sole custody of the girl was problematic. Investigators decided that it was not because John was no longer living with Phoebe's mother; therefore the domestic violence was apparently deemed irrelevant.

Of course, the investigators' assumptions were ridiculous. First, they ignored the consistent and broad overlap between domestic violence and child abuse. Second, they dismissed domestic violence as a relationship problem, as opposed to a crime committed by an abuser against a partner.[30]

Batterers don't make good parents—a simple proposition, but one that custody judges, even child protective service investigators, apparently find difficult to accept. Even if one were naively to believe that a child witnessing his mother beaten, raped, and otherwise abused is unaffected, the fact is the majority of child witnesses also suffer maltreatment, including neglect, sexual abuse, and psychological abuse. More than a third of the child witnesses are also victims of physical abuse. Even if the non-abusing parent is able to extricate herself and her children from the abuser, child witnesses run a greatly increased risk of continued mistreatment, including custodial interference.[31]

As a result, custody and visitation presents a major no-win dilemma for battered women. Batterers seek custody more frequently than do non-battering fathers. Batterers win custody of their children with greater frequency than one might assume. Despite howls of complaint from fathers' rights groups that family courts are biased in favor of the mother in custody awards, the higher percentage of mothers with custody over fathers is a result of the extremely low percent of fathers who ask for custody. A Pew poll in 2011 found that 91 percent of child custody after divorce is decided with no interference from the family court system. Only 9 percent are contested, and in these cases, court bias goes the other way. Numerous state commissions on the status of women in the last decade of the twentieth century documented that courts were biased *against* women in general and specifically when it comes to custody. For example, a Massachusetts Gender Bias Study commissioned by that state's supreme judicial court looked at over 2,000 custody cases in dispute. It found that fathers win sole custody more than three times as often as mothers, and win joint custody almost three-quarters of the time when it is contested.[32] More recent research reveals these patterns persist today.

If they don't get custody, batterers are also much less likely to pay child support. In fact, the same fathers' rights groups that complain loudly about man-hating courts depriving children of their loving fathers instruct those fathers on how to avoid paying child support. Child support awards represent 40 percent of many poor women's income, and batterers ordered to pay child support are much less apt to pay than non-batterers. The national payment rate was less than two-thirds of what was ordered for the 2011 financial year, according to the federal Office of Child Support Enforcement. Among the states with the lowest collection rates are many with the highest domestic violence rates. In 2011, according to the U.S. Census, $14.3 billion ordered in child support to custodial parents went unpaid.

Parents who were never married or were separated were the least likely to pay what was ordered.

Battered mothers are at a severe disadvantage when challenged for custody by their abuser. As a result of the domestic violence, the mother's parental authority may have been severely compromised. Custody evaluators observing this conclude that the mother is unfit to parent. Batterers manipulate their children to persuade them that the mother is responsible for the abuse he visits on her. Children often take the side of the more powerful parent, the abuser, not the victim. At the very least, children may not reveal to evaluators the abuse within the household.

Psychological evaluations widely utilized by courts to assist in custody decisions are slanted toward the batterer. The mother, frequently left with trauma from her abuse, appears to be unstable in the tests, and at the very least paranoid. Evaluators, relied upon to help courts decide parental fitness, often have little or no grasp of domestic violence or its effects on children. If anything, they dismiss indications of intimate partner violence as part and parcel of "high-conflict" divorces. Many have backgrounds in mental health counseling, a profession that historically has failed dismally when it comes to identifying domestic violence. In fact, studies in the 1990s found that up to 91 percent of custody evaluators fail to identify domestic violence when it is presented to them, and 40 percent did not consider it important even if they did.[33]

Fast-forward to the twenty-first century, and court evaluators have gotten somewhat better. A content analysis of court evaluators' reports in one court circuit found that more than a decade later, only 60 percent of the reports over a two-year period found that child and maternal safety were compromised by failure of the evaluators to consider evidence of domestic violence or even child abuse.[34] A decade after this, researchers interviewed a number of court evaluators with an average of fourteen years on the job. Some got it and some did not. Some dismissed domestic violence as mutual, situational violence, irrelevant in their recommendations on custody. Others understood domestic violence to be part of chronic abuse and coercive control requiring their attention. The former generally did not believe women who claimed to be victims, and thought preservation of the father-child bond outweighed any consideration of domestic violence. The latter found false allegations of domestic violence to be rare, and put victim safety over maintaining father-child bonds.

To compound this, batterers generally (unlike Crystal's husband in California) have financial resources behind them. They can simply hire the better lawyer. Not only can the battered woman not afford an attorney, but once she leaves her abuser, she may be only able to offer her children

housing in a domestic violence or homeless shelter, and that only temporarily. Domestic violence is a major cause of homelessness for women with
children.

Fear of losing custody or of unsupervised visitation by the abusive father
is a major factor that prevents victims from leaving their abusers. They may
also fear calling police when they are abused because the police might call
child protective services if there are children in the household. The battered
mothers are rightly afraid. If alerted, child protective services will often take
children away from mothers even if it is obvious that the mistreatment is
caused by the abusive father. The system will blame the mother for failing
to protect the children from the father, even though she cannot protect
herself. The state and courts simply find it easier to remove the children or
grant custody to the abuser than to remove the abuser from the household.

WHEN THE SYSTEM FAILS TO ACT, VICTIMS MUST

Bertram Lee was convicted three times for abusing his wife, Ynes, dating back to 2000 in Kent County, Michigan. The last conviction was
for slamming her hand in a closet door, then taking the phone from
her when she tried to call for help. As Ynes revealed in her application
for a protective order following the third conviction, Bertram's dozen
years of abuse had included stalking Ynes, calling her at home and
work, and leaving messages threatening to kill her and then himself.

Ynes eventually got the protective order because even after Bertram's third conviction, the prosecutor reduced the charges from
domestic violence and interfering with communications to attempted
domestic violence. Bertram was placed on probation and told to have
no contact with his estranged wife, who was then filing for divorce.

As soon as his probation ended, Bertram went right back to Ynes.
That was when she stabbed him with a steak knife as they struggled.
Bertram died a week later in the hospital from his wound. Because
Ynes had a prior conviction for first degree retail fraud in 1988, she
was prosecuted as a habitual offender. She pled guilty to manslaughter and, being a habitual offender, in order to avoid a charge of second
degree murder, getting sentenced to twenty-two and a half years in
July 2014. If Bertram had been held appropriately accountable for
his non-lethal domestic violence, he would undoubtedly be alive and
Michigan would not be paying room and board for Ynes for the next
four to twenty-two years.*

> **Note**
>
> *Deiter, B., "Man Fatally Stabbed Had 3 Domestic Violence Convictions, Court Records Show," *The Grand Rapids Press*, August 29, 2013; Deiter, B., "Abused Wife Pleads No Contest to Manslaughter in Husband's Fatal Stabbing," *The Grand Rapids Press*, July 14, 2014.

Prosecutors in the cited case announced that they took domestic violence murders seriously. However, if they took non-lethal domestic violence at all seriously, the case would never have arisen.

INCREASING CRIMINAL JUSTICE AGENCIES' ATTENTION SPANS

Perhaps unfairly, perhaps not, both the good and bad examples sprinkled throughout this text were selected to illustrate the range of criminal justice responses to domestic violence. While some of the latter illustrate agencies acting in ways that can make your skin crawl, even the worst agencies can transform themselves. Issues claimed to be insurmountable barriers one day evaporate the next when a new chief takes over, prosecutor is elected, or judge assigned. Unfortunately, the reverse is also true. Good, even outstanding agencies one year can become examples of the opposite the next.

A final challenge facing the criminal justice system in protecting victims and holding abusers accountable is overcoming criminal justice agencies' historically short attention spans when it comes to domestic violence. Every decade, for example, new domestic violence law enforcement programs are heralded as the final word for policing domestic violence. Within a decade, they fade away. Currently, there are two programs so heralded making the rounds: the Lethality Assessment Program (LAP), pioneered in Maryland; and an abuser-targeting program, the Offender-Focused Domestic Violence Initiative, pioneered in North Carolina. On paper, the two strategies could not be more diametrically opposite. The former is victim focused and the latter abuser focused. But they both work. Where adopted, the two strategies have paid off, far better than what the same law enforcement agencies were accomplishing before adopting these programs. Neither, of course, offers a magic bullet to stop domestic violence, but both save lives.

LETHALITY ASSESSMENT PROGRAM (LAP) AND TARGETING HIGH-RISK ABUSERS

Law enforcement Lethality Assessment Programs consist of two steps. First, when police arrive at the scene of a domestic violence incident, they ask the victim a series of eleven questions that help them determine her risk of being murdered by her abuser. The questions are based on a slightly larger fifteen-question danger assessment developed in a 1986 study and revised in 2003 by researchers that examined domestic violence homicides and attempted homicides around the country, analyzing common characteristics involved in all of them. They looked at 220 intimate homicides and 356 abused women who survived almost lethal attacks by intimates.[35]

Before LAP, responding officers would simply hand out a small card with some victim information on it. Now, if the victim is found to be at risk based on the lethality assessment questions, officers are instructed to talk with her, call the local women's shelter or hotline, and encourage the woman to make arrangements to receive services. The hotline tries to reinforce the findings of the lethality assessment and convince the woman that she is at risk and should engage in immediate safety planning. The hotline also offers her services from participating domestic violence advocacy and service agencies, including access to a shelter facility.

The questions come in two series. A positive response to any of the first three questions triggers the police to act. These three questions include: 1) Has he ever used a weapon against you or threatened you with a weapon? 2) Has he threatened to kill you or your children? 3) Do you think he might try to kill you? A positive response to at least half of the following eight questions also prompts the police to act even if the answer is negative to the first three questions: 1) Does he have a gun or can he get one easily? 2) Has he ever tried to choke you? 3) Is he violently or constantly jealous of you and does he control most of your daily activities? 4) Have you left him or separated after living together or being married? 5) Is he unemployed? 6) Has he ever tried to kill himself? 7) Do you have a child that he knows is not his? 8) Does he follow or spy on you or leave threatening messages? In addition, officers are told they can ignore negative findings of risk if their intuition tells them that the woman is in danger.

The official forms are gender neutral, although the research was limited to female victims of male intimate perpetrators (hence the male pronoun used here). There is no scientific evidence that the scale is accurate for other victims and perpetrators. By scoring the responses as it does, research found that the scale correctly identified more than 80 percent of the lethal abusers researched. However, to accomplish this, it also identified 40 percent of the victims' abusers as lethal who did not kill their victims.

In implementing lethality assessments, some police departments go farther. If identified as high risk, the next day police personnel follow up with victims who did not connect with services and/or get advocates to call the victims offering further assistance.

According to the Maryland Network Against Domestic Violence, between 2006 and 2012, of the 56,000 victims the program screened, more than half (53 percent) scored as high risk for lethality. The majority, 57 percent, talked to an advocate at the scene, and 31 percent followed up with domestic violence services. Where advocates got back to victims who did not enroll in services initially, the proportion rose to 56 percent. As a result of the program, according to the coalition, domestic violence homicides in the state went down 41 percent. The number of victims connecting to services rose dramatically, from 4 percent in 2004 to 31 percent of the high-risk victims identified by police a decade later.[36]

LAP has spread quickly. From three jurisdictions, the program spread to sixty-six law enforcement agencies in twenty-one of Maryland's counties, and it didn't stop there. The program proved so popular that the Justice Department's Office on Violence Against Women funded its replication across the country. In March 2013, the attorney general of the United States proclaimed that the program had helped to prevent domestic violence homicides for the twenty-five thousand high-danger victims of domestic violence the police had identified across Maryland.

Other jurisdictions have joined Maryland to claim similar successes. Anoka County, Minnesota, began its program with federal funds in 2010. According to police officials, between September 2010 and February 2012, officers completed 609 risk assessments with victims; 68 percent were determined to be at high risk for homicide at the hands of their partner. Of those, 77 percent received or were receiving ongoing services from the area's domestic violence assistance agencies. Similar results were produced in Kansas City, which began its program in June 2009 after training all nine hundred of its patrol officers. According to the police chief, domestic homicides were reduced by a quarter and aggravated assaults by 7 percent over one year. Shelter occupancy also rose by sixteen more women a day, and hotline calls increased by almost 20 percent. Between June 2009 and May 2011, officers screened over two thousand victims. Nearly 69 percent were scored high danger, and more than half spoke to a domestic violence counselor. Twenty percent enrolled in services. A similar pilot in the District of Columbia claimed a 50 percent domestic violence homicide reduction.

The number of domestic homicides dropped from five to two between 2013 and 2014 in Pittsburgh, Pennsylvania, while other nondomestic homicides soared. Police attribute the decline to adoption in December 2013 of the Lethality Assessment Program. Those found to be high risk in the city are connected to the Women's Center & Shelter of Greater Pittsburgh. In 2014, police assessed 1,767 victims and found 1,266 to be at high risk. They got 873 to speak to the hotline. Police did follow-ups with victims who did not contact the hotline to show their concern for these victims' safety. Authorities say the victim-centered approach has encouraged more victims to testify against their abusers as well as seek shelter. Eighty police departments across Pennsylvania have now instituted lethality programs.

Lethality Assessment Programs have spilled over to the rest of the criminal justice system too. Bail commissioners, judges, and prosecuting attorneys are adopting lethality assessments in their work making charging and bail decisions. In Anoka, for example, the sheriff's office now includes their lethality assessments in the paperwork they send to the county attorney after making an arrest, and the probation office informs the judge of the abuser's purported risk.

In May 2011, Oklahoma's governor signed a law mandating eight hours of domestic violence and stalking training for new police officers, including learning how to use the lethality assessment. Oklahoma is also where the first formal comprehensive evaluation of the LAP was completed, funded by the U.S. Justice Department's National Institute of Justice, the research arm of the department. The evaluation substantiated the claims of the many jurisdictions that have adopted the program, in part.[37]

Researchers compared victim impact data from the seven Oklahoma jurisdictions that had implemented LAP with victims from other jurisdictions that operated as they always had in regard to domestic violence. Victims in both groups were interviewed immediately after the police intervention and then around seven months later. Most of the women in both groups were scored as high risk. Women in the LAP jurisdictions reported using significantly more protective strategies both immediately after the indexed event (e.g., seeking services, removing/hiding their partner's weapons) and at follow-up (e.g., applying for and receiving an order of protection, establishing a code with family and friends). In addition, women who participated in the LAP intervention were significantly more satisfied with the police response and were likely to report that the advocate was at least somewhat helpful.

In regard to reabuse, the findings were more mixed. "There were no significant differences in the presence or absence of intimate partner violence or severe intimate partner violence between the LAP intervention and high-violence comparison groups at follow up." However, the LAP intervention group was less likely to experience abuse (i.e., verbal/psychological, physical, and/or sexual abuse) as determined by something called the conflict tactics scale, a gender neutral scale developed by sociologists. In regard to homicides, the researchers found that domestic violence homicides declined in both the LAP and non-LAP jurisdictions during the study.

The researchers commented that given the high level of violence and abuse the victims had experienced before the study incidents, it is not realistic to expect miracles—decreases in violence and abuse, yes, but their elimination, no. The reduction in frequency and/or severity of violence that the LAP afforded women, researchers concluded, may provide victims the opportunity to use services aimed to assist with the process of breaking free from a violent relationship.

In April 2015, the governor of Arkansas signed into law legislation dubbed Laura's Law, after Laura Aceves, a twenty-one-year-old mother of three murdered by her ex-boyfriend in 2012. The law requires police to use lethality assessments when responding to domestic violence incidents. The legislative sponsor said he submitted the bill after learning about its success in neighboring Oklahoma. Laura's mother commented to the *Huffington Post* that law enforcement "treated my daughter's case like a traffic violation," but she expressed the hope that with this bill, domestic violence victims are "not going to be invisible anymore."[38]

OFFENDER-FOCUSED DOMESTIC VIOLENCE INITIATIVE

High Point is a small city of about 109,000 people in North Carolina. In 2009, its police department adopted a crime-fighting model for domestic violence that had been successfully deployed to tackle gang violence in Boston more than a decade earlier. The department focused on domestic violence, according to police chief Marty Sumner, because when his detectives examined a list of fifty-eight homicides in the five years before 2009, they found domestic violence lay behind the largest portion of them. The last homicide, in fact, had been a twenty-seven-year-old mother, bound, gagged, and strangled to death by her husband. Prior strangulation had prompted the victim to secure a protective order against him two months before her body was found.

The department's aim differed from that of Lethality Assessment Programs. It focused on stopping offenders, as opposed to encouraging victims to get services after they were attacked. As one of the criminologists who helped pioneer the original Boston program explained, "What it was designed to do was to protect the most vulnerable women at the greatest risk from the most dangerous men. If we know that this guy is systematically abusing this woman, then our response to that should be to make him stop, not to make her leave her home and go into a shelter with her kids."[39] The department identified one thousand high-risk abusers to target.

The program classifies all known abusers into four tiers based on their number of prior domestic violence arrests and criminal histories, weapons use in the domestic crimes, and so on. Abusers in Tier A are the most violent, with lengthy rap sheets complete with violent crimes and at least three domestic violence arrests. Tier B contains those with two domestic violence arrests, and Tier C contains those with one domestic violence arrest. Tier D have never been arrested for domestic abuse but have had officers respond to their homes for incidents.

Police scrutinize all the abusers in Tier A to see if they can immediately arrest them for an outstanding warrant or on fresh warrants after detectives reinvestigate old cases. Tier B abusers are called into the station for collective meetings to warn them they need to shape up or feel the heat of law enforcement. Within the domestic violence context, these meetings often feature mentions of offenders in Tier A as examples for what could happen if they continue their violent ways. Tier C abusers get one-on-one chats with investigators who warn them of their fates if they continue on their violent paths, namely, a jail cell.

The first Tier B call in was held on February 21, 2012. A dozen former domestic violence offenders sauntered into High Point City Hall. As the police chief explained, they were the same violent people his department was used to dealing with, violent inside the relationship, and violent outside of it. Community members sat behind the offenders. Each offender received a flyer with mug shots of other offenders recently convicted for domestic assault, including one who had been sentenced to eight years in federal prison and another scheduled for deportation. Facing them on the podium were ministers, volunteers, and seven members of the motorcycle club Street Dreamz, clad in leather jackets, a group that had met with police for years, sharing information on gang members, drug dealers, and, most recently, domestic violence offenders. A pastor of a Baptist church in a depressed neighborhood leads the club. Officials from the FBI, ATF (the drug enforcement agency), and Crimestoppers joined the group. Their message was simple: "As of tonight, our A-game is on."

A county assistant district attorney addressed the audience. Since the domestic violence initiative launched, he related how his office now seeks to lengthen sentences using the felony charge of habitual misdemeanor assault. He told the audience that before, if you punched a partner in the face, you got up to 150 days only. Now, a bleeding lip can be prosecuted like an armed robbery. He also proclaimed that the case would go forward with or without the victim. He concluded that his office already had the paperwork filed to prosecute any reoffenders.

An assistant U.S. Attorney followed and told the men that if the county prosecutor's office lacked evidence for probable cause, he was prepared to use undercover agents to buy drugs from them or sell guns to them, just to stop them from hitting their girlfriends. Under federal law, offenders convicted for domestic assaults, along with individuals under protective orders, cannot possess firearms, meaning that the audience would be set up for federal charges. He concluded, "You put your hands on her again, we're going to turn your life upside down."[40]

When officers respond to a domestic violence incident where the abuser is absent and not already classified, they leave a notice on the door that the abuser is now in Tier D.

By keeping tabs on these abusers, police have files ready for prosecutors and courts to make better-informed decisions. The initiative has demonstrated some of the same successful stats as the LAP. From 2009 to 2013, after the program was initiated, only one homicide was attributed to domestic violence. Injurious assaults were down dramatically, as were arrests and demand for services. Only 9 percent of the 1,024 offenders notified and watched reoffended as of April 2014, according to a University of North Carolina Greensboro study. The results occurred despite fifteen arrests of A-listers among a group of twenty-seven. From 2013 to May 2015, there were no domestic violence murders in the county at all. Police pointed to small video cameras they carry, which they use to record statements at the scene so that stories can't be changed later in court. They also describe how they file charges based on the evidence, not on the wishes of the victim. Police show up in court at arraignment to inform judges of the circumstances so that bails are set higher for repeat abusers.

Although a more recent program than LAP, the Offender-Focused Domestic Violence Initiative is also spreading across the country. Roanoke, Virginia, announced it was adopting the High Point program at the end of 2014. The U.S. Justice Department *Community Policing Dispatch* newsletter featured the High Point program in its September 2014 issue.

What can we make of these two diametrically opposite approaches?

What these programs prove is as fundamental as it is simple. It really doesn't matter what programs police adopt. Commitment to making domestic violence a priority is the key. Doing so and taking it seriously will improve victim safety and increase offender accountability. Training obviously helps, but training alone is meaningless if not backed up by command staff paying attention to how officers and deputies do their jobs. This means checking to make sure they are arresting suspects and suspects only, not their victims. It means reviewing incident reports to make sure the responding officers and deputies are capturing the pertinent information prosecutors will need to extract guilty pleas. It means collaborating with local domestic violence service agencies to support victims in need.

On paper, LAP appears to be exactly the wrong approach. Connecting victims to services is, of course, extremely important, but if that's all that's done, it keeps the onus of protection on the victims, meanwhile hardly deterring their abusers from further violence. Yet the genius of the LAP program is that through victims, it in effect clues in responding officers that the domestic violence incident, no matter how minor it may appear to police, is in fact deadly serious. By ratcheting up the false positives—in other words, overpredicting lethality—the scale prompts the responding officers to do more than make calls to hotlines for victims. Rather than officers viewing the abuser as a misdemeanant of little consequence, the abuser's status is elevated to that of a potential murderer. The misdemeanor arrest is recast as homicide prevention, which police are far more likely to take seriously. Thus, the result is the same as the abuser-targeted program. Jurisdictions see increased arrests, higher bails, more prosecutions of abusers, more prosecutions specifically for strangulation, and other, more-serious domestic violence charges.

The increased safety afforded victims can be explained better by the fact that LAP made the officers using it perform better investigations, which eventually led to more prosecutions and more jail for abusers. The researchers of the Oklahoma LAPs focused on the programs' victim impact, but it also hinted at its equally important offender impact. Buried in the evaluation is the finding that women in the LAP intervention group had a 48.59 percent "chance of their partner going somewhere where he could not find or see the participant," while women in the comparison group had only a 27.24 percent chance of their partners going away. Of the LAP-involved women whose partners "went somewhere he could not find them," more than two-thirds (68.2 percent) reported that their partners were in *jail*!

In short, police actions, not victim actions, provide the program's protective impact. As mentioned before, if victim safety were under the control of the victim, she wouldn't be a victim. No one chooses to be a victim of domestic violence.

Historically, there have been a number of criminal justice initiatives that have boasted similar successes. Truth be told, an initiative that combined both the LAP and Offender-Focused Domestic Violence Initiative programs was originally established by the Colorado Springs police department back in 1996, called Domestic Violence Enhanced Response Team (DVERT). It, too, targeted serious domestic violence cases referred from advocates, shelters, prosecutors, and county and local police. It was both victim and offender focused. It, too, boasted great successes and was copied around the country. It, too, was promoted by federal funding for its replication at the time, until the feds moved on to promote the next promising program.

Nor is DVERT the only program that has dramatically lowered reabuse. Specialized law enforcement domestic violence units featuring more extensive inquiries by police department dispatchers, more evidence gathering at the scene, and more direct assistance to victims have also been found to significantly reduce reabuse. For example, a North Carolina study found that abusers handled by its specialized law enforcement unit reabused significantly less than those handled by regular patrol units over a two-year period. The odds ratio for reoffending was halved by the unit's involvement. This reduction was even more telling because the specialized unit handled only the more serious cases of offenders with prior offenses.[41]

Similarly, in 2007, New York City police attributed a dramatic 32 percent decline in its annual city domestic violence homicides from seventy to forty-eight as a result of its police follow-up home visitation program. That year, New York City police doubled the number of such visitations from 33,400 in 2001 to 76,602, apparently reaching the tipping point. While the New York City police program went largely unnoticed in the United States, across the Atlantic Ocean, the British government announced it would replicate NYPD Blue. The Home Secretary announced Her Majesty's government would confer with New York's Mayor Bloomberg to examine how New York's approach could be implemented across England.[42]

Specialized prosecution, court, and probation supervision programs focusing on domestic violence have also boasted great results, as have coordinated community responses, uniting criminal justice and domestic violence agencies to combat domestic violence.[43] While the criminal justice system is not a true "system" with interconnecting parts designed to work together, if one agency makes domestic violence a priority, it generally spurs on the other agencies to enhance their responses too. If police do a better job, it makes it easier for prosecutors to follow. If prosecutors do a better job, it encourages police to do a better job because they see their domestic violence cases being taken seriously. And if prosecutors do a better job, it presses judges to approve better plea bargains, and so on. While the Office on Violence Against Women and local advocates are big on interagency task forces and collaboration, often jurisdictions do better when the criminal justice agencies compete with each other, intent on shielding their particular agency from blame if the next domestic violence case ends up making headlines. Instead of racing to the bottom, they race to the top in holding offenders accountable and protecting victims.

IF IT WORKS, KEEP ON DOING IT

The challenge is not adopting one program or another. It is keeping the good ones going.

In 2014, for example, New York police announced a new domestic violence pilot program in northern Manhattan. The *Daily News* found out the department's new pilot was, in fact, the elimination of random home visits at victims' homes to do safety and accountability checks, substituting pre-scheduled meetings only, to save on police resources. Advocates expressed immediate outrage, pointing out that victims in poor and minority neighborhoods would never agree to such visits, as they would be afraid of being labeled snitches. Sadly, where the department is conducting its "new" pilot, there has been a 12 percent jump from the same period the year before in domestic violence felony crimes. As late as 2013, a head of the city's domestic violence unit was quoted in the *New York Times* saying that home visits were "the cornerstone of our response to domestic violence." In the same article, the prosecutor who leads the domestic violence unit for the Queens district attorney estimated that three-quarters of domestic violence defendants violate an order of protection within seventy-two hours by phone calls or text messages or by returning to the residence. The unannounced home visits by the police, he explained, make the abuser wary about moving back in because "[t]he victim is telling the defendant, 'The officers keep coming by to ask if you're here, checking on you.'" Providing advance warning will obviously not serve as a similar deterrent.[44]

New York police are not alone in dropping a widely hailed model domestic violence program.

GETTING POLICE TO EXCEL

Historically, the Nashville police department was a model criminal justice agency, not only for Tennessee but the nation. It too exemplified the best . . . for a while. Nashville followed San Diego, one of the first cities to create a specialized police domestic violence unit in 1992. Nashville created its unit two years later. The unit grew to twenty-five officers with special domestic violence training. After less than one year in operation, Nashville's Domestic Violence Division was recognized nationally. An article in the local *Tennessean* boasted that, at the same time a Los Angeles judge was considering whether to allow evidence that O. J. Simpson had a history of abusing his wife, Nichole Brown Simpson, Nashville was also making the national news. Journalist Bill Moyers had spotlighted Nashville's effort in a recent PBS television special titled, "What Can We Do About Violence?"

At that time, the department's Domestic Violence Division was the largest single investigative unit in the United States dealing with domestic violence. Its intent was to offer an even application of equal protection of the law to all victims of domestic violence by administering quality investigations, victim and suspect assessment, counseling and assistance, safety planning, enhanced prosecution, and police and public education. By the end of 1995, domestic violence homicides in Nashville had dropped 65 percent, from thirty-two in 1993 to fifteen in 1995. The number dropped further to twelve in 1995, a year that saw other homicides in the city increase. U.S. attorney general Janet Reno praised the department in 1996.

Before Nashville's unit was created, only one detective was assigned to follow up on the eighteen thousand domestic violence calls per year. Patrol officers dealt with domestic cases. With its new unit, every *precinct* had at least one investigator just for domestic violence. It launched its first city-wide warrant sweep in 1995, arresting 113 of the worst abusers, including at least one wanted for murder and half a dozen for stalking, a newly enacted state law. Detectives got creative, initiating special programs like "stalking the stalker" where they believed a victim was at a high risk of being harmed. This included stalking the batterer, putting a trace on his phone, videotaping his actions, and contacting the victim's employer to notify the police if the offender was seen nearby.[45]

The officers in the division were all specially trained to respond to victims. They were told three things to say: "I'm sorry this happened to you, it's not your fault, and we're going to help you." Building victim trust enabled the police to get the information they needed to make a better case.

Early on, Casey Gwinn, then the city prosecutor in San Diego, whose own city had pioneered the domestic violence response program Nashville had copied, cautioned that Nashville's early successes had to be put into context. "You can't look at the score at the end of the first quarter and conclude you won the game," he told Moyers. "While I think it's incredibly positive that homicides have dropped so significantly in Nashville, it's naive to think the problem has been solved. The challenge is what's going to happen over the next five or ten years."[46]

Ten years later, Gwinn proved to have been prescient.

Through 2005, the department was consistently clearing domestic violence cases by arresting suspects. In 2001, it only "exceptionally cleared" 134 cases, meaning that although there was sufficient evidence to arrest the suspect, the police could not do so due to forces beyond its control, like the suspect's absence. However, in 2005, police exceptionally cleared 3,866 of domestic violence cases. That year they only arrested 1,352 abusers for either aggravated or simple assaults out of 10,306 assault incidents. At 13 percent, this was as low an arrest rate as could be found across the country. Also that year, police responded to 103 incidents coded as stalking and arrested only eighteen.

And then things got worse. Exceptionally cleared domestic violence cases continued to rise through 2009. In 2009, it rose to fifty-six hundred. At that time, a Nashville police officer admitted to a county domestic violence fatality review team that things were grim in the department. He told them, "We have actually had to lock the doors (of the police domestic violence unit) because we did not have sufficient personnel to keep the facility open to the public. The cases are basically put on hold; the victims are put on hold."

Questioned in 2010 about the diminished number of domestic violence arrests, the police did what all criminal justice officials do when confronted with poor domestic violence performance. They blamed victims for not cooperating. Police, they explained, had to exceptionally clear cases because of victim refusal to cooperate. The *Tennessean*, however, wouldn't let the brass off so easily. Reporters interviewed victims who were eager to press charges against their abusers but unable to do so because police detectives had already closed the cases. The official records indicated they were closed due to lack of victim cooperation. The newspaper found the department was so eager to close cases that it did not wait for victims to get out of hospitals or respond to letters. Police reports were incomplete. One failed to include a man's threats to stab his wife to death, which he did two days after the police report was taken.

The newspaper offered an explanation for the dismal police performance. The most recent police chief had been big on traffic enforcement and the revenue it brought into the city coffers. He called traffic duty "Mission One." A recently retired officer told reporters that detectives were urged to speed up domestic violence investigations so they could concentrate more time to more-lucrative traffic enforcement. Advocates revealed worse. In January 2010, a boy called 911 to say that his father was trying to kill his mother. Responding officers made a quick call to the house and reported the situation "resolved" because the mother told them she had not been abused. When the man killed the boy's mother two days later, an investigation revealed that the responding officers had not written up an incident report, nor had they notified the prosecutor. The prosecutor said his office would have prosecuted the case based on the boy's call alone, had it been informed. (Easy to declare after the fact.) A sergeant was suspended for two days for his failure to write up a report.

By 2010, the number of officers assigned the domestic violence unit had been reduced to eight. Nashville reached a tipping point in 2011. Mayor Karl Dean initiated a domestic violence safety and accountability assessment. More than one hundred individuals representing Metro departments and community organizations came together to examine gaps in safety and services for victims of domestic violence. After painstaking work, they presented the assessment to the mayor and residents of Nashville in 2013 and released a report the next year. Actually, officials only released twenty-two pages of the report, squelching 162 other pages that documented how far the police, prosecutors, and judges had fallen. Ironically, the authors of the report had written what "a bold step for the city [it was] to put itself under the microscope and examine where the gaps in processes and systems exist." But the city wasn't as bold when it came to releasing the report. The full report finally did come out, but only as a result of an open records request months later. It did not reveal a pretty picture of city police, prosecutors, or judges.

According to the report, victims had to wait up to four hours for police response, although the average response time was twenty minutes; judges and night court commissioners regularly blamed victims; police didn't bother to photograph victim injuries, probably because they knew prosecutors or judges would drop two-thirds of the cases; some officers believed promotions were more likely rewards for traffic stops than domestic violence arrests. The report included the story of one victim who waited an hour for police after being assaulted with a screwdriver. She then waited hours for detectives to complete their investigation. All the while, she reported, her abuser was only a few feet away, preventing her from communicating with the officers. In the end, the officers told her abuser to stay somewhere else to cool off. The abuse persisted until she finally got the courage to leave and seek an order of protection. Gaining confidence after working with advocates, she decided to pursue charges for the screwdriver incident. She went to night court only to have the night court commissioner lambaste her for waiting so long to file charges. A complaint against her abuser was issued, but she left the courtroom in tears. The same night court commissioner surfaced elsewhere in the report for telling a victim who reported stalking by her court-restrained abuser to come back when "something real happens." The same victim obtained video footage of the abuser violating the court order, lurking outside her house. Although it had taken police forty-four minutes to get to her, they caught the abuser running away from the house. Despite the video, stalking, and violation of the court order, the prosecutor eventually successfully prosecuted the abuser only for petty vandalism.

As one of the commission members, Mark Wynn, a former Nashville detective who had helped make Nashville a model for its domestic violence program years earlier, explained to the *Tennessean*, "It's bad enough that victims are too afraid to call. But if a service in the City has done something to discourage that victim from calling, somebody needs to answer for that." To his credit, the Metro Nashville police chief, Steve Anderson, while defending his department, vowed to do better. An assistant to the mayor admitted that there was "a little bit more energy" around domestic violence formerly because "O.J. Simpson had just happened and all of that." A judge reported that the night court commissioners had since been given sensitivity training. The prosecutor doubled the number of domestic violence prosecutors from two to four, but said reduction of charges, as alleged in the report, was justified. Finally, the courts announced the creation of a specialized domestic violence court. By 2014, the number of domestic violence prosecutors rose to eight, in addition to two investigators and six staffers working in victim support, representing more people than any other division in the prosecutor's office.[47]

The Metro Police department's domestic violence unit expanded to a few more than a dozen detectives, assigned upward of twelve thousand domestic violence cases each year, according to agency statistics. Meanwhile, the detectives began to tackle the huge backlog of unserved warrants.

Detectives in the past had complained of crushing caseloads made worse by pressure to perform traffic stops. While detectives on occasion would find time to run out and try to execute a warrant, time was scarce. With the division expanded once again, officers were able to rotate each week, giving them a chance to take two days to pick off the top suspects on the list. They also visited victims with orders of protection to check in and make sure suspects weren't violating those terms. Metro Police supervisors began reviewing every domestic violence case, and officers have been recognized for their enthusiasm and professionalism at the street level. As for the future, Metro Police chief Steve Anderson is hoping for the establishment of a full-blown family justice center that will offer collaborative services and support to a broader spectrum of crime victims. By 2013, Nashville police were arresting domestic violence offenders again. Out of almost 10,000 simple and aggravated assault cases, they cleared a little over 8,000, or 80 percent, topping the statewide domestic violence clearance rate of 55.4 percent. Although not all cleared cases were cleared by an arrest, most were. The initiative gained plaudits from domestic violence advocates, even those who were critical of the department in the past.

The rest of the county's criminal justice system stepped up too. In September 2014, Courtroom 4B opened, Davidson County's new domestic violence court. For the first time, all domestic violence cases come to this courtroom, where specialized judges (working in a three-judge rotation), prosecutors, and security staff work. The large majority of cases stay there, while more serious felony cases end up sent to criminal court. In addition to the new domestic violence court, an advocacy center opened in the same building. The center includes a secure set of offices where victims can meet with advocates, police, or prosecutors to get help with orders of protection, filing charges, or getting other kinds of help, such as emergency housing. It's all designed to make victims feel safer and more comfortable seeking help in abusive situations.[48]

PORTLAND POLICE FADE

The Portland, Oregon, police department similarly proved to have a limited attention span when it comes to domestic violence. In 2013, the Multnomah County district attorney's office (Portland, Oregon) pressed charges in less than half the domestic violence cases it reviewed, according to local press. A major factor preventing more prosecutions was the deterioration in the quality of police investigations provided the prosecutors. Over the past decade, the Portland Police Bureau's two major specialized domestic violence teams, the Domestic Violence Enhanced Response Team (DVERT) and Domestic Violence Reduction Unit (DVRU), had been cut in half, leaving only five officers assigned to the DVRU and two officers plus a Multnomah County sheriff's office detective assigned to DVERT. With a population of over half a million people, Portland is Oregon's largest city. As a result of the cutbacks, the specially trained officers investigated less than 10 percent of domestic violence reports received by the department each year. In 2013, that meant out of a total of 8,179 domestic violence reports, officers trained to handle them were assigned to only 586.[49]

WHAT THE CRIMINAL JUSTICE SYSTEM CAN AND SHOULD DO

No one program or segment of the criminal justice system alone can turn the tide, identifying all domestic violence victims and their abusers, assisting the former while stopping the latter. By the time many abusers come to the attention of courts and police, it may be that little will stop that abuser short of prison or tightly controlled probation supervision. However, the criminal justice system can do a lot, even if it fails to deter all abusers.

NORM SETTING

When children first learn right from wrong, step one consists in identifying appropriate behavior. This means defining for them both good and bad behavior. These identifications are reinforced by rewards offered for the former and punishments for the latter. As children become moral adults, they don't need their choices reinforced by rewards and punishments because they have inculcated a moral code. They choose certain behaviors because they believe they are the right things to do.

The problem with many batterers is that they have yet to identify their abusive behavior as bad. In fact, it works for them. It gets them what they want, at least in the short term, which is as far as most criminals think ahead. That is also why many batterers are unfazed by batterer intervention programs. Such programs present them with the now-famous "power and control wheel," which illustrates that abusive, controlling behaviors include much more than just physical assaults. To many, it provides a learning guide to expand their repertoire of abusive behaviors. As one batterer explained to the author, the program taught him that he "didn't have to hit her to make her do what he wanted!"

Further, batterers often surround themselves with others who support them. If summoned to appear in court, it is not unusual for them to be accompanied by family members, even new girlfriends, not to mention their buddies and even clergy or employers. Nor do abusers have to be too selective to find many cues in popular culture that promote violence against women.

Against all this, the criminal justice system can (and certainly should) provide a concrete, unambiguous message that domestic violence is unacceptable, period. Presently, that message is compromised, inconsistent, and incomplete. It may be a message too late for the most hardened batterers, but it is a message that can reach everyone else. After all, the criminal justice system offers two types of deterrence, specific and general. The former focuses on the individual wrongdoer. It addresses him specifically and fashions a response that will stop him from doing it again or remove him from the community so he can't do it again. The latter, however, is aimed at the general community. It works because it helps establish social or cultural norms.

Examples are plentiful. The civil rights movement of the 1960s did not successfully change the attitudes of every racist in the country. It changed laws that then changed behaviors. Attitudes gradually caught up for most people. The crackdown of drunk drivers two decades later offered perhaps a better example. Thanks to Mothers Against Drunk Driving, legislatures enacted laws promoting the criminalization of drunk driving, among other things making drunk driving motor vehicle homicides a specific crime, rather than just an unfortunate but forgivable mistake. Drunk driving deaths decreased dramatically across the country. While the laws did not keep the chronic drunk drivers off the roads, they did influence the rest. Laws helped changed social and cultural norms—what is considered acceptable behavior. They supported new behaviors including the creation of designated drivers, responsible service in bars and even among social hosts, and, in at least one state, the elimination of happy hour reduced-price alcohol service. Sociologists call this "social norming"—making these behaviors the norm, not the exception.

For domestic violence, the criminal justice system forms a foundation for creating these requisite social and cultural norms. Abusers who don't yet understand that their behavior is immoral and ultimately self-destructive can at least learn it is criminal and punishable by law. That is a necessary first step in the learning process.

It is a step that the criminal justice systems of the United States and its many subdivisions—state, county, and local—have not boldly taken. Police have to do better than 50 percent in arresting perpetrators; prosecutors have to follow suit and reinforce legitimate arrests with the realistic threat of prosecution, even if it means actually going to trial with or without the victim. Judges have to do more than rubber stamp bargain-basement plea deals. They must insist on sanctions that fit the crime. The "going rate" for a "simple assault" has to be consistently greater than it is for the various misdemeanors that are not devastating crimes again persons. Otherwise, abusers will be no more deterred from assaulting their partners than they will be from littering on state highways.

Legislatures can assist by making stalking, strangulation, and domestic assaults all felonies and eliminate once and for all legislatively authorized diversion programs. Prosecutors can assist by following the spirit as well as the letter of the law and enhance sentences for repeat abusers.

Some studies purport to find that prosecuting and even jailing abusers doesn't stop them.[50] While these specific studies are no doubt accurate, it is not accurate to conclude that prosecuting and sentencing abusers is useless. It is like the old saw about throwing a bucket of water on a forest fire and concluding that water doesn't put out fire. It all depends on the quality of the prosecution and the sanctions imposed. If the severity of prosecutions and sentencing is less for interpersonally devastating crimes, that is, domestic violence, than that for nondomestic, nonviolent crimes, it sends abusers a message—that the law doesn't take domestic violence very seriously.

Examples illustrating this appear in the local press every day. Three, from three different states, made headlines that surfaced in a *Google News* search for "domestic violence" in February and March 2015 alone, initially reported by D. Moran in the *Grand Rapids Press*, Michigan; D. Kennard in the *Daily Herald*, Utah; and C. Robinson in the *Birmingham News*, Alabama.

NOT TAKING DOMESTIC VIOLENCE CRIMES SERIOUSLY IN MICHIGAN

Perry Freemon of Ypsilanti Township, Michigan, was arrested for shooting his ex-girlfriend in February 2015. At the time, she was installing new locks on her home to keep him away and protect her four children. He found her there and shot her. Her recovery from the wounds, it was reported, will not be quick or easy. Freemon was subsequently arraigned for assault with intent to murder, two counts of assault with a dangerous weapon, and three weapons charges.

Freemon had previously been prosecuted and even jailed for domestic violence, but this clearly did not deter him from committing it again.[*]

Note

[*]Counts, J., "Ypsilanti Township Man Accused of Shooting Ex-Girlfriend Charged with 7 Felonies," MLive.com, February 28, 2015.

In Michigan, a first domestic violence assault is a misdemeanor, punishable by jail time of up to ninety-three days and/or a fine of $500. A second offense is also a misdemeanor, punishable by jail time of up to a year and/or a fine of $1,000; a third offense is a felony, punishable by two to five years in prison and/or a fine of $5,000. In 2013, Perry Freemon had been prosecuted for a domestic assault and sentenced to a jail term of thirty-nine days for his *third* domestic violence offense, along with two years of probation. In fact, at the time of the 2015 shooting of his ex-girlfriend, he was in violation of that probation for repeatedly missing court-ordered payments.

No wonder the victim was changing her locks at the time of the attack. If the Michigan prosecutors and courts were concerned with her safety, they were certainly not employing even the most tepid sanctions provided by state lawmakers.

Tepid prosecution and lenient sentencing doesn't deter chronic abusers.

NOT TAKING DOMESTIC VIOLENCE SERIOUSLY IN UTAH

Elwin Hitesman, thirty-three, from Eagle Mountain, Utah, was similarly featured in his local paper. As reported, at the start of March 2015, he had been arrested on and off for domestic violence for fourteen years. Although many of the charges had been dismissed, he was convicted for domestic assaults at least three times, in September 2000, June 2001, and June 2007. Despite these successful prosecutions, he was arrested again in February 2015 for domestic violence . . . apparently undeterred by prior prosecutions.

The charges arose from a domestic violence incident involving his wife. She had been stopped on the last day of January for speeding. According to the trooper, she was frantic because she was late and was afraid her husband would be angry. A few hours later, police were summoned to Hitesman's home. A third party reported seeing him drag his wife out of the car as she attempted to lock the door to stop him. He then dragged her into the house. The Good Samaritan tried to intervene, and Hitesman assaulted the man, throwing his phone out a window when he tried to call 911.

By the time police arrived, they heard crashing noises and yelling in the house. The Good Samaritan met the police outside and urged them to hurry to save the woman inside. Although hysterical, the wife begged police not to arrest her husband because she feared he would lose his job. Nonetheless, as they should have, police arrested Hitesman again, charging him with assault, unlawful detention, and interrupting a communication device.*

Note

*Romero, M., "Police Piecing Together Background of Domestic Violence-Related Shooting," *Deseret News*, March 2, 2015.

Utah, like Michigan, has a domestic violence enhancement law for repeat domestic violence (77-36-1.1), where a third offense is bumped up to a felony, punishable by up to five years in prison and a fine up to $5,000. However, in Utah, the prior conviction has to be within the last five years. Of course, the sentencing judge, noting the prior criminal history, can still legally impose a more severe sentence. The sunset provision just means the judge doesn't have to.

However, the sunset provision kept all of Elwin Hitesman's 2015 domestic violence charges as misdemeanors. The maximum penalty for a domestic assault in Utah is no more than six months in jail, the same punishment provided by the Utah legislature for shoplifting under $300, being a public nuisance, or committing a number of traffic offenses! Hitesman pled not guilty that February and was released—after all, he was only charged with misdemeanors.

Three prior convictions and Hitesman was still abusing his wife. More proof that minimally prosecuting domestic violence doesn't work? This minimal prosecution resulted in deadly consequences. On February 27, Hitesman's wife called police herself to report she had shot her husband, killing him. Police held her for questioning, but released her to care for the couple's four children. The officers told the media they did not believe the suspect was a threat or would flee. Further, there were indications, they revealed, that the shooting may have been self-defense.

If Hitesman had been punished more severely than your average shoplifter, perhaps he would still be alive. Instead, Utah sunsetting enhancement laws for domestic violence convictions at five years and multiple judges' failure to increase sanctions for repeat offenses left Hitesman free to continue his decade-plus-long campaign of abuse.

NOT TAKING DOMESTIC VIOLENCE SERIOUSLY IN ALABAMA

Over in Birmingham, Alabama, in the first week of March, Willie Stevens was shot and killed when police said he went to his ex-girlfriend's house and attacked her. When the woman's current boyfriend intervened, a fight ensued, and the woman's boyfriend ended up shooting Stevens. The boyfriend was subsequently charged with manslaughter.

Court records show Stevens had at least two prior convictions for domestic violence cases involving different women. In 2008, he was convicted of third-degree domestic violence and third-degree burglary, receiving a one-year suspended sentence. Again in 2012, he was convicted of domestic violence and burglary for breaking into an ex-girlfriend's home through a window, then assaulting her about the face, according to court records. He pleaded guilty to two misdemeanors and received another one-year suspended sentence.*

Note

*Robinson, C., "Man Killed after Slapping Ex-Girlfriend Had History of Domestic Violence, Court Records Show," Al.com, March 5, 2015.

Alabama law provides for enhancement of sentences for repeat domestic violence. As a first offense, domestic violence in the third degree is punishable by not more than one year in jail. For a second offense of domestic violence in the third degree, the punishment is a minimum sentence of forty-eight hours in a city or county jail or detention facility. The Alabama law, unlike Utah's, has no sunset provision after five years.

Burglary in the third degree, on the other hand, is a class C felony with a minimum sentence of no less than one year and one day and no more than ten years. In order for Willie Stevens to have avoided jail time for two sets of prior domestic violence and burglary, the burglary charges had to be dropped and the second domestic assault charged as a first offense. Perhaps if prosecutors and judges had sentenced Stevens consistent with at least the intent of the state law, the Good Samaritan boyfriend of the woman he assaulted would not be facing imprisonment, and Stevens's life would not have ended at age thirty.

Domestic violence–related offenses should be felonies and prosecuted and, if convicted or pled out, sentenced as such. To assault a stranger is bad, to assault an intimate worse. They are not comparable crimes with comparably harmful impacts. Nor should the impact of domestic assault be measured by physical injuries alone. The emotional, social, financial, psychological, and health impacts are far worse. A domestic assault, for that reason, should always be considered an aggravated assault, a felony, by nature of the relationship of the parties. It goes without saying that strangulation, violation of protective orders, and stalking should also be felonies for the same reasons. In fact, considering the levels of trust violated and psychological impact left on victims, it is difficult to see any crime perpetrated against an intimate partner not being a felony.

While enlightened criminal justice practitioners recognize misdemeanor domestic violence arrests constitute homicide prevention, making these crimes felonies will engage the (all too many) unenlightened practitioners, too. If we have to wait for the criminal justice system to work when all its practitioners become so enlightened, it is a wait already much too long. Thus, what should and can be demanded is that police, prosecutors, judges, and probation officers do their jobs competently and take domestic violence seriously. That is asking enough.

The problem here is not know-how, it is will. Police know how to arrest suspected criminals. Prosecutors know how to prosecute, even with "uncooperative" victims. After all, prosecutors win murder trials every day without cooperative victims! What the criminal justice system lacks is motivation and commitment when it comes to protecting victims of domestic violence, as was seen in Nashville during its particularly dark days of domestic violence enforcement, when traffic stops trumped victim safety.

It is time to go back to the Model Domestic Violence Code fashioned in 1995 and redo it based on what has been learned in the last twenty years. The most important takeaway is that we made a fundamental error in our effort to get police to arrest abusers. We gave them the authority to arrest a non-witnessed misdemeanor, rather than make the crime a felony to achieve the same result. What has become abundantly clear is that the criminal justice system won't hold abusers accountable and protect women with the keystone charge being a misdemeanor assault.

We have also learned over the last twenty years that good laws aren't enough. We have to hold those charged with their enforcement accountable. The biggest challenge has proven to lie with prosecutors. Their failure discourages law enforcement officers from doing their job and compromises judges from doing theirs. Officers aren't going to expend the resources and energy needed to investigate crimes that prosecutors routinely divert or dismiss. Judges can't begin to protect victims if they are presented with lethal defendants and maximum sentences of sixty days. State attorneys general should be charged with overseeing local prosecutors and intervening when they find prosecutors who, by their actions, collaborate with criminals and fail America's victims, whether they be gay, straight, transgender, cisgender, men, women, adults, or children. The U.S. attorney general should exercise the same oversight, in turn, over both state attorneys general as well as U.S. Attorneys. The failure of U.S. Attorneys to enforce federal firearm prohibitions to prevent the arming of convicted and court-restrained batterers is not only a continuing disgrace, but it also represents a continuing national danger.

Due to the gravity of this danger, the U.S. attorney general should bring civil rights cases against prosecutors who endanger their citizens through failure to enforce the law. While an individual prosecution decision may be explained by unique exigencies, patterns of prosecutors reveal whether or not a prosecutor's office is doing the job. The patterns are apparent. As revealed in the preceding chapters, we are not talking about comparing subtle nuances when it comes to the performance of the criminal justice system. We are talking stark contrasts. There is probably no criminal justice agency that cannot do better. The problem is there are far too many that can hardly do any worse!

How do we get there? We focus more on prosecuting violent crimes, like domestic violence, and less on nonviolent, minimal impact crimes, like most drug offenses that currently clog our courts and correctional institutions.

After several decades, let us declare an end to the war on drugs and turn it over to the public health system where it belongs, not the criminal justice system. While at the highest levels, the drug trade comprises unspeakable violence, it's the lower end where the mass of incarcerations in this country are taking place, among the street addicts and small-time pushers, those more victimized by the drug trade than those making victims through it. The experts tell us that addiction is a brain disease. It should be treated as such instead of being criminalized. This hopeless and hapless American war on drugs has perverted and distorted the American criminal justice system, draining it of resources to deal with domestic violence. It has made America the number one nation when it comes to numbers of incarcerated citizens. Over the last four decades, we have increased our prison population 500 percent. The surge has not been in response to an equal surge in crime or a crackdown on perpetrators of domestic violence, but the demonization of drug use.

Half the current federal prison population is there for drugs, with more than a fourth there for marijuana! In 1970, the proportion incarcerated for drugs was just 16 percent. In addition to locking up hundreds of thousands for drugs, millions have been branded as felons for drug crimes, disproportionately affecting minorities and the poor. In 2013, more than a million and a half Americans were arrested for drug crimes, with only 17.7 percent for selling or manufacturing drugs. In a breakdown from the year before, half the arrests were for marijuana, all but 91,593 for possession, not trafficking or sale.[51]

The resources committed to arresting persons for marijuana possession alone are staggering. According to researchers, a basic misdemeanor arrest for marijuana possession in New York City takes from two or three hours for one offender and up to five-plus hours for multiple offenders.[52] During this time, police return to the station with the handcuffed arrestees and book them, taking photographs and fingerprints, gathering other information, and writing it all up. They then send the personal data to be checked against the state's criminal databases and wait to receive the arrestees' criminal records, if the database searches find any. Arresting officers regularly take suspects to the central booking jail, are interviewed by assistant district attorneys, and appear in court where, if unionized, they get time and a half pay. Using the most conservative time estimate of two and a half hours, the researchers multiplied this by the number of lowest-level marijuana possession arrests (NYS Penal Law 221.10) for each year since 2002 through 2012. In those eleven years, the NYPD made a total of 439,056 possession-only arrests. Multiplied by two and a half hours of police time per arrest, that equals approximately one million hours of police officer time. That is the equivalent of having thirty-one police officers working eight hours a day, 365 days a year, for eleven years, making only marijuana possession arrests.

Those same officers could have instead repeatedly visited every address across the city where domestic violence is suspected.

Apart from big city police departments like New York's, nine out of ten sheriff's offices regularly perform drug enforcement functions. More than a third operate a special unit for drug enforcement, with one or more officers assigned full-time. A majority of sheriff's offices serving a population of 250,000 or more residents have a full-time drug enforcement unit, nationwide employing 4,031 officers full-time to drug enforcement units, ranging from twenty-seven in jurisdictions with one million or more residents to two in those with fewer than fifty thousand residents.[53] Think how many protective orders could be successfully and routinely served, arrests made, and investigations completed if these resources went to special domestic violence investigation teams.

The symbiotic bond between drug cartels and criminal justice must be ended once and for all. The drug cartels need the American criminal justice system to add value to the cartel's products, and the American criminal justice system needs the cartel to continue to justify its disproportionate concentration on drug crimes, not to mention its lucrative forfeitures of drug defendants' assets. The country has, in effect, a national and state bounty system for drug offenses. In 2011, the U.S. Justice Department's asset forfeiture fund was $1.8 billion, according to the federal General Accounting Office. That year, almost $500 million was shared with local law enforcement. California got the most, $80 million in 2011, mostly from assets that state, local, and federal law enforcement seized from medical marijuana dispensaries. In addition to the federal program, states have their own asset forfeitures. Michigan law enforcement, for example, in 2012 made ten thousand forfeitures totaling $7.8 million by local police agencies, $4 million by multi-jurisdictional task forces, $500,000 by state police, and $1.5 million by sheriff's departments. Add Michigan's federal share and the state received $22.3 million once administrative costs were subtracted. The forfeitures went, in turn, to pay for more drug enforcement and related activities, including fifty-one personnel, overtime for drug investigations, sixty-three vehicles, informant fees, and buy money to ensure the arrest of the next year's batch of drug defendants and forfeitures. New York State reported $16.9 million forfeited and distributed in 2012 pursuant to state forfeiture statutes. At least $2.2 million went to the general fund for investigations, $800,000 went for prosecutors, and $6.9 million went to pay for damages/restitution for those agencies that listed where the money was spent.[54]

Drug asset forfeitures have actually supplanted drug arrest and prosecutions. Suspects who agree not to contest drug asset forfeitures are given a bye in court! If the criminal justice system got a bounty for domestic violence felony arrests, state domestic violence laws would not have to be enhanced. If the system similarly seized the assets of abusers, no domestic violence shelter would ever have to turn away another victim and her children fleeing their abuser.

There are plenty of prison cells, police, judges, probation officers, and prosecutors available if we adopt the eradication of domestic violence as our first priority. After voters in California passed Proposition 47 in 2014, which lets low-level offenders apply to be resentenced, 2,923 inmates were released by March 2015. That's plenty of room for the criminal justice system to lock up the most dangerous abusers to give their victims and their children a chance to begin their lives fresh without violence and abuse. Colorado showed what criminal justice resources could be made available by reforming state drug laws. In 2011, Colorado legalized marijuana possession of an ounce or less. A Drug Policy Alliance report released in 2015 found that the total number of charges filed in state courts for marijuana possession, distribution, and cultivation fell by nearly 95 percent across the state, from 38,878 in 2010 to just 2,036 in 2014. Of course, there is no guarantee that the freed-up resources will be used for domestic violence.

Seattle has demonstrated another low-cost alternative to the current criminal justice obsession with perpetuating the endless war on drugs. Instead of locking addicts up, they enroll them in something called Law Enforcement Assisted Diversion, offering housing, counseling, job training, even yoga, instead of jail. The results have been so encouraging that it is being picked up in other cities. As one criminal justice official has written, "This is a big deal—bigger reductions than are seen in almost any criminal justice interventions. This makes the case for 'system as usual' processing (even with drug courts) very weak." Billionaire George Soros's Open Society Foundation announced in 2015 that it would give five jurisdictions up to $200,000 each to help them copy it. In Seattle, just providing housing for chronic alcoholics has saved millions on emergency response and hospital costs.[55]

Perhaps the criminal justice system can do both, drugs and domestic violence. But a one-front campaign is bound to be more successful than a two-front campaign. So what should take precedence for the criminal justice system—locking up addicts better served in addiction recovery programs, or locking up abusers to protect their vulnerable victims?

As the prior pages make clear, many law enforcement officers, prosecutors, and courts have demonstrated they can do the job. They have the know-how. They have and are doing the job, here and there. The challenge is making these efforts the rule, not the exception, and sustaining them across the country.

NOTES

INTRODUCTION

1. *State v. Black*, 60 NC 266, 267 (1864).
2. *State v. Oliver*, 90 NC 60 (1874).
3. In July 2015, an arbitrator ruled that the NFL's ten-game suspension for Hardy was too severe and dropped it to four games, the same Tom Brady later initially received for his role for playing with an underinflated football.
4. The new law, however, allows all but the worst abusers to get their firearms back after three to ten years, in violation of federal law that calls for permanent prohibition. Further it instructs the state police to request the FBI to remove the names of convicted batterers from the national registry used to enforce the federal firearm prohibitions.
5. *United States v. Castleman*, 572 U.S.___(2014).

CHAPTER 1

1. Truman, J., and Langton, L., *Criminal Victimization, 2013*, U.S. Department of Justice, Bureau of Justice Assistance, NCJ 247648, September 2014; see also Catalano, S., *Intimate Partner Violence, 1993–2010*, U.S. Department of Justice, Bureau of Justice Assistance, NCJ 239203, November 2012.
2. Zahn, M., "Intimate Partner Homicide: An Overview," in *Intimate Partner Homicide*, *NIJ Journal*, No. 250, eds. J. Hernon and D. Tompkins, U.S. Department of Justice, National Institute of Justice, November 2003, 2–4.

3. Ohio Family Health Survey Research Team, *Ohio Family Health Survey, 2010*, Interact for Health, March 2011.

4. Lewis, K., and Burd-Sharps, S., *A Portrait of California 2014–2015*, Measure of America of the Social Science Research Council, 2015.

5. *Up to Us: Lessons Learned and Goals for Change After Thirteen Years of the Washington State Domestic Violence Fatality Review*, Washington State Coalition Against Domestic Violence, December 2010, http://dvfatalityreview.org/portfolio/up-to-us-2010/, downloaded October 5, 2015.

CHAPTER 2

1. Berk, R., Newton, P., and Berk, S., "What a Difference a Day Makes: An Empirical Study of the Impact of Shelters for Battered Women," *Journal of Marriage and the Family* 48, 1986, 481–90; Maneta, E., "APA: Abused as Kids, Women More Likely to Abuse Partners," American Psychiatric Association, ed. J. Gever, reported in *MedPage Today*, May 18, 2011; Sullivan, C., and Bybee, D., "Reducing Violence Using Community-Based Advocacy for Women with Abusive Partners," *Journal of Consulting and Clinical Psychology*, 67(1), 1999, 43–53; Tutty, L., Bidgood, B., and Rothery, M., "Support Groups for Battered Women: Research on Their Efficacy," *Journal of Family Violence* 8(4), 1993, 325–43.

2. Bybee, D., and Sullivan, C., "Predicting Re-victimization of Battered Women Three Years After Exiting a Shelter Program," *American Journal of Community Psychology* 36(1–2), September 2005, 85–96; Sullivan, C., and Bybee, D., "Reducing Violence Using Community-Based Advocacy for Women with Abusive Partners," *Journal of Consulting and Clinical Psychology*, 67(1), 1999, 43–53; Sullivan, C., Tan, C., Basta, J., Rumptz, M., and Davidson, W., "An Advocacy Intervention Program for Women with Abusive Partners: Initial Evaluation," *American Journal of Community Psychology* 20, 1992, 209–332.

3. Thompson, R., Rivara, F. P., Thompson, D. C., Barlow, W. E., Sugg, N. K., Maiuro, R. D., and Rubanowice, D. M., "Identification and Management of Domestic Violence: A Randomized Trial," *American Journal of Preventive Medicine* 19(4), 2000, 253–63.

4. Dienemann, J., Campbell, J., Landenburger, K., and Curry, M., "The Domestic Violence Survivor Assessment: A Tool for Counseling Women in Intimate Partner Violence Relationships," *Patient Education and Counseling* 46(3), 2002, 221–28.

5. Baker, C., Cook, S., and Norris, F., "Domestic Violence and Housing Problems: A Contextual Analysis of Women's Help Seeking, Received Informal Support, and Formal System Response," *Violence Against Women* 9(7), July 2003, 754–83; Donnelly, D. A., Cook, K. J., Van Ausdale, D., and Foley, L., "White Privilege, Color Blindness, and Services to Battered Women," *Violence Against Women* 11(1), January 2005, 6–37; Gordon, J. "Community Services for Abused Women:

A Review of Perceived Usefulness and Efficacy," *Journal of Family Violence* 11(4), 1996, 315–29; Zweig, J., Schlichter, K., and Burt, M., "Assisting Women Victims of Violence Who Experience Multiple Barriers to Services," *Violence Against Women* 8(2), February 2002, 162–80.

6. Humphreys, C., and Thiara, R., "Mental Health and Domestic Violence: 'I Call It Symptoms of Abuse,'" *The British Journal of Social Work* 33(2), 2003, 209–26; Zweig, J., and Burt, M., "Predicting Women's Perceptions of Domestic Violence and Sexual Assault Agency Helpfulness," *Violence Against Women* 13(11), November 2007, 1149–78.

7. Dawson, S., Neylon, N., and Hart, T., *Experiences of Battered Women in Ohio: A Community Focus Group Report*, U.S. Department of Justice, Office on Violence Against Women and U.S. Department of Health and Human Services Administration for Children and Families, Columbus, Ohio: Ohio Domestic Violence Network, October 2003.

8. National Domestic Violence Fatality Review Initiative, http://www.ndvfri. org/about.php, downloaded October 1, 2015.

9. Catalano, S., Smith, E., Snyder, H., and Rand, M., *Female Victims of Violence*, U.S. Department of Justice, Publications and Materials Paper 7, 2009; Macy, R. J., Nurius, P. S., Kernic, M. A., and Holt, V. L., "Battered Women's Profiles Associated with Service Help-Seeking efforts: Illuminating Opportunities for Intervention," *Social Work Research*, 29(3), 2005, 137–50.

10. Baker, C., Cook, S., and Norris, H., "Domestic Violence and Housing Problems: A Contextual Analysis of Women's Help Seeking, Received Informal Support, and Formal System Response," *Violence Against Women* 9(7), July 2003, 754–83; Donnelly, D. A., Cook, K. J., Van Ausdale, D., and Foley, L., "White Privilege, Color Blindness, and Services to Battered Women," *Violence Against Women* 11(1), January 2005, 6–37; Gordon, J., "Community Services for Abused Women: A Review of Perceived Usefulness and Efficacy," *Journal of Family Violence* 11(4), 1996, 315–29; Zweig, J., Schlichter, K., and Burt, M., "Assisting Women Victims of Violence Who Experience Multiple Barriers to Services," *Violence Against Women* 8(2), February 2002, 162–80.

CHAPTER 3

1. §18-6101.

2. West Virginia Code §48-27-503.

3. §18.2-60.4.

4. §33.1-346.

5. Miller, N., *What Does Research and Evaluation Say About Domestic Violence Laws? A Compendium of Justice System Laws and Related Research Assessments*, Institute for Law and Justice, December 2005.

6. *Domestic Violence Dashboard Project, 2013 Data*, New York State Office for the Prevention of Domestic Violence, 2014, http://www.opdv.ny.gov/statistics/nydata/2013/nys2013data.pdf, downloaded October 7, 2015.

7. Miller, N., *Domestic Violence: A Review of State Legislation Defining Police and Prosecution Duties and Powers*, Institute for Law and Justice, 33–34, June 2004, http://ilj.org/publications/docs/Domestic_Violence_Legislation.pdf, downloaded October 7, 2015.

8. Norman-Eady, S., "Restraining Orders," *OLR Research Report*, 2005-R-0861, December 8, 2005; Pines, Z., *2004 Caseload Statistics of the Unified Judicial System of Pennsylvania*, December 13, 2005, http://www.aopc.org/Index/Aopc/Research/caseloads/2004report.pdf, downloaded October 7, 2015; Crime Commission Family Violence Sub-Committee, *Protective Orders in Virginia: FY 2003*, State of Virginia, Virginia Crime Commission, November 2003.

9. "Annual Statistical Report for FY 2011," Vermont Judiciary, State of Vermont, 2012.

10. Logan, T., Walker, R., Hoyt, W., and Faragher, T., *The Kentucky Civil Protective Order Study*, U.S. Department of Justice, National Institute of Justice, 2009.

11. Palmer, J., "Hurdles Exist for Women Attempting to Leave Abusive Relationships," *The Oklahoman*, October 27, 2014.

12. Czekalinski, S., Riepenhoff, J., and Wagner, M., "Day One: Repeat Domestic-Violence Offenders Get Off Easy in Ohio," *Columbus Dispatch*, October 25, 2010.

13. DV in the News, *National Bulletin on Domestic Violence Prevention* 21(7), July 2015, 7.

14. *2013 Report on Lesbian, Gay, Bisexual, Transgender, Queer, and HIV-Affected Intimate Partner Violence*, National Coalition of Anti-Violence Programs, October 15, 2014.

15. Jung, T., "Southern Arizona DV Unit Seizes Initiative," *Arizona Daily Star*, January 10, 2015.

16. In Oklahoma, for example, although 7.95 percent of the subsequent murderers had orders taken out against them by their homicide victims, 20.4 percent of them had orders taken out against them by other victims at some point. From *Domestic Violence Homicide in Oklahoma, A Report of the Oklahoma Domestic Violence Fatality Review Board 2013*, on National Domestic Violence Fatality Review Initiative website: http://www.ndvfri.org/about.php, downloaded October 1, 2015.

17. Klein, A., *The Criminal Justice Response to Domestic Violence*, Belmont, CA: Wadsworth Thomson Learning, 2004, 21.

18. Klein, A. et al., *An Exploratory Study of Juvenile Orders of Protection as a Remedy for Dating Violence*, U.S. Department of Justice, National Institute of Justice, April 29, 2013.

19. "New Ala. Law Allows Death in Protection Cases," *Montgomery Advertiser*, May 19, 2014.

20. Carlson, M., Harris, S., and Holden, G., "Protective Orders and Domestic Violence: Risk Factors for Reabuse," *Journal of Family Violence* 14(2), 1999,

205–26; Harrell, A., and Smith, B., "Effects of Restraining Orders on Domestic Violence Victims," in *Do Arrest and Restraining Orders Work?* eds. E. Buzawa and C. Buzawa, Thousand Oaks, CA: Sage, 1996: 214–43; Logan, T., and Walker, R., "Civil Protective Order Effectiveness: Justice or Just a Piece of Paper?" *Violence & Victims* 25(3), 2010, 332–48.

21. There is evidence that judicial demeanor has a lot to do with whether or not victims return to courts for final, longer-lasting protective orders, regardless of the seriousness of the abuse that brought them to court. If victims feel the court is hostile, or bureaucratic and uncaring, they are less likely to return to court for a final order, and more likely to agree with what their abusers have drummed into them—that the orders are just pieces of paper. Ptacek, J., *Battered Women in the Courtroom: The Power of Judicial Responses*, Northeastern Series on Gender, Crime, and Law, Boston, MA: Northeastern University Press, 1999.

22. Proctor, J., "Stalker's Record Was Not Available," *Albuquerque Journal*, March 12, 2010.

CHAPTER 4

1. *Family Violence: A Model State Code* was drafted by the advisory committee of the Conrad N. Hilton Foundation Model Code Project of the Family Violence Project, then headed by Merry Hofford, National Council of Juvenile and Family Court Judges, based in Reno, Nevada. The original publication is undated but was released in 1994. Every year since, the National Council releases a *Family Violence Legislative Update*. As of this writing, it is up to volume 19, covering the 2013 legislative sessions. The National Council website has a section on domestic violence, http://www.ncjfcj.org/our-work/domestic-violence *Family Violence: A Model State Code*, National Council of Juvenile and Family Court Judges, Reno, NV, 1994.

2. Smith, S., "Family Violence, Legislative Update," National Council of Juvenile and Family Court Judges, Reno, NV, 2014.

CHAPTER 5

1. Hart, B., "Impact of VAWA," *National Bulletin on Domestic Violence Prevention* 20(10), October 2014, 4.

2. National Law Enforcement Officers Memorial Fund, http://www.nleomf.org/newsroom/news-releases/law-enforcement-officer.html, downloaded October 5, 2015.

3. Baker, K., *Report on the District of Columbia Police Response to Domestic Violence*, D.C. Coalition Against Domestic Violence and the Women's Law and Public Policy Fellowship Program at Georgetown University Law Center, Nov. 3, 1989, 44.

4. *2013 Domestic Violence, Rape, and Stalking Statistics*, State of Kansas, Kansas Bureau of Investigation, http://www.accesskansas.org/kbi/stats/stats_dvrape. shtml, downloaded October 1, 2105.

5. *Thurman v. Torrington*, 595 F. Supp. (DC Conn. 1994).

6. Canfield. K., "Judge Spares Thurman Prison Time," *Hartford Courant*, January 27, 2000.

7. *Washburn v. City for Federal Way*, No. 87906-1. (WA. S. Ct., October 17, 2013).

8. "Groups Seek Justice for Domestic Violence Survivor and Policy Reforms at Hearing," ACLU Press Release, October 27, 2014.

9. In 2015, the Obama White House appointed Caroline Bettinger-López as the new White House advisor on Violence Against Women in the office of Vice President Joe Biden. Prior to joining the University of Miami Law School (her immediate previous position), she was the deputy director of the Columbia Law School Human Rights Institute where she joined other human rights lawyers representing Jessica (Gonzales) Lenahan against the City of Castle Rock. After the Colorado Supreme Court denied Ms. Lenahan's appeal of the lower court's refusal to find that the police had a duty to enforce the protection order, she assisted the ACLU in seeking justice in the U.S. Supreme Court on Jessica's behalf and leading the legal team that petitioned the Inter-American Commission on Human Rights seeking a declaration that the United States (and by extension, the state of Colorado and the City of Castle Rock) failed in its obligations of "due diligence" in protecting victims of domestic violence and in enforcing the constitutional rights of victims.

10. Robles, Y., "Brighton Firefighter Sentenced, Wife Settles Civil Claim against City," *Denver Post*, March 4, 2015.

11. Sherman, L., Smith, D., Schmidt, J., and Rogan, D., "Crime, Punishment, and Stake in Conformity: Legal and Informal Control of Domestic Violence," *American Sociological Review* 57, 407–17, 1992.

12. Felson, R., Messner, S., Hoskin, A., and Deane, G., "Reasons for Reporting and Not Reporting Domestic Violence to the Police," *Criminology*, 40(3), 2002, 617–48.

13. All these stats are from state public safety or law enforcement websites that are updated annually.

14. Wagner, M., Riepenhoff, J., and Czekalinksi, S., "Repeat Domestic Violence Offenders Get Off Easy," "Some Abusers Repeatedly Violate Restraining Orders, and the Legal System Often Lets Them Get Away with It," and "Repeat Domestic Violence Offenders Demean and Brutalize Victims While Frustrating Judges," *Columbus Dispatch*, October 5, 15, 25, 2015.

15. In February 2015, the *Columbus Dispatch* reported an interesting case where the court upheld the right of a victim to file a civil suit against her abusive husband whom she had divorced and who was sentenced to prison for assaulting her. She explained that unlike the divorce, which was designed to divide the property, or the criminal case, which was prosecuted by the state to prove a crime was committed,

her suit was designed for her to tell her story as she wanted it told in order to make her whole and help her recover from the trauma of her ex-husband's abuse.

16. Family Violence Council, *Report on Domestic Violence for 2013 for Lincoln/Lancaster County*, Lincoln Medical Foundation, Inc., 2014.

17. Diedrich, J., and Barton, G., "Brown Deer Police Failed to Protect Public, Officials Say," *Milwaukee Journal Sentinel*, October 23, 2012.

18. Buzawa, E., Hotaling, G., Klein, A., and Byrnes, J. *Response to Domestic Violence in a Pro-Active Court Setting*, U.S. Department of Justice, National Institute of Justice, NCJ 181427, July 1999.

19. Hirschel, D., and Buzawa, E. "Intimate Partner Violence Offenders Who Flee the Scene Are Likely to Avoid Arrest," *Domestic Violence Report* 20(2), December/January 2015.

20. Ibid.

21. The Baltimore City Domestic Violence Fatality Review Team (BCDVFRT), *2014 Recommendations*, City of Baltimore, undated,http://www.ndvfri.org/reports/maryland/Maryland_BaltimoreCity_AnnualReport_2014.pdf, downloaded October 5, 2015.

22. Messing, J., Campbell, J., Wilson, J., Brown, S., Patchell, B., and Shall, C., *Police Department's Use of the Lethality Assessment Program: A Quasi-Experimental Evaluation*, National Institute of Justice, NCR 247456, 2014, https://www.ncjrs.gov/pdffiles1/nij/grants/247456.pdf, downloaded October 4, 2015.

23. S. Sorenson, Sivitz, E., and Joshi, M. et al., "A Systematic Review of Epidemiology of Nonfatal Strangulation, a Human Rights and Health Concern," *American Journal of Public Health*, 2014.

24. Glass, N. et al., "Non-Fatal Strangulation Is an Important Risk Factor for Homicide of Women," *Journal of Emergency Medicine* 35, 2008.

25. Strack, G., McClane, G., and Hawley, D., "A Review of 300 Attempted Strangulation Cases, Part II: Clinical Evaluation of the Surviving Victim," *Journal of Emergency Medicine* 21(3), 2001, 311.

26. Volochinsky, B., "Obtaining Justice for Victims of Strangulation in Domestic Violence: Evidence Based Prosecution and Strangulation-Specific Training." *Legal Case Review* 4(10), 2012.

27. New York State Division of Criminal Justice Services, "New Strangulation Statute Proving an Effective Tool for Law Enforcement," press release, April 7, 2011.

28. Stern, R., "Maricopa County Attorney's Office Gets Award for New Approach in Strangulation Cases; Prosecutions Way Up," *Phoenix New Times*, June 12, 2013.

29. Domestic Violence Strangulation Project, Maricopa Association of Governments, Azmag.gov, downloaded December 7, 2014.

30. *Update on 2013 Domestic Violence Statistics for King County*, Prosecuting Attorney's Office, King County, April 2, 2014.

31. Simmons, L. "New Strangulation Law Leads to More Than 100 Arrests around Hampton Roads," WGNT, Hampton Roads, VA, January 15, 2013; Hench,

D., "Charges Go Way Up in Maine after Law Change on Strangling," *Portland Press Herald*, September 1, 2014.

32. McKay, K., "A Closer Look at Strangulation Cases," *The Prosecutor* 44(1), January-February 2014.

33. McFarlane, J., Campbell, J., Wilt, S., Sachs, C., Ulrich, Y., and Xu, X., "Stalking and Intimate Partner Femicide," *Homicide Studies*, 3(4), November 1999, 300–16.

34. Mohandie, K., Meloy, J. R., McGowan, M., and Williams, J., "The RECON Typology of Stalking: Reliability and Validity Based upon a Large Sample of North American Stalkers." *Journal of Forensic Sciences* 51, January 2006, 147–55, 153.

35. Logan, T., and Walker, R., "Civil Protective Order Outcomes: Violations and Perceptions of Effectiveness," *Journal of Interpersonal Violence* 24(4), 2009, 675–92; Logan, T., and Walker, R., "Civil Protective Order Effectiveness: Justice or Just a Piece of Paper?" *Violence and Victims*, 25(3), 2010, 332–48.

36. S. Catalano, *Stalking Victims in the United States – Revised*, U.S. Department of Justice, Bureau of Justice Statistic, NCJ 224527, September 2012.

37. Kane, R., "Police Responses to Restraining Orders in Domestic Violence Incidents: Identifying the Custody-Threshold Thesis," *Criminal Justice and Behavior*, vol. 27, no. 2, 2000, 561.

38. Klein, A., Salomon, A., Huntington, N., Dubois, J., and Long, D., *Statewide Study of Stalking and Its Criminal Justice Response*, U.S. Department of Justice, National Institute of Justice NCJ 228354, May 2009.

39. Bufkin, S., "Rep. Katherine Clark Wants Online Threats Against Women to be Taken Seriously by the Feds," *Bustle*, March 11, 2015.

40. Brewster, M., "Legal Help—Seeking Experiences of Former Intimate-Stalking Victims," *Criminal Justice Policy Review* 12(2), June 2001, 91–112; Jasinski, J., and Mustaine, E., "Police Response to Physical Assault and Stalking Victimization: A Comparison of Influential Factors," *American Journal of Criminal Justice* 26(1), 2001, 23–41.

41. Logan, T., and Walker, R., "Civil Protective Order Effectiveness: Justice or Just a Piece of Paper?" *Violence and Victims* 25(3), 2010, 332–48.

42. Caponera, B., *Incidence and Nature of Domestic Violence In New Mexico VIII: An Analysis of 2007 Data From The New Mexico Interpersonal Violence Data Central Repository*, Office of Injury Prevention, Injury and Behavioral Epidemiology Bureau, Epidemiology and Response Division, New Mexico Department of Health, July 2008.

43. Klein, A., Salomon, A., Huntington, N., Dubois, J., and Long, D. *Statewide Study of Stalking and Its Criminal Justice Response*, U.S. Department of Justice, National Institute of Justice, NCJ 228354, May 2009.

44. Tjaden, P., and Thoennes, N., *Stalking: Its Role in Serious Domestic Violence Cases*, Final Report for National Institute of Justice, U.S. Department of Justice, National Institute of Justice, NCJ 187346, January 2001.

45. Colo. Rev. Stat. Ann. §18-9-111(4)(a) (2005).

46. Logan, T., Walker, R., Hoyt, W., and Faragher, T., *The Kentucky Civil Protective Order Study: A Rural and Urban Multiple Perspective Study of Protective Order Violation Consequences, Responses & Costs*, Final Report for National Institute of Justice, U.S. Department of Justice, National Institute of Justice, 2009.

47. Banner, A., "Failure to Protect Laws Punish Victims of Domestic Violence," *Huffington Post*, December 4, 2014.

48. Hirschel, J. D., Buzawa, E., Pattavina, A., Faggiani, D., and Reuland. M., *Explaining the Prevalence, Context, and Consequences of Dual Arrest in Intimate Partner Cases*, Final Report for National Institute of Justice, U.S. Department of Justice, National Institute of Justice, NCJ 218355, April 2007.

49. Unlike many straight, male pro ball players who get infamously minimal punishments on the court, field, or rink for their domestic violence—not to mention in the criminal courts—Brittney Griner and Glory Johnson were both suspended for seven WNBA games without pay.

50. Amnesty International, *Stonewalled—Still Demanding Respect: Police Abuses Against Lesbian, Gay, Bisexual and Transgender People in the USA*, London: Amnesty International Publications, 2006.

51. Fawcett, J., *Up to Us: Lessons Learned and Goals for Change After Thirteen Years of the Washington State Domestic Violence Fatality Review*, Washington State Coalition Against Domestic Violence, December 2010.

52. "Officer Defends Giving Boy Back to Dahmer," *New York Times*, August 25, 1991.

53. Amnesty International, *Stonewalled—Still Demanding Respect: Police Abuses Against Lesbian, Gay, Bisexual and Transgender People in the USA*, Amnesty International Publications, 2006.

54. Finneran, C., and Stephenson, R., "Intimate Partner Violence Among Men Who Have Sex with Men: A Systematic Review," *Trauma Violence Abuse 14*, 2013, 168–85.

55. Chibbaro Jr., L., "D.C. Police Officers Save Life of Lesbian Domestic Violence Victim," *Washington Blade*, September 17, 2014.

56. Amnesty International, *Stonewalled—Still Demanding Respect: Police Abuses Against Lesbian, Gay, Bisexual and Transgender People in the USA*, Amnesty International Publications, 2006.

CHAPTER 6

1. Rakoff, J., "Why Innocent People Plead Guilty," *New York Review of Books*, November 20, 2014.

2. See, e.g., Klein, A., and Tobin, T., "Longitudinal Study of Arrested Batterers, 1995-2005: Career Criminals," *Violence Against Women 14(2)*, February 2008, 136–57; Hartley, C., and Frohmann, L., *Cook County Target Abuser Call (TAC): An Evaluation of a Specialized Domestic Violence Court*, Final Report for National

Institute of Justice, U.S. Department of Justice, National Institute of Justice, NCJ 202944, August 2003; Labriola, M., Rempel, M., and Davis, R., *Testing the Effectiveness of Batterer Programs and Judicial Monitoring: Results From a Randomized Trial at the Bronx Misdemeanor Domestic Violence Court*, Final Report for National Institute of Justice, New York: Center for Court Innovation, National Institute of Justice, November 2005.

3. Nunley, K., "Kern County D.A. Plans Domestic Violence Diversion Program," KBAK, September 22, 2014.

4. Attorney General's Task Force on Local Criminal Justice Response to Domestic Violence, *Keeping the Promise-Victim Safety and Batterer Accountability*, California, Office of the Attorney General, July 2005.

5. Domestic Violence Crisis Center, "A Victim Centered Perspective on CT's Diversionary Practice," *Verve* 2(3), March 30, 2012.

6. Domestic Violence Coordinating Council, "Examining CT's Domestic Violence Courts," *Verve* 2(4), April 2012.

7. Ventura, L., and Davis, G., "Domestic Violence: Court Case Conviction and Recidivism," in *Violence Against Women* 11(2), February 2005, 255–77.

8. Reed, E., "Toledo Domestic Violence Report Released," NBC 24, May 5, 2012.

9. Czekalinski, S., Riepenhoff, J., and Wagner, M., "Day One: Repeat Domestic-Violence Offenders Get Off Easy in Ohio," *Columbus Dispatch*, October 25, 2010.

10. Klein, A., "DV Arrest and Conviction Rates May Be Less Than Meets the Eye," *National Bulletin on Domestic Violence Prevention*, 19(10), October 2013.

11. *Georgia Domestic Violence Fatality Review Project 10 Annual Report*, Georgia Commission on Family Violence, Georgia Coalition Against Domestic Violence, March 2013.

12. Martin, A., "Day 5: Special Report on Domestic Violence: State Stuck Without Victims' Help," *Galesburg Register-Mail*, May 21, 2015.

13. Bocko, S., Cicchetti, C., Lempicki, L., and Powell, A., *Restraining Order Violations, Corrective Programming and Recidivism*, Massachusetts Trial Court, Office of the Commissioner of Probation, 2004.

14. Hirschel, J. D. et al., *Explaining the Prevalence, Context, and Consequences of Dual Arrest in Intimate Partner Cases*, Final Report for National Institute of Justice, U.S. Department of Justice, National Institute of Justice, NCJ 218355, April 2007.

15. Garner, J., and C. Maxwell, C., *Prosecution and Conviction Rates for Intimate Partner Violence*, Shepherdstown, WV: Joint Centers for Justice Studies, 2008, 49.

16. Smith, E., and Farole, D., *Profile of Intimate Partner Violence Cases in Large Urban Counties*, Special Report, U.S. Department of Justice, Bureau of Justice Statistics, NCJ 228193, 2009.

17. Peak, C., "San Francisco Trails Bay Area in Domestic Violence Prosecutions," *San Francisco Public Press*, September 24, 2012.

18. Bradberry, C., and McManus, R., *Criminal Domestic Violence (CDV) in South Carolina: An Examination of the Effects of ACT 166 of 2005*, Report by the Office of Research and Statistics of the Budget and Control Board to the Department of Public Safety, South Carolina, November 2007.

19. Hirschel, J. et al., *Explaining the Prevalence, Context, and Consequences of Dual Arrest in Intimate Partner Cases*, Final Report for National Institute of Justice, U.S. Department of Justice, National Institute of Justice, NCJ 218355, April 2007.

20. Ibid.

21. Brown, J., "Domestic Violence Habitual Offender Law Languishes in Colorado," *Denver Post*, May 17, 2015.

22. Chibbaro Jr., L., "Lesbian Gets 8 Years in D.C. Domestic Violence Case," *Washington Blade*, November 23, 2014.

23. *2013 Report on Lesbian, Gay, Bisexual, Transgender, Queer, and HIV-Affected Intimate Partner Violence*, National Coalition of Anti-Violence Programs, October 15, 2014.

24. Charing, S., "Northeast Baltimore Suffers Another Gay Murder," *Gay Life*, November 1, 2014; Cousins, J., "Body Found in Baltimore Home; Man Arrested," WBALTV, October 13, 2014; Hager, J., "Baltimore City Police Make Arrests in Two Murders," ABC, WMAR Baltimore, October 13, 2014.

25. Shwayder, M., "A Same-Sex Domestic Violence Epidemic Is Silent," *The Atlantic*, November 5, 2013.

26. Amnesty International, *Stonewalled—Still Demanding Respect: Police Abuses Against Lesbian, Gay, Bisexual and Transgender People in the USA*, Amnesty International Publications, 2006.

27. Klein, A., Centerbar, D., Koller, S., and Klein, J., *Impact of Differential Sentencing Severity for Domestic Violence Offenses and All Other Offenses Over Abusers' Life Spans*, U.S. Department of Justice, National Institute of Justice, September 2013.

28. George, T., *Domestic Violence Sentencing Conditions and Recidivism*, Olympia, WA: Washington State Center for Court Research, Administrative Office of the Courts, 2012.

29. Barchenger, S., "Nashville DA's Domestic Violence Team Seizes First Gun," *The Tennessean*, May 12, 2015.

30. Smith, B., Davis, R., Nickles, L., and Davies, H., *Evaluation of Efforts to Implement No-Drop Policies: Two Central Values in Conflict*, Final Report for National Institute of Justice, U.S. Department of Justice, National Institute of Justice, NCJ 187772, March 2001.

31. Maxwell, C., Robinson, A., and Klein, A., "The Prosecution of Domestic Violence Across Time," in E. Stark and E. Buzawa, eds., *Violence Against Women in Families and Relationships, Vol III, Criminal Justice and the Law*, Santa Barbara, CA: Praeger, 2009, 69–91.

32. Hartley, C., and Frohmann, L., *Cook County Target Abuser Call (TAC): An Evaluation of a Specialized Domestic Violence Court*, Final Report for National Institute of Justice, U.S. Department of Justice, National Institute of Justice, NCJ 202944, August 2003.

33. Harrell, A., Schaffer, M., DeStefano, C., and Castro, J., *The Evaluation of Milwaukee's Judicial Oversight Demonstration*, Final Report for National Institute of Justice, U.S. Department of Justice, National Institute of Justice and The Urban Institute, April 2006.

34. "DA Almost Eliminates DV Dismissals," *National Bulletin on Domestic Violence Prevention* 16(12) December 2010.

35. Family Violence Council, *Report on Domestic Violence for 2015 for Lincoln/ Lancaster County*, Lincoln Medical Foundation, Inc., 2015.

36. Peterson, R., "Evaluation of Brooklyn's video statement program for DV cases," *Research in Brief, No. 29*, New York City Criminal Justice Agency, May 2012,

37. Newmark, L., Rempel, M., Diffily, K., and Kane, K., *Specialized Felony Domestic Violence Courts: Lessons in Implementation and Impacts of the Kings County Experience*, Urban Institute, Washington, D.C., 2001.

38. Davis, D., "Updated: Minnesota Cities Apply to Make Police Body Camera Videos Private," *Grand Forks Herald*, September 15, 2015.

39. Klein, A., *The Criminal Justice Response to Domestic Violence*, Belmont, CA: Wadsworth Thomson Learning, 2004, 137–39.

40. Stevenson, P., and Bileski, M., *Domestic Violence Arrest and Case Processing Data: An Analysis of the Information in Arizona's Computerized Criminal History Record System*, Arizona Criminal Justice Commission, 2013.

41. Belknap, J., Graham, D., Hartman, J., Lippen, V., Allen, G., and Sutherland, J., *Factors Related to Domestic Violence Court Dispositions in a Large Urban Area: The Role of Victim/Witness Reluctance and Other Variables*, Executive Summary for National Institute of Justice, U.S. Department of Justice, National Institute of Justice, NCJ 184112, August 2002; Hirschel, J., and Hutchison, I., "The Relative Effects of Offense, Offender, and Victim Variables on the Decision to Prosecute Domestic Violence Cases," *Violence Against Women* 7(1), January 2001, 46–59.

42. *Pretrial Innovations: Supporting Safety and Case Integrity*, in *Enhancing Responses to Domestic Violence, Promising Practices from the Judicial Oversight Demonstration Initiative*, Office on Violence Against Women, National Institute of Justice, Urban Institute, and Vera Institute of Justice, 2006.

43. Buzawa, E., Hotaling, G., Klein, A., and Byrnes, J., *Response to Domestic Violence in a Pro-Active Court Setting*, Final Report for National Institute of Justice, U.S. Department of Justice, National Institute of Justice, NCJ 181427, July 1999; Newmark, L. et al., *Specialized Felony Domestic Violence Court: Lessons on Implementation and Impacts from the Kings County Experience*, Final Report for National Institute of Justice, U.S. Department of Justice, National Institute of Justice, NCJ 191861, 199723, October 2001 and 2004.

44. Woods, D., "Vineland Domestic Violence Suspect Released and Then Arrested Again, Police Say," *South Jersey Times*, January 14, 2015.

45. "Milford Man Held on $1.1 Million Bond on Domestic Violence Charges," *Milford Mirror*, January 19, 2015.

46. McNamara. P., and Jung, Y., "Logistical Challenges Abound, but Task Force Is Tackling Them," *Arizona Daily Star*, Tucson, AZ, January 11, 2015.

47. In June 2015, the charges against Chase were dismissed. The prosecutors declared that the victim had been inconsistent under oath. A witness, for example, testified that the victim had stumbled out of the apartment shared with Chase, but the victim had said that Chase dragged her out. Subsequently, Chase filed a federal lawsuit against the Metro government and a dozen officers involved in his arrest for violating his civil rights.

48. Smith, B. et al., *Evaluation of Efforts to Implement No-Drop Policies: Two Central Values in Conflict*, Final Report for National Institute of Justice, U.S. Department of Justice, National Institute of Justice, NCJ 187772, March 2001.

49. Peterson, R., "Evaluation of Brooklyn's Video Statement Program for DV Cases," *Research in Brief*, no. 29, p. 3, New York City Criminal Justice Agency, May 2012.

50. *Keeping the Promise: Victim Safety and Batterer Accountability*, Report to the California Attorney General from the Task Force on Local Criminal Justice Response to Domestic Violence, June 2005.

51. Smith, B. et al., *Evaluation of Efforts to Implement No-Drop Policies: Two Central Values in Conflict*, Final Report for National Institute of Justice, U.S. Department of Justice, National Institute of Justice, NCJ 187772, March 2001.

CHAPTER 7

1. *Keeping the Promise: Victim Safety and Batterer Accountability*, Report to the California Attorney General from the Task Force on Local Criminal Justice Response to Domestic Violence, June 2005.

2. Klein, A., Centerbar, D., Keller, S., and Klein, J., *Impact of Differential Sentencing Severity for Domestic Violence Offenses and All Other Offenses Over Abusers' Life Spans*, U.S. Department of Justice, National Institute of Justice, September 2013.

3. Smith, E., and Farole, D., *Profile of Intimate Partner Violence Cases in Large Urban Counties*, Special Report, Bureau of Justice Statistics, NCJ 228193, October 2009.

4. *Domestic Violence Incident Report (DAIR) for the Period of January 1, 2012– December 31, 2012*, Wisconsin Department of Justice, Office of Crime Victim Services.

5. Prather, S., "Domestic Violence Convictions Up Sharply in Minnesota," *Star Tribune*, August 15, 2015.

6. *Domestic Violence Fatality Review Commission Report*, State of Vermont, 2014.

7. George, T., *Domestic Violence Sentencing Conditions and Recidivism*, Olympia, WA: Washington State Center for Court Research, Administrative Office of the Courts, 2012.

8. Newmark, L., Rempel, M., Diffily, K., and Kane, K., *Specialized Felony Domestic Violence Courts: Lessons in Implementation and Impacts of the Kings County Experience*, Final Report for National Institute of Justice, U.S. Department of Justice, National Institute of Justice, NCJ 191861, 199723, October 2001 and 2004.

9. Smith, E., Durose, M., and Langan, P., *State Court Processing of Domestic Violence Cases*, Special Report, U.S. Department of Justice, Bureau of Justice Statistic, NCJ 214993, 2008.

10. Klein, A., Centerbar, D., Keller, S., and Klein, J., *Impact of Differential Sentencing Severity for Domestic Violence Offenses and All Other Offenses Over Abusers' Life Spans*, Final Report for National Institute of Justice, U.S. Department of Justice, National Institute of Justice, September 2013.

11. Pfaff, J., "The Causes of Growth in Prison Admissions and Populations," *Social Science Research Network*, January 23, 2012; Ghandnoosh, N., *Black Lives Matter: Eliminating Racial Inequity in the Criminal Justice System*, The Sentencing Project, 2015.

12. "New Michigan DV Court to Save Third-Time Felony Abusers from Jail," *National Bulletin on Domestic Violence Prevention* 20(9), September 2014, 8.

13. Petroski, W., "Branstad Wants Get-Tough Legislation on Domestic Violence," *The Des Moines Register*, January 14, 2015.

14. Parole is similar to probation but applies to prisoners who are released early by parole boards or other paroling authorities. If they fail their parole, they are returned to prison to serve the remainder of their sentences. The state or county administers parole agencies, while many probation departments are administered by the courts. In some states, probation and parole are combined and may be part of a larger department of corrections.

15. Klein, A., Wilson, D., Crowe, A., and DeMichele, M., *Evaluation of the Rhode Island Probation Specialized Domestic Violence Supervision Unit*, Final Report for National Institute of Justice, U.S. Department of Justice, National Institute of Justice, March 31, 2005.

16. Harrell, A., Castro, J., Newmark, L., and Vishers, C., *Final Report on the Evaluation of the Judicial Oversight Demonstration*, Executive Summary for National Institute of Justice, U.S. Department of Justice, National Institute of Justice, NCJ 219386, 2007.

17. Mederos, F., "Changing Our Visions of Intervention: The Evolution of Programs for Physically Abusive Men," in E. Aldarondo and F. Mederos, eds., *Programs for Men Who Batter*, Civil Research Institute, Kingston, NJ, 2002, 1–26.

18. Klein, A., and Tobin, T., "Longitudinal Study of Arrested Batterers, 1995-2005: Career Criminals," *Violence Against Women*, 14(2), February 2008, 136–57.

19. This is not quite as low as it appears. If it can be assumed that 40 percent of the referred abusers are not going to reabuse anyway, and 30 percent are going to reabuse no matter what, that means only 30 percent of the referred abusers may or may not be influenced by the treatment. So a 5 percent treatment effect for this population may actually mean a 15 percent treatment effect for those referred abusers who would otherwise do it again but are not beyond hope. See, e.g., Babcock, J., Green, C., and Robie, C., "Does Batterers' Treatment Work? A Meta-Analytic Review of Domestic Violence Treatment," *Clinical Psychology Review* 23(8), January 2004, 1023–53.

20. See, e.g., Zador, P., "Statistical Evaluation of the Effectiveness of 'Alcohol Safety Action Projects'," *Accident Analysis & Prevention* 8(1), February 1976, 61–66.

21. Davis, R., Taylor, B., and Maxwell, C., *Does Batterer Treatment Reduce Violence? A Randomized Experiment in Brooklyn*, Final Report for National Institute of Justice, U.S. Department of Justice, National Institute of Justice, NCJ 180772, January 2000.

22. Block, C., *Risk Factors for Death or Life-Threatening Injury for Abused Women in Chicago*, Final Report for National Institute of Justice, U.S. Department of Justice, National Institute of Justice, NCJ 199732, 2004.

CHAPTER 8

1. Hemenway, D., and Richardson, E., "Homicide, Suicide, and Unintentional Firearm Fatalities: Comparing the United States with Other High-Income Countries," *Journal of Trauma* 70, 2011, 238–42.

2. Everytown for Gun Safety, *Analysis of Recent Mass Shootings*, July 2014, http://bit.ly/1mqcMR8, downloaded October 8, 2015.

3. Adam, S., *Serial Batterers*, Commonwealth of Massachusetts, Office of the Commissioner of Probation, Boston, MA, 1999.

4. Campbell, J. et al., "Assessing Risk Factors for Intimate Partner Homicide," *NIJ Journal* 250, 2003, 14–19.

5. Adams, D., *Why Do They Kill? Men Who Murder Their Intimate Partners*, Nashville, TN: Vanderbilt University Press, 2007.

6. Sorenson S., and Wiebe, D., "Weapons in the Lives of Battered Women," *American Journal of Public Health* 94(8), 2004, 1412–17; Rothman, E. F., Hemenway, D., Miller, M., and Azrael, D., "Batterers' Use of Guns to Threaten Intimate Partners," *Journal of the American Medical Women's Association* 60, 2005, 62–68.

7. "These Abusers Aren't Allowed to Own Guns. So Why Aren't States Removing Them?" *Huffington Post*, October 14, 2014.

8. Karberg, J., Frandsen, R., Durso, J., and Lee, A., *Background Checks for Firearm Transfers, 2012 - Statistical Tables*, U.S. Department of Justice, Bureau of Justice Statistics, NCJ 247815, December 2014.

9. Brandl, S., *An Evaluation of the Firearm Surrender Pilot in Wisconsin: Final Report*, University of Wisconsin-Milwaukee, March 20, 2012.

10. *Crime Gun Trace Reports* (1999, 2000, 2002), Washington, D.C.: Bureau of Alcohol, Tobacco and Firearms, 2000; Wintemute G., Romero M., Wright M., and Grassel K., "The Life Cycle of Crime Guns: A Description Based on Guns Recovered from Young People in California," *Annual of Emergency Medicine* 43(6), 2004, 733–42.

11. Frandsen, R., *Enforcement of the Brady Act, 2010: Federal and State Investigations and Prosecutions of Firearm Applicants Denied by a NICS Check in 2010*, U.S. Department of Justice, National Institute of Justice, NCJ 239272, August 2012, 6.

12. *Survey of State Criminal History Information Systems, 2010*, Washington, D.C.: Bureau of Justice Statistics, 2010.

13. Gerney, A., and Parsons, C., "How Gun Violence Affects Women and Four Policy Solutions to Better Protect Them," *Domestic Violence Report* 20(1), October/November 2014.

14. *A Census of Domestic Violence Gun Homicides in Arizona*, Everytown for Gun Safety and the Arizona Coalition to End Sexual & Domestic Violence, undated, http://everytown.org/documents/2015/05/census-of-domestic-violence-gun-homicides-in-az.pdf, downloaded October 5, 2015.

15. McFarlane, J. et al., "Stalking and Intimate Partner Femicide," *Homicide Studies* 3(4), November 1999, 300–316.

16. FindLaw, "Ocean Springs Woman Took Action to Keep Ex-Boyfriend Away Before Shooting," available at http://legalpronews.findlaw.com/article/6c15d1aaf9 75224ac1851c816c87d7b6#.U4iInybD-71, last accessed June 2014; Campbell, A., "Michelle Hahn Gunned Down at Walmart, Allegedly by Stalker Ex-Boyfriend Charles Fickentsher," *Huffington Post*, November 14, 2012.

17. Milkovits, A., "In R.I. Domestic Violence Cases, Suspects Often Keep Guns," *Providence Journal*, June 16, 2015.

18. Mervosh, S., "Domestic Abusers Now Required to Hand Over Firearms in Dallas County," *The Dallas Morning News*, May 5, 2015.

19. Bernstein, M., "Lax Enforcement Leaves Guns in Hands of Oregon Abusers," *The Oregonian*, November 15, 2015.

20. Vigdor, E., and Mercy, J., "Do Laws Restricting Access to Firearms by Domestic Violence Offenders Prevent Intimate Partner Homicide?" *Evaluation Review* 30(3), June 2006, 313–46.

21. Wintemute, G. et al., "Identifying Armed Respondents to Domestic Violence Restraining Orders and Recovering Their Firearms: Process Evaluation of an Initiative in California," *American Journal of Public Health*, 2013.

22. Klein, A., *Enforcing Domestic Violence Firearm Prohibitions, A Report on Promising Practices*, Office on Violence Against Women and National Center on Full Faith and Credit, September, 2006.

23. Ibid.

24. Ibid.

25. Ibid.

26. *In re: The Seizure of Weapons from Apurba Nath*, Docket No. A–4645–11T4, Decided: March 4, 2014.

27. Gerney, A., and Parsons, C., "How Gun Violence Affects Women and Four Policy Solutions to Better Protect Them," *Domestic Violence Report* 20(1), October/November 2014; see also Frandsen, R., *Enforcement of the Brady Act, 2009: Federal and state investigations and prosecutions of firearm applicants denied by a NICS Check in 2009*, U.S. Department of Justice, National Institute of Justice, NCJ 234173, April 2011; Kertscher, T., "U.S. Files Criminal Charges in Fraction of Gun Denial Cases, Mayors Against Illegal Guns Says," *Politifact*, February 3, 2013.

28. La. Rev. Stat. Ann §§9:361-9:366B.

29. Miller, A., "Colorado Passes Milestone Child Custody Law Reform," *Domestic Violence Report*, 19(1), October/November 2013.

30. Menzel, M., "Case Examines Domestic Violence," *Tallahassee Democrat*, February 14, 2015.

31. Bancroft, L., and Silverman, J., *The Batterer as Parent, Addressing the Impact of Domestic Violence on Family Dynamics*, Thousand Oaks, CA: Sage, 2002.

32. Gender Bias Study Committee, Gender Bias Study of the Court System in Massachusetts, *New England Law Review* 24(3), 1990, 745–856.

33. Harway, M., and Hansen, M., "Therapist Conceptions of Family Violence," in M. Harway and M. Hansen, eds., *Battering and Family Therapy: A Feminist Perspective*, Newbury Park, CA: Sage, 1993, 42–53; Gondolf, E., *Assessing Woman Battering in Mental Health Services*, Thousand Oaks, CA: Sage, 1999.

34. Horvath, L., Logan, T., and Walker, R., "Child Custody Cases: A Content Analysis of Evaluation Practices," *Professional Psychology: Research and Practice* 33(6), 2002, 557–65.

35. Campbell, J., "Nursing Assessment for Risk of Homicide with Battered Women," *Advances in Nursing Science* 8(4), 36–51; Campbell, J. et al., "Risk Factors for Femicide in Abusive Relationships: Results from a Multi-Site Case Control Study," *American Journal of Public Health*, 2003, 1089–97.

36. *Maryland Annual Report Summary, January–December 2014*, Lethality Assessment Program: Maryland Model (LAP), http://mnadv.org/_mnadvWeb/wp-content/uploads/2015/09/2014-LAP-Maryland-Annual-Report-Summary.pdf, downloaded October 7, 2015.

37. Messing, J. et al., *Police Department's Use of the Lethality Assessment Program: A Quasi-Experimental Evaluation*, U.S. Department of Justice, National Institute of Justice, 2004, 4.

38. Jeltsen, M., "This Is How a Domestic Violence Victim Falls Through the Cracks," *Huffington Post*, June 16, 2014, updated March 27, 2015.

39. Tucker, J., "Can Police Prevent Domestic Violence Simply by Telling Offenders to Stop?" *Indy Weekly*, November 13, 2013; see also Broussard, R., "EBR Prosecutors Take New Tack in Domestic Violence Prosecutions," *The Advocate*, August 18, 2014; Weaver, E., "Enough Is Enough, Agencies Unite Against Domestic Violence," *Times-News*, January, 16, 2015.

40. Tucker, J., "Can Police Prevent Domestic Violence Simply by Telling Offenders to Stop?" *Indy Weekly*, November 13, 2013.

41. Friday, P., Lord, V., Exum, M., and Hartman, J., *Evaluating the Impact of a Specialized Domestic Violence Police Unit*, Final Report for National Institute of Justice, U.S. Department of Justice, National Institute of Justice, NCJ 215916, May 2006.

42. "NYC Policing DV: Is Success Miracle or Fluke?" *National Bulletin on Domestic Violence Prevention* 16(9), September 2010, 1.

43. Klein, A., *Practical Implications of Current Domestic Violence Research: For Law Enforcement, Prosecutors and Judges*, Special Report, U.S. Department of Justice, National Institute of Justice, June 2009.

44. Weichselbaum, S., "Exclusive: New NYPD Policing Plan Will Change How Cops Handle Domestic Violence Crimes across Most of Manhattan," *New York Daily News*, April 8, 2014.

45. Gipson, C., *History of the Domestic Violence Division Metro Nashville Police Department: A Decade of Services to Victims of Family Violence*, Metro Nashville Police Department, March 2004.

46. Spaid, E., "How Police Stalk Stalkers in Nashville," *Christian Science Monitor*, November 10, 1995.

47. Haas, B., and Rau, N., "Nashville Police Drop Thousands of Domestic Violence Cases," *The Tennessean*, August 10, 2010; Conte, A., "Progress Against Domestic Violence Has Come Slowly," *The Tennessean*, November 3, 2014.

48. Pleasant, J., "Nashville Adds Domestic Violence Coordinator to Better Protect Victims," WKRN-TV, September 24, 2013; "Nashville Opens Advocacy Center for Domestic Violence Victims," Nashville.gov, posted September 25, 2014.

49. Green, E., "Now Understanding the Neurobiology of Trauma Helps Portland Police Work with Domestic Violence Survivors," *Street Roots News*, January 20, 2015.

50. Garner, J., and Maxwell, C., *Prosecution and Conviction Rates for Intimate Partner Violence*, Shepherdstown, WV: Joint Centers for Justice Studies, 2008, 49.

51. Pfaff, J., "The Causes of Growth in Prison Admissions and Populations," *Social Science Research Network*, January 23, 2012; see also Ghandnoosh, N., *Black Lives Matter, Eliminating Racial Inequity in the Criminal Justice System*, The Sentencing Project, 2015.

52. Levine, H., Siegel, L., and Sayegh, G., "One Million Police Hours: Making 440,000 Marijuana Possession Arrests in New York City, 2002–2012," *Drug Policy Alliance and Marijuana Arrest Research Project*, New York City, NY, March 2013, 2.

53. Hickman, M., and Reaves, B., *Sheriffs' Offices 2003*, U.S. Department of Justice, Bureau of Justice Statistics, NCJ 211361, May 2006, 15.

54. *New York State Asset Forfeiture 2012 Annual Report*, NY State Division of Criminal Justice Services, Albany, New York.

55. "Seattle Attempt to Keep Addicts Out of Jail in Study," Associated Press, April 8, 2015.

BIBLIOGRAPHY

A Census of Domestic Violence Gun Homicides in Arizona, Everytown for Gun Safety and the Arizona Coalition to End Sexual & Domestic Violence, undated, http://everytown.org/documents/2015/05/census-of-domestic-violence-gun-homicides-in-az.pdf, downloaded October 5, 2015.

Adam, S. *Serial Batterers*, Commonwealth of Massachusetts, Office of the Commissioner of Probation, Boston, MA, 1999.

Adams, D., *Why Do They Kill? Men Who Murder Their Intimate Partners*, Nashville, TN, Vanderbilt University Press, 2007.

Amnesty International, *Stonewalled—Still Demanding Respect: Police Abuses Against Lesbian, Gay, Bisexual and Transgender People in the USA*, Amnesty International Publications, 2006.

Analysis of Recent Mass Shootings, Everytown for Gun Safety, July 2014, http://bit.ly/1mqcMR8, downloaded October 8, 2015.

Anderson, A., "Cardeilhac Jury Watches Strangulation Video, Learns About Choke Holds," *KOTA Territory News*, November 18, 2014.

Annual Statistical Report for FY 2011, Vermont Judiciary, State of Vermont, 2012.

Attorney General Task Force on Local Criminal Justice Response to Domestic Violence, *Keeping the Promise: Victim Safety and Batterer Accountability*, California, Office of the Attorney General, July 2005.

Babcock, J., Green, C., and Robie, C., "Does Batterers' Treatment Work? A Meta-Analytic Review of Domestic Violence Treatment," *Clinical Psychology Review* 23(8), January 2004, 1023–53.

Baker, C., Cook, S., and Norris, F., "Domestic Violence and Housing Problems: A Contextual Analysis of Women's Help Seeking, Received Informal Support, and Formal System Response," *Violence Against Women* 9(7), July 2003, 754–83.

Baker, K., *Report on District of Columbia Police Response to Domestic Violence*, D.C. Coalition Against Domestic Violence and the Women's Law and Public Policy Fellowship Program at Georgetown University Law Center, November 3, 1989, 44.

Baltimore City Domestic Violence Fatality Review Team (BCDVFRT), *2014 Recommendations*, City of Baltimore, undated, http://www.ndvfri.org/reports/maryland/Maryland_BaltimoreCity_AnnualReport_2014.pdf, downloaded October 5, 2015.

Bancroft, L., and Silverman, J., *The Batterer as Parent: Addressing the Impact of Domestic Violence on Family Dynamics*, Thousand Oaks, CA: Sage, 2002.

Banner, A., "Failure to Protect Laws Punish Victims of Domestic Violence," *Huffington Post*, December 4, 2014.

Barchenger, S., "Nashville DA's Domestic Violence Team Seizes First Gun." *The Tennessean*, May 12, 2015.

Bartos, L., "Contra Costa County Aims to Stop Domestic Violence Homicides Before They Happen," *California Health Report*, February 9, 2015.

Belknap, J., Graham, D., Hartman, J., Lippen, V., Allen, G., and Sutherland, J., *Factors Related to Domestic Violence Court Dispositions in a Large Urban Area: The Role of Victim/Witness Reluctance and Other Variables*, Executive Summary for National Institute of Justice, U.S. Department of Justice, National Institute of Justice, NCJ 184112, August 2002.

Berk, R., Newton, P., and Berk, S. "What a Difference a Day Makes: An Empirical Study of the Impact of Shelters for Battered Women." *Journal of Marriage and the Family* 48, 1986, 481–90.

Bernstein, M., "Lax Enforcement Leaves Guns in Hands of Oregon Abusers," *The Oregonian*, November 15, 2015.

Besonen, J., "A New Crime, But Convictions Are Elusive," *New York Times*, February 16, 2013, downloaded October 20, 2014.

Bishop, T., "45 Year Sentence Sets Precedent for Future Domestic Violence Rulings," *Fox 21 News*, May 27, 2015.

Block, C., *Risk Factors for Death or Life-Threatening Injury for Abused Women in Chicago*, Final Report for National Institute of Justice, U.S. Department of Justice, National Institute of Justice, NCJ 199732, 2004.

Bocko, S., Cicchetti, C., Lempicki, L., and Powell, A., *Restraining Order Violators, Corrective Programming and Recidivism*, Massachusetts Trial Court, Office of the Commissioner of Probation, November 2004.

Bradberry, C., and McManus, R., *Criminal Domestic Violence (CDV) in South Carolina: An Examination of the Effects of ACT 166 of 2005*, Report by the Office of Research and Statistics of the Budget and Control Board to the Department of Public Safety, South Carolina, November 2007.

Brandl, S., *An Evaluation of the Firearm Surrender Pilot Project in Wisconsin: Final Report*, University of Wisconsin-Milwaukee, March 20, 2012.

Brewster, M., "Legal Help—Seeking Experiences of Former Intimate-Stalking Victims," *Criminal Justice Policy Review* 12(2), June 2001, 91–112.

Broussard, R., "EBR Prosecutors Take New Tack in Domestic Violence Prosecutions," *The Advocate*, August 18, 2014.

Brown, J., "Domestic Violence Habitual Offender Law Languishes in Colorado," *Denver Post*, May 17, 2015.

Bufkin S., "Rep. Katherine Clark Wants Online Threats Against Women to be Taken Seriously by the Feds," *Bustle*, March 11, 2015.

Buzawa, E., Hotaling, G., Klein, A., and Byrnes, J., *Response to Domestic Violence in a Pro-Active Court Setting*, Final Report for National Institute of Justice, U.S. Department of Justice, National Institute of Justice, NCJ 181427, July 1999.

Bybee, D., and Sullivan, C., "Predicting Re-Victimization of Battered Women Three Years After Exiting a Shelter Program," *American Journal of Community Psychology* 36(1-2), September 2005, 85–96.

Campbell, A., "Michelle Hahn Gunned Down at Walmart, Allegedly by Stalker Ex-Boyfriend Charles Fickentsher," *Huffington Post*, November 14, 2012.

Campbell, J., "Nursing Assessment for Risk of Homicide with Battered Women," *Advances in Nursing Science* 8(4), 36–51.

Campbell, J. et al., "Assessing Risk Factors for Intimate Partner Homicide," *NIJ Journal* 250, 2003, 14–19.

Campbell, J. et al., "Risk Factors for Femicide in Abusive Relationships: Results from a Multi-Site Case Control Study," *American Journal of Public Health*, 2003, 1089–97.

Canfield, K., "Judge Spares Thurman Prison Time," *Hartford Courant*, January 27, 2000.

Caponera, B., *Incidence and Nature of Domestic Violence in New Mexico VIII: An Analysis of 2007 Data from the New Mexico Interpersonal Violence Data Central Repository*, Office of Injury Prevention, Injury and Behavioral Epidemiology Bureau, Epidemiology and Response Division, New Mexico Department of Health. July, 2008.

Carlson, M., Harris, S., and Holden, G., "Protective Orders and Domestic Violence: Risk Factors for Reabuse," *Journal of Family Violence* 14(2), 1999, 205–26.

Casey, M., and Nichols, L., "Goodyear Murder Suspect Has History of Domestic Violence," *Arizona Republic*, March 28, 2015.

Catalano, S., *Stalking Victims in the United States—Revised*, U.S. Department of Justice, Bureau of Justice Statistic, NCJ 224527, September 2012.

Catalano, S., Smith, E., Snyder, H., and Rand, M., *Female Victims of Violence*, U.S. Department of Justice, Publications and Materials Paper 7, 2009.

Charing, S., "Northeast Baltimore Suffers Another Gay Murder," *Gay Life*, November 1, 2014.

Chibbaro Jr., L., "D.C. Police Officers Save Life of Lesbian Domestic Violence Victim," *Washington Blade*, September 17, 2014.

Chibbaro Jr., L., "Lesbian Gets 8 Years in D.C. Domestic Violence Case," *Washington Blade*, November 23, 2014.

Clem, D., "Canton Domestic Violence Warrant Requests Disappeared," *Detroit Free Press*, September 23, 2015.

Conte, A., "Progress Against Domestic Violence Has Come Slowly," *The Tennessean*, November 3, 2014.

Counts, J., "Ypilsanti Township Man Accused of Shooting Ex-Girlfriend Charged with 7 Felonies," MLive.com, February 28, 2015.

Cousins, J., "Body Found in Baltimore Home; Man Arrested," WBALTV, October 13, 2014.

Crime Commission Family Violence Sub-Committee, *Protective Orders in Virginia: FY 2003*, State of Virginia, Virginia Crime Commission, November 2003.

Crime Gun Trace Reports (1999, 2000, 2002), Washington, DC: Bureau of Alcohol, Tobacco and Firearms, 2000.

Czekalinski, S., Riepenhoff, J., and Wagner, M., "Day One: Repeat Domestic-Violence Offenders Get Off Easy in Ohio," *Columbus Dispatch*, October 25, 2010.

"DA Almost Eliminates DV Dismissals," *National Bulletin on Domestic Violence Prevention* 16(12), December 2010.

Daniels III, F., "Judge Casey Moreland Offers a Lesson." *The Tennessean*, July 22, 2015.

Davis, D., "Updated: Minnesota Cities Apply to Make Police Body Camera Videos Private," *Grand Forks Herald*, September 15, 2015.

Davis, R., Taylor, B., and C. Maxwell, C., *Does Batterer Treatment Reduce Violence? A Randomized Experiment in Brooklyn*, Final Report for National Institute of Justice, U.S. Department of Justice, National Institute of Justice, NCJ 180772, January 2000.

Dawson, S., Neylon, N., and Hart, T., *Experiences of Battered Women in Ohio: A Community Focus Group Report*, U.S. Department of Justice, Office on Violence Against Women and U.S. Department of Health and Human Services Administration for Children and Families, Columbus, Ohio: Ohio Domestic Violence Network, October 2003.

Diedrich, J., "Radcliffe Haughton Sidestepped Brown Deer Police for Years," *Milwaukee Journal Sentinel*, October 22, 2012.

Diedrich, J., and Barton, G., "Brown Deer Police Failed to Protect Public, Officials Say," *Milwaukee Journal Sentinel*, October 23, 2012.

Dienemann, J., Campbell, J., Landenburger, K., and Curry, M., "The Domestic Violence Survivor Assessment: A Tool for Counseling Women in Intimate Partner Violence Relationships," *Patient Education and Counseling* 46(3), 2002, 221–28.

Deiter, B., "Abused Wife Pleads No Contest to Manslaughter in Husband's Fatal Stabbing," *The Grand Rapids Press*, July 14, 2014.

Deiter, B., "Man Fatally Stabbed Had 3 Domestic Violence Convictions, Court Records Show," *The Grand Rapids Press*, August 29, 2013.

Domestic Violence Coordinating Council, "Examining CT's Domestic Violence Courts," *Verve* 2(4), April 2012.

Domestic Violence Crisis Center, "A Victim Centered Perspective on CT's Diversionary Practice," *Verve* 2(3), March 30, 2012.

Domestic Violence Dashboard Project, 2013 Data, New York State Office for the Prevention of Domestic Violence, 2014, http://www.opdv.ny.gov/statistics/ny-data/2013/nys2013data.pdf, downloaded October 7, 2015.

Domestic Violence Fatality Review Commission Report, State of Vermont, 2014.

Domestic Violence Incident Report (DAIR) for the Period of January 1, 2012–December 31, 2012, Wisconsin Department of Justice, Office of Crime Victim Services, 2013.

Domestic Violence Strangulation Project, Maricopa Association of Governments, Azmag.gov, downloaded December 7, 2014.

Donnelly, D. A., Cook, K. J., Van Ausdale, D., and Foley, L., "White Privilege, Color Blindness, and Services to Battered Women." *Violence Against Women* 11(1), January 2005, 6–37.

"DV in the News," *National Bulletin on Domestic Violence Prevention* 21(7), July 2015.

Family Violence: A Model State Code, National Council of Juvenile and Family Court Judges, Reno, NV, 1994.

Family Violence Council, *Report on Domestic Violence for 2013 for Lincoln/Lancaster County*, Lincoln Medical Foundation, Inc., 2014.

Family Violence Council, *Report on Domestic Violence for 2015 for Lincoln/Lancaster County*, Lincoln Medical Foundation, Inc., 2015.

Fawcett, J., *Up to Us: Lessons Learned and Goals for Change After Thirteen Years of the Washington State Domestic Violence Fatality Review*, Washington State Coalition Against Domestic Violence, December 2010, http://dvfatalityreview.org/portfolio/up-to-us-2010/, downloaded October 5, 2015.

Felson, R., Messner, S., Hoskin, A., and Deane, G., "Reasons for Reporting and Not Reporting Domestic Violence to the Police," *Criminology*, 40(3), 2002, 617–48.

Figueroa, T., and Sifuentes, E., "Suspect in Schabarth Slaying Found Dead," *North County Times*, March 4, 2012.

Finneran, C., and Stephenson, R., "Intimate Partner Violence Among Men Who Have Sex with Men: A Systematic Review," *Trauma Violence Abuse* 14, 2013, 168–85.

Frandsen, R., *Enforcement of the Brady Act, 2009: Federal and State Investigations and Prosecutions of Firearm Applicants Denied by a NICS Check in 2009*, U.S. Department of Justice, National Institute of Justice, NCJ 234173, April 2011.

Frandsen, R., *Enforcement of the Brady Act, 2010: Federal and State Investigations and Prosecutions of Firearm Applicants Denied by a NICS Check in 2010*, U.S. Department of Justice, National Institute of Justice, NCJ 239272, August 2012.

Friday, P., Lord, V., Exum, M., and Hartman, J., *Evaluating the Impact of a Specialized Domestic Violence Police Unit*, Final Report for National Institute of Justice, U.S. Department of Justice, National Institute of Justice, NCJ 215916, May 2006.

Garner, J., and Maxwell, C., *Prosecution and Conviction Rates for Intimate Partner Violence*, Shepherdstown, WV: Joint Centers for Justice Studies, 2008, 49.

Gender Bias Study Committee, Gender Bias Study of the Court System in Massachusetts, *New England Law Review*, 24(3), 1990, 745–856.

George, T., *Domestic Violence Sentencing Conditions and Recidivism*, Olympia, WA: Washington State Center for Court Research, Administrative Office of the Courts, 2012.

"Georgia Domestic Violence Fatality Review Project 10 Annual Report," Georgia Commission on Family Violence, Georgia Coalition Against Domestic Violence, March 2013.

Gerney, A., and Parsons, C., "How Gun Violence Affects Women and Four Policy Solutions to Better Protect Them," *Domestic Violence Report* 20(1), October/November 2014.

Ghandnoosh, N., *Black Lives Matter, Eliminating Racial Inequity in the Criminal Justice System*, The Sentencing Project, 2015.

Gipson, C., *History of the Domestic Violence Division Metro Nashville Police Department: A Decade of Services to Victims of Family Violence*, Metro Nashville Police Department, March 2004.

Glass, N. et al., "Non-Fatal Strangulation Is an Important Risk Factor for Homicide of Women," *Journal of Emergency Medicine* 35, 2008.

Gondolf, E., *Assessing Woman Battering in Mental Health Services*, Thousand Oaks, CA: Sage, 1999.

Gonzalez, T., "Judge Casey Moreland Reprimanded by State Judicial Board," *The Tennessean*, October 24, 2014.

Gordon, J., "Community Services for Abused Women: A Review of Perceived Usefulness and Efficacy," *Journal of Family Violence* 11(4), 1996, 315–29.

Green, E., "Now Understanding the Neurobiology of Trauma Helps Portland Police Work with Domestic Violence Survivors," *Street Roots News*, January 20, 2015.

"Groups Seek Justice for Domestic Violence Survivor and Policy Reforms at Hearing," ACLU Press Release, October 27, 2014.

Haas, B., and Rau, N., "Nashville Police Drop Thousands of Domestic Violence Cases," *The Tennessean*, August 10, 2010.

Hager, J., "Baltimore City Police Make Arrests in Two Murders," ABC, WMAR Baltimore, October 13, 2014.

Harrell, A., Castro, J., Newmark, L., and Vishers, C., *Final Report on the Evaluation of the Judicial Oversight Demonstration*, Executive Summary for National Institute of Justice, U.S. Department of Justice, National Institute of Justice, NCJ 219386, 2007.

Harrell, A., Schaffer, M., DeStefano, C., and Castro, J., *The Evaluation of Milwaukee's Judicial Oversight Demonstration*, Final Report for National Institute of Justice, U.S. Department of Justice, National Institute of Justice and The Urban Institute, April 2006.

Harrell, A., and Smith, B., "Effects of Restraining Orders on Domestic Violence Victims," in *Do Arrest and Restraining Orders Work?* eds. E. Buzawa and C. Buzawa, Thousand Oaks, CA: Sage, 1996, 214–43.

Hart, B., "Impact of VAWA," *National Bulletin on Domestic Violence Prevention* 20(10), October 2014, 4.

Hartley, C., and Frohmann, L., *Cook County Target Abuser Call (TAC): An Evaluation of a Specialized Domestic Violence Court*, Final Report for National Institute of Justice, U.S. Department of Justice, National Institute of Justice, NCJ 202944, August 2003.

Harway, M., and Hansen, M., "Therapist Conceptions of Family Violence," in M. Harway and M. Hansen, eds., *Battering and Family Therapy: A Feminist Perspective*, Newbury Park, CA: Sage, 1993, 42–53.

Hemenway, D., and Richardson, E., "Homicide, Suicide, and Unintentional Firearm Fatalities: Comparing the United States with Other High-Income Countries," *Journal of Trauma* 70, 2011, 238–42.

Hench, D., "Charges Go Way Up in Maine after Law Change on Strangling," *Portland Press Herald*, September 1, 2014.

Hickman, M., and Reaves, B., *Sheriffs' Offices 2003*, U.S. Department of Justice, Bureau of Justice Statistics, NCJ 211361, May 2006.

Highland, D., "Man Could Get Death Penalty in Domestic Shooting Case," *Bowling Green Daily News*, July 17, 2015.

Hirschel, D., and Buzawa, E., "Intimate Partner Violence Offenders Who Flee the Scene Are Likely to Avoid Arrest," *Domestic Violence Report* 20(2), December/January 2015.

Hirschel, J. D., Buzawa, E., Pattavina, A., Faggiani, D., and Reuland, M., *Explaining the Prevalence, Context, and Consequences of Dual Arrest in Intimate Partner Cases*, Final Report for National Institute of Justice, U.S. Department of Justice, National Institute of Justice, NCJ 218355, April 2007.

Hirschel, J., and Hutchison, I., "The Relative Effects of Offense, Offender, and Victim Variables on the Decision to Prosecute Domestic Violence Cases," *Violence Against Women* 7(1), January 2001, 46–59.

Horvath, L., Logan, T., and Walker, R., "Child Custody Cases: A Content Analysis of Evaluation Practices," *Professional Psychology: Research and Practice*, 33(6), 2002, 557–65.

Humphreys, C., and Thiara, R., "Mental Health and Domestic Violence: 'I Call It Symptoms of Abuse,'" *The British Journal of Social Work* 33(2), 2003, 209–26.

Jasinski, J., and Mustaine, E., "Police Response to Physical Assault and Stalking Victimization: A Comparison of Influential Factors," *American Journal of Criminal Justice* 26(1), 2001, 23–41.

Jeltsen, M., "This Is How a Domestic Violence Victim Falls Through the Cracks," *Huffington Post*, June 16, 2014, updated March 27, 2015.

Jung, T., "Southern Arizona DV Unit Seizes Initiative," *Arizona Daily Star*, January 10, 2015.

Kane, R., "Police Responses to Restraining Orders in Domestic Violence Incidents: Identifying the Custody-Threshold Thesis," *Criminal Justice and Behavior*, vol. 27, no. 2, 2000.

Karberg, J., Frandsen, R., Durso, J., and Lee, A., *Background Checks for Firearm Transfers, 2012 - Statistical Tables*, U.S. Department of Justice, Bureau of Justice Statistics, NCJ 247815, December 2014.

Kertscher, T., "U.S. Files Criminal Charges in Fraction of Gun Denial Cases, Mayors Against Illegal Guns Says," *Politifact*, February 3, 2013.

Klein, A., *The Criminal Justice Response to Domestic Violence*, Belmont, CA: Wadsworth Thomson Learning, 2004.

Klein, A., "Determined Prosecutor Pursues Justice," *National Bulletin on Domestic Violence Prevention* 16(6), June 2010.

Klein, A., "DV Arrest and Conviction Rates May Be Less Than Meets the Eye," *National Bulletin on Domestic Violence Prevention*, 19(10), October 2013.

Klein, A., *Enforcing Domestic Violence Firearm Prohibitions, A Report on Promising Practices*, Office on Violence Against Women and National Center on Full Faith and Credit, September 2006.

Klein, A., *Practical Implications of Current Domestic Violence Research: For Law Enforcement, Prosecutors and Judges*, Special Report, U.S. Department of Justice, National Institute of Justice, June 2009.

Klein, A., Centerbar, D., Keller, S., and Klein, J., *Impact of Differential Sentencing Severity for Domestic Violence Offenses and All Other Offenses Over Abusers' Life Spans*, U.S. Department of Justice, National Institute of Justice, September 2013.

Klein, A., Salomon, A., Elwyn, L., Barasch, A., Powers, J., Maley, M., Gilmer, J., Pirchner, M., Harris, I. et al., *An Exploratory Study of Juvenile Orders of Protection as a Remedy for Dating Violence*, U.S. Department of Justice, National Institute of Justice, April 29, 2013.

Klein, A., Salomon, A., Huntington, N., Dubois, J., and Long, D., *Statewide Study of Stalking and Its Criminal Justice Response*, U.S. Department of Justice, National Institute of Justice, NCJ 228354, May 2009.

Klein, A., and Tobin, T., "Longitudinal Study of Arrested Batterers, 1995-2005: Career Criminals," *Violence Against Women* 14(2), February 2008, 136–57.

Klein, A., Wilson, D., Crowe, A., and DeMichele, M., *Evaluation of the Rhode Island Probation Specialized Domestic Violence Supervision Unit*, Final Report for National Institute of Justice, U.S. Department of Justice, National Institute of Justice, March 31, 2005.

Krell, A., "5 Requests for Restraining Orders Against Man Accused of Fleeing Police," *News Tribune*, Tacoma, WA, January 5, 2015.

Labriola, M., Rempel, M., and Davis, R., *Testing the Effectiveness of Batterer Programs and Judicial Monitoring: Results From a Randomized Trial at the Bronx Misdemeanor Domestic Violence Court*, Final Report for National Institute of Justice, New York: Center for Court Innovation, National Institute of Justice, November 2005.

Law, V., "Domestic Violence Victims in NY Prisons May Get Some Relief," *Aljazeera America*, January 1, 2015.

Leung, R., "Gonzales Vs. Castle Rock, Supreme Court To Decide If Mother Can Sue Her Town And Its Police," CBS News, March 17, 2005.

Levine, H., Siegel, L., and Sayegh, G., "One Million Police Hours: Making 440,000 Marijuana Possession Arrests in New York City, 2002–2012," *Drug Policy Alliance and Marijuana Arrest Research Project*, New York City, NY, March 2013.

Lewis, K., and Burd-Sharps, S., *A Portrait of California, 2014-2015*, Measure of America of the Social Science Research Council, 2015.

Logan, T., and Walker, R., "Civil Protective Order Effectiveness: Justice or Just a Piece of Paper?" *Violence & Victims* 25(3), 2010, 332–48.

Logan, T., and Walker, R., "Civil Protective Order Outcomes: Violations and Perceptions of Effectiveness," *Journal of Interpersonal Violence*, 24(4), 2009, 675–92.

Logan, T., Walker, R., Hoyt, W., and Faragher, T., *The Kentucky Civil Protective Order Study: A Rural and Urban Multiple Perspective Study of Protective Order Violation Consequences, Responses, & Costs*, Final Report for National Institute of Justice, U.S. Department of Justice, National Institute of Justice, 2009.

Low, R., "Wife Says 30 Days for Domestic Violence Just Slap of Hand for Repeat Offender," *Fox 31*, Denver, CO, August 18, 2015.

Luthern, A., "Police, Prosecutors Use New Tools to Help Domestic Violence Victims," *Milwaukee Journal Sentinel*, December 25, 2014.

Lynds, J., "Mars Hill Man Arrested, Denied Bail for Alleged Domestic Violence," *Bangor Daily News*, March 13, 2015.

Macy, R. J., Nurius, P. S., Kernic, M. A., and Holt, V. L., "Battered Women's Profiles Associated with Service Help-Seeking Efforts: Illuminating Opportunities for Intervention," *Social Work Research*, 29(3), 2005, 137–50.

Maneta, E., "APA: Abused as Kids, Women More Likely to Abuse Partners," American Psychiatric Association, ed. J. Gever, reported in *MedPage Today*, May 18, 2011.

"Man with History of Domestic Violence Convicted of Assaulting Girlfriend," WHBQ, Memphis, TN, January 29, 2015.

Martin, A., "Day 5: Special Report on Domestic Violence: State Stuck Without Victims' Help," *Galesburg Register-Mail*, May 21, 2015.

Maryland Annual Report Summary, January–December 2014, Lethality Assessment Program: Maryland Model (LAP), http://mnadv.org/_mnadvWeb/wp-content/uploads/2015/09/2014-LAP-Maryland-Annual-Report-Summary.pdf, downloaded October 7, 2015.

Maxwell, C., Robinson, A., and Klein, A., "The Prosecution of Domestic Violence Across Time," in E. Stark and E. Buzawa, eds., *Violence against Women in Families and Relationships: Vol III, Criminal Justice and the Law*, Santa Barbara, CA: Praeger, 2009, 69–91.

McCabe, F., "Man Sentenced to Prison for Killing Ex-Girlfriend," *Las Vegas Review-Journal*, February 24, 2012.

McDonald, T., and Hankerson, M., "NC Domestic Violence Order Doesn't Allow Police to Search Accused for Guns," *The News and Observer*, May 6, 2014.

McFarlane, J., Campbell, J., Wilt, S., Sachs, C., Ulrich, Y., and Xu, X., "Stalking and Intimate Partner Femicide," *Homicide Studies*, 3(4), November 1999, 300–316.

McKay, K., "A Closer Look at Strangulation Cases," *The Prosecutor* 44(1), January-February 2014.

McNamara, P., and Jung, Y., "Logistical Challenges Abound, but Task Force Is Tackling Them," *Arizona Daily Star*, Tucson, AZ, January 11, 2015.

Mederos, F., "Changing Our Visions of Intervention: The Evolution of Programs for Physically Abusive Men," in E. Aldarondo and F. Mederos, eds., *Programs for Men Who Batter*, Civil Research Institute, Kingston, NJ, 2002, 1–26.

Menzel, M., "Case Examines Domestic Violence," *Tallahassee Democrat*, February 14, 2015.

Mervosh, S., "Domestic Abusers Now Required to Hand Over Firearms in Dallas County," *The Dallas Morning News*, May 5, 2015.

Messing, J. et al., *Police Department's Use of the Lethality Assessment Program: A Quasi-Experimental Evaluation*, U.S. Department of Justice, National Institute of Justice, 2004, 4.

Messing, J., Campbell, J., Wilson, S., Brown, B., Patchell, and Shall, C., *Police Department's Use of the Lethality Assessment Program: A Quasi-Experimental Evaluation*, National Institute of Justice, NCR 247456, 2014, https://www.ncjrs.gov/pdffiles1/nij/grants/247456.pdf, downloaded October 4, 2015.

"Milford Man Held on $1.1 Million Bond on Domestic Violence Charges," *Milford Mirror*, January 19, 2015.

Milkovits, A., "In R.I. Domestic Violence Cases, Suspects Often Keep Guns," *Providence Journal*, June 16, 2015.

Miller, A., "Colorado Passes Milestone Child Custody Law Reform," *Domestic Violence Report* 19(1), October/November 2013.

Miller, N., *Domestic Violence: A Review of State Legislation Defining Police and Prosecution Duties and Powers*, Institute for Law and Justice, 33–34, June 2004, http://ilj.org/publications/docs/Domestic_Violence_Legislation.pdf, downloaded October 7, 2015.

Miller, N., *What Does Research and Evaluation Say About Domestic Violence Laws? A Compendium of Justice System Laws and Related Research Assessments*, Institute for Law and Justice, December 2005.

Mohandie, K., Meloy, J. R., McGowan, M., and Williams, J., "The RECON Typology of Stalking: Reliability and Validity Based upon a Large Sample of North American Stalkers," *Journal of Forensic Sciences* 51, January 2006, 147–55, 153.

"Nashville Opens Advocacy Center for Domestic Violence Victims," Nashville.gov, posted September 25, 2014.

National Domestic Violence Fatality Review Initiative website: http://www.ndvfri.org/about.php, downloaded October 1, 2015.

National Law Enforcement Officers Memorial Fund, http://www.nleomf.org/newsroom/news-releases/law-enforcement-officer.html, downloaded October 5, 2015.

"New Ala. Law Allows Death in Protection Cases," *Montgomery Advertiser*, May 19, 2014.

"New Michigan DV Court to Save Third-Time Felony Abusers from Jail," *National Bulletin on Domestic Violence Prevention* 20(9), September 2014.

New York State Asset Forfeiture 2012 Annual Report, NY State Division of Criminal Justice Services, Albany, New York.

New York State Division of Criminal Justice Services, "New Strangulation Statute Proving an Effective Tool for Law Enforcement," press release, April 7, 2011.

Newmark, L., Rempel, M., Diffily, K., and Kane, K., *Specialized Felony Domestic Violence Courts: Lessons in Implementation and Impacts of the Kings County Experience*, Final Report for National Institute of Justice, U.S. Department of Justice, National Institute of Justice, NCJ 191861, 199723, October 2001 and 2004.

"Nine Strikes and Then Out," *National Bulletin on Domestic Violence Prevention* 14(7), July 2009.

Norman-Eady, S., "Restraining Orders," *OLR Research Report*, 2005-R-0861, December 8, 2005.

Nunley, K., "Kern County D.A. Plans Domestic Violence Diversion Program," KBAK, September 22, 2014.

"NYC Policing DV: Is Success Miracle or Fluke?" *National Bulletin on Domestic Violence Prevention* 16(9), September 2010, 1.

"Ocean Springs Woman Took Action to Keep Ex-Boyfriend Away Before Shooting," available at http://legalpronews.findlaw.com/article/6c15d1aaf975224ac1851c816c87d7b6#.U4iInybD-71, last accessed June 2014.

"Officer Defends Giving Boy Back to Dahmer," *New York Times*, August 25, 1991.

Ohio Family Health Survey Research Team, *Ohio Family Health Survey, 2010*, Interact for Health, March 2011.

"Orange County Woman Relieved after Accused Stalker Arrested," WFTV News, January 8, 2015.

"Orange County Woman Worries Law Isn't Protecting Her from Stalker," WFTV News, January 7, 2015.

Palmer, J., "Hurdles Exist for Women Attempting to Leave Abusive Relationships," *The Oklahoman*, October 27, 2014.

Peak, C., "San Francisco Trials Bay Area in Domestic Violence Prosecutions," *San Francisco Public Press*, September 24, 2012.

Perez-Trevino, E., "District Attorney Stresses Pro-Victim Stance in Domestic Violence Cases," *The Herald*, August 9, 2015.

Peterson, R., "Evaluation of Brooklyn's Video Statement Program for DV Cases," *Research in Brief*, no. 29, p. 3, New York City Criminal Justice Agency, May 2012.

Petroski, W., "Branstad Wants Get-Tough Legislation on Domestic Violence," *The Des Moines Register*, January 14, 2015.

Pfaff, J., "The Causes of Growth in Prison Admissions and Populations," *Social Science Research Network*, January 23, 2012.

Pines, Z., *2004 Caseload Statistics of the Unified Judicial System of Pennsylvania*, December 13, 2005, http://www.aopc.org/Index/Aopc/Research/caseloads/2004report.pdf, downloaded October 7, 2015.

Pleasant, J., "Nashville Adds Domestic Violence Coordinator to Better Protect Victims," WKRN-TV, September 24, 2013.

"Police: Changed locks Led Suspect to Break In, Kill 8," *USA Today*, August 9, 2015.

Prather, S., "Domestic Violence Convictions Up Sharply in Minnesota," *Star Tribune*, August 15, 2015.

Pretrial Innovations: Supporting Safety and Case Integrity, in *Enhancing Responses to Domestic Violence, Promising Practices from the Judicial Oversight Demonstration Initiative*, Office on Violence Against Women, National Institute of Justice, Urban Institute, and Vera Institute of Justice, 2006.

Proctor, J., "Stalker's Record Was Not Available," *Albuquerque Journal*, March 12, 2010.

Ptacek, J., *Battered Women in the Courtroom: The Power of Judicial Responses*, Northeastern Series on Gender, Crime, and Law, Boston, MA: Northeastern University Press, 1999.

Pulkkinen, L., "Supreme Court Faults Police for Failing to Protect Murdered Federal Way Woman from Abuser," *Seattle Post Intelligencer*, October 17, 2013.

Rakoff, J., "Why Innocent People Plead Guilty," *New York Review of Books*, November 20, 2014.

"Recent History of Mass Shootings in the United States," *The Oregonian*, October 2, 2015.

Reed, E., "Toledo Domestic Violence Report Released," NBC 24, May 5, 2012.

Robinson, C., "Man Killed after Slapping Ex-Girlfriend Had History of Domestic Violence, Court Records Show," Al.com, March 5, 2015.

Robles, Y., "Brighton Firefighter Sentenced, Wife Settles Civil Claim Against City," *Denver Post*, March 4, 2015.

Romero, M., "Police Piecing Together Background of Domestic Violence-Related Shooting," *Deseret News*, March 2, 2015.

Rothman, E. F., Hemenway, D., Miller, M., and Azrael, D., "Batterers' Use of Guns to Threaten Intimate Partners," *Journal of the American Medical Women's Association* 60, 2005, 62–68.

Roush, S., "Man Awaits Rape Trial after Domestic Violence Clearance," *Eagle Gazette*, Lancaster, OH, December 11, 2014.

"Seattle Attempt to Keep Addicts Out of Jail in Study," Associated Press, April 8, 2015.

Sherman, L., Smith, D., Schmidt, J., and Rogan, D., "Crime, Punishment, and Stake in Conformity: Legal and Informal Control of Domestic Violence," *American Sociological Review* 57, 1992, 407–17.

Shwayder, M., "A Same-Sex Domestic Violence Epidemic Is Silent," *The Atlantic*, November 5, 2013.

Simmons, L., "New Strangulation Law Leads to More Than 100 Arrests around Hampton Roads," WGNT, Hampton Roads, VA, January 15, 2013.

Smith, B., Davis, R., Nickles, L., and Davies, H., *Evaluation of Efforts to Implement No-Drop Policies: Two Central Values in Conflict*, Final Report for National Institute of Justice, U.S. Department of Justice, National Institute of Justice, NCJ 187772, March 2001.

Smith, C., "Beating. Strangulation. Released without bond?" KGUN9-TV, Florence, Arizona, January 6, 2015.

Smith, E., Durose, M., and Langan, P., *State Court Processing of Domestic Violence Cases*, Special Report, U.S. Department of Justice, Bureau of Justice Statistic, NCJ 214993, 2008.

Smith, E., and Farole, D., *Profile of Intimate Partner Violence Cases in Large Urban Counties*, Special Report, Bureau of Justice Statistics, NCJ 228193, October 2009.

Smith, S., "Family Violence, Legislative Update," National Council of Juvenile and Family Court Judges, Reno, Nevada, 2014.

Smith, T., "Authorities: Man Assaulted Daughter, 5, Wife," *Times Daily*, January 16, 2015.

Sorenson, S., Sivitz, E., and Joshi, M. et al., "A Systematic Review of Epidemiology of Nonfatal Strangulation, a Human Rights and Health Concern," *American Journal of Public Health*, 2014.

Sorenson S., and Wiebe, D., "Weapons in the Lives of Battered Women," *American Journal of Public Health* 94(8), 2004, 1412–17.

Spaid, E., "How Police Stalk Stalkers in Nashville," *Christian Science Monitor*, November 10, 1995.

Stern, R., "Maricopa County Attorney's Office Gets Award for New Approach in Strangulation Cases; Prosecutions Way Up," *Phoenix New Times*, June 12, 2013.

Stevenson, P., and Bileski, M., *Domestic Violence Arrest and Case Processing Data: An Analysis of the Information in Arizona's Computerized Criminal History Record System*, Arizona Criminal Justice Commission, 2013.

Stout, S., "Domestic Violence Suspect Arrested Twice in Two Days," KPHO, January 6, 2015.

Strack, G., McClane, G., and Hawley, D., "A Review of 300 Attempted Strangulation Cases, Part II: Clinical Evaluation of the Surviving Victim," *Journal of Emergency Medicine*, 21(3), 2001.

Sullivan, C., and Bybee D., "Reducing Violence Using Community-Based Advocacy for Women with Abusive Partners," *Journal of Consulting and Clinical Psychology*, 67(1), 1999, 43–53.

Sullivan, C., Tan, C., Basta, J., Rumptz, M., and Davidson, W., "An Advocacy Intervention Program for Women with Abusive Partners: Initial Evaluation," *American Journal of Community Psychology* 20, 1992, 209–332.

Sutton, J., "Girl, 11, Shoots Man Attacking Mother in Southeast Oklahoma City," *The Oklahoman*, September 24, 2014.

Survey of State Criminal History Information Systems, 2010. Washington, DC: Bureau of Justice Statistics, 2010.

"These Abusers Aren't Allowed to Own Guns. So Why Aren't States Removing Them?" *Huffington Post*, October 14, 2014.

Thompson, R., Rivara, F. P., Thompson, D. C., Barlow, W. E., Sugg, N. K., Maiuro, R. D., and Rubanowice, D. M., "Identification and Management of Domestic Violence: A Randomized Trial," *American Journal of Preventive Medicine* 19(4), 2000, 253–63.

Tjaden, P., and Thoennes, N., *Stalking: Its Role in Serious Domestic Violence Cases*, Final Report for National Institute of Justice, U.S. Department of Justice, National Institute of Justice, NCJ 187346, January 2001.

Truman, J., and Langton, L., *Criminal Victimization, 2013*, U.S. Department of Justice, Bureau of Justice Assistance, NCJ 247648, September 2014; see also Catalano, S., *Intimate Partner Violence, 1993-2010*, U.S. Department of Justice, Bureau of Justice Assistance, NCJ 239203, November, 2012.

Tucker, J., "Can Police Prevent Domestic Violence Simply by Telling Offenders to Stop?" *Indy Weekly*, November 13, 2013.

Tutty, L., Bidgood, B., and Rothery, M., "Support Groups for Battered Women: Research on Their Efficacy," *Journal of Family Violence* 8(4), 1993, 325–43.

2013 Domestic Violence, Rape, and Stalking Statistics, State of Kansas, Kansas Bureau of Investigation, http://www.accesskansas.org/kbi/stats/stats_dvrape.shtml, downloaded October 1, 2015.

2013 Report on Lesbian, Gay, Bisexual, Transgender, Queer, and HIV-Affected Intimate Partner Violence, National Coalition of Anti-Violence Programs, October 15, 2014.

Update on 2013 Domestic Violence Statistics for King County, Prosecuting Attorney's Office, King County, April 2, 2014.

Ventura, L., and Davis, G., "Domestic Violence: Court Case Conviction and Recidivism," in *Violence Against Women* 11(2), February 2005, 255–77.

Vigdor, E., and Mercy, J., "Do Laws Restricting Access to Firearms by Domestic Violence Offenders Prevent Intimate Partner Homicide?" *Evaluation Review* 30(3), June 2006, 313–46.

Volochinsky, B., "Obtaining Justice for Victims of Strangulation in Domestic Violence: Evidence Based Prosecution and Strangulation-Specific Training," *Legal Case Review* 4(10), 2012.

Wagner, M., Riepenhoff, J., and Czekalinksi, S., "Repeat Domestic Violence Offenders Demean and Brutalize Victims While Frustrating Judges," *Columbus Dispatch*, October 25, 2015.

Wagner, M., Riepenhoff, J., and Czekalinksi, S., "Repeat Domestic Violence Offenders Get Off Easy," *Columbus Dispatch*, October 5, 2015.

Wagner, M., Riepenhoff, J., and Czekalinksi, S., "Some Abusers Repeatedly Violate Restraining Orders, and the Legal System Often Lets Them Get Away with It," *Columbus Dispatch*, October 15, 2015.

Waterman, C., "Prosecution Dismisses Felony Domestic Violence Charge Against Essexville Man," *MLive*, Bay City, MI, April 1, 2015.

Weaver, E., "Enough Is Enough, Agencies Unite Against Domestic Violence," *Times-News*, January 16, 2015.

Weichselbaum, S., "Exclusive: New NYPD Policing Plan Will Change How Cops Handle Domestic Violence Crimes across Most of Manhattan," *New York Daily News*, April 8, 2014.

Whale, R., "Grieving Mother Sues State over Daughter's 2012 Murder," *Auburn Reporter News Reporter*, December 11, 2014.

Wilson, A., "Ray Rice's Domestic Violence Charges Dismissed by New Jersey Judge," *The Baltimore Sun*, May 21, 2015.

Wintemute, G. et al., "Identifying Armed Respondents to Domestic Violence Restraining Orders and Recovering Their Firearms: Process Evaluation of an Initiative in California," *American Journal of Public Health*, 2013.

Wintemute, G., Romero, M., Wright, M., and Grassel, K., "The Life Cycle of Crime Guns: A Description Based on Guns Recovered from Young People in California," *Annual of Emergency Medicine*, 43(6), 2004, 733–42.

Woods, D., "Vineland Domestic Violence Suspect Released and Then Arrested Again, Police Say," *South Jersey Times*, January 14, 2015.

Zador, P., "Statistical Evaluation of the Effectiveness of 'Alcohol Safety Action Projects'," *Accident Analysis & Prevention* 8(1), February 1976, 61–66.

Zahn, M., "Intimate Partner Homicide: An Overview," in *Intimate Partner Homicide, NIJ Journal*, No. 250, eds. J. Hernon and D. Tompkins, U.S. Department of Justice, National Institute of Justice, November 2003, 2–4

Zweig, J., and Burt, M., "Predicting Women's Perceptions of Domestic Violence and Sexual Assault Agency Helpfulness," *Violence Against Women* 13(11), November 2007, 1149–78.

Zweig, J., Schlichter, K., and Burt, M., "Assisting Women Victims of Violence Who Experience Multiple Barriers to Services," *Violence Against Women* 8(2), February 2002, 162–80.

COURT CASES

Carrie Arteaga v. Town of Waterford et al., No. HHD X07 CV 5014477S (March 16, 2010)

Estate of Macias v. Ihde, 219 F.3d 1018 (9th Cir. 2000)

Grenier et al. v. West Haven et al., U.S. District Ct, Case 3:11-cv-00808-JAM, September 17, 2012

In re Marriage of Crystal and Shawn H., 2013 WL 2940952 (Cal. App. 4th Dist. 2013)

In re The Seizure of Weapons from Apurba Nath, Docket No. A–4645–11T4, Decided: March 4, 2014

State v. Black, 60 NC 266, 267 (1864)
State v. Oliver, 90 NC 60 (1874)
Thurman v. Torrington, 595 F. Supp. (DC Conn. 1994)
United States v. Castleman, 572 U.S.___(2014)
Washburn v. City for Federal Way, No. 87906-1. (WA. S. Ct., October 17, 2013)

INDEX

ABOUT THE AUTHORS

Andrew R. Klein has served as a principal investigator on numerous research and evaluation grants for multiple federal, state, and county government and non-profit agencies covering a diverse range of areas from family violence, Temporary Assistance for Needy Families (TANF), victim rights, batterer intervention programming, faith-based rural domestic violence programming, elder abuse, and residential prison substance abuse treatment. Editor and columnist for Thomson-West's *National Bulletin on Domestic Violence Prevention*, he is also the author of major texts such as *Alternative Sentencing* (1988), *Intermediate Sanctions and Probation* (1997), and *The Criminal Justice Response to Domestic Violence* (2003). As a nationally recognized expert in the study of domestic violence and criminal justice, he has served on numerous national commissions and advisory boards on development of domestic violence courts, sentencing and supervision of youthful drunk drivers, probation, and more. He has provided technical assistance, headlined conferences, and provided professional training in his areas of expertise in almost every state of the Union and United States military bases abroad as well as the US Coast Guard.

Jessica L. Klein is a rape crisis and domestic violence victim advocate for Beth Israel Hospital, New York City, providing advocacy, counseling, safety planning, and service referrals to patients admitted to the emergency department after experiencing sexual assault or intimate partner violence.

She is also a rape crisis counselor on a hotline for the Anti-Violence Project, a New York-based organization that services LGBTQ and HIV-affected people across New York City. She has provided training at the Judicial Domestic Violence Training for Hawaiian Judges, training judges on the basic warning signs/components of intimate partner violence. She is a contributor for Thomson-West's *National Bulletin on Domestic Violence Prevention*.